13-02-91

IN.

CLIST Programming

Other McGraw-Hill Books of Interest

ISBN	AUTHOR	TITLE
0-07-006551-9	Bosler	*CLIST Programming*
0-07-044129-4	Murphy	*Assembler for COBOL Programmers: MVS, VM*
0-07-006533-0	Bookman	*COBOL II for Programmers*
0-07-046271-2	McGrew, McDaniel	*In-House Publishing in a Mainframe Environment*
0-07-051265-5	Ranade et al.	*DB2: Concepts, Programming, and Design*
0-07-054594-4	Sanchez, Canton	*IBM Microcomputers: A Programmer's Handbook*
0-07-002467-7	Aronson, Aronson	*SAS® System: A Programmer's Guide*
0-07-002673-4	Azevedo	*ISPF: The Strategic Dialog Manager*
0-07-007248-5	Brathwaite	*Analysis, Design, and Implementation of Data Dictionaries*
0-07-009816-6	Carathanassis	*Expert MVS/XA JCL: A Guide to Advanced Techniques*
0-07-015231-4	D'Alleyrand	*Image Storage and Retrieval Systems*
0-07-016188-7	Dayton	*Integrating Digital Services*
0-07-017606-X	Donofrio	*CICS: Debugging, Dump Reading, and Problem Determination*
0-07-018966-8	Eddolls	*VM Performance Management*
0-07-033571-0	Kavanagh	*VS COBOL II for COBOL Programmers*
0-07-040666-9	Martyn, Hartley	*DB2/SQL: A Professional Programmer's Guide*
0-07-050054-1	Piggott	*CICS: A Practical Guide to System Fine Tuning*
0-07-050686-8	Prasad	*IBM Mainframes: Architecture and Design*
0-07-051144-6	Ranade, Sackett	*Introduction to SNA Networking: Using VTAM/NCP*
0-07-051143-8	Ranade, Sackett	*Advanced SNA: A Professional's Guide to VTAM/NCP*

Database Experts Series

ISBN	AUTHOR	TITLE
0-07-020631-7	Hoechst et al.	*Guide to Oracle®*
0-07-033637-7	Kageyama	*CICS Handbook*
0-07-016604-8	DeVita	*The Database Experts' Guide to FOCUS*
0-07-055170-7	IMI Systems, Inc.	*DB2 and SQL/DS: A User's Reference*
0-07-023267-9	Larson	*The Database Experts' Guide to DATABASE 2*
0-07-039002-9	Lusardi	*Database Experts' Guide to SQL*
0-07-048550-X	Parsons	*The Database Experts' Guide to IDEAL*

Communications Series

ISBN	AUTHOR	TITLE
0-07-055327-0	Schlar	*Inside X.25 A Manager's Guide*
0-07-005075-9	Berson	*APPC: Introduction to LU6.2*
0-07-034242-3	Kessler	*ISDN: Concepts, Facilities, and Services*
0-07-071136-4	Wipfler	*Distributed Processing in CICS*
0-07-002394-8	Arnell, Davis	*Handbook of Effective Disaster/Recovery Planning*
0-07-009783-6	Cap Gemini America	*DB2 Applications Development Handbook*
0-07-009792-5	Cap Gemini America	*Computer Systems Conversion*

CLIST Programming

Kurt Bosler

McGraw-Hill, Inc.

New York   St. Louis   San Francisco   Auckland   Bogotá
Caracas   Hamburg   Lisbon   London   Madrid
Mexico   Milan   Montreal   New Delhi   Paris
San Juan   São Paulo   Singapore
Sydney   Tokyo   Toronto

Library of Congress Cataloging-in-Publication Data

Bosler, Kurt.
CLIST programming / Kurt Bosler

    p.   cm.
    ISBN 0-07-006551-9
    1. CLIST (Computer program language) I. Title.
    QA76.73.C235867   1990
    005.13'3—dc20   90-38566
                                                    CIP

1 2 3 4 5 6 7 8 9 0   DOC/DOC   9 6 5 4 3 2 1 0

ISBN 0-07-006551-9

*The sponsoring editor for this book was Theron Shreve, and the
production supervisor was Suzanne W. Babeuf. It was set in Century
Schoolbook by Archetype, Inc.*

Printed and bound by R. R. Donnelley & Sons Company.

*Subscription information to BYTE Magazine:
Call 1-800-257-9402, or write Circulation Dept.,
One Phoenix Mill Lane, Peterborough, NH 03458.*

Contents

Preface

The CLIST language is one of the most powerful and least utilized of the OS programmer's tools. This book is designed to present the facilities of the CLIST language and develop an understanding of their use. Data-management concepts are a key to this understanding and are discussed with certain CLIST functions.

Job Control Language (JCL) is also discussed since it is, in part, the background counterpart of the CLIST language and shares many of the same functions. It is not necessary, however, to know JCL to benefit from the material presented.

The book is designed to provide a complete coverage of the CLIST language and requires no prior experience with CLISTs. A knowledge of fundamental programming concepts and some exposure to the Time-Sharing Option (CLISTs run under TSO) is desirable. The book is also appropriate for CLIST programmers who want to gain a better understanding of the language.

More detail is given to concepts that are less obvious. The amount of detail has also been determined from classroom experience, and readers should not be overwhelmed by the length of some chapters. Conversely, readers should feel free to skip the subjects that are already familiar to them. CLIST examples are provided that perform utility functions. They can be transcribed and run with little or no change.

Those who have not used CLISTs before will be pleased to find out how simple the language really is. They will also find that there is minimal preparation to start using CLIST and the language can be directed to provide unique application solutions. The first chapter of the book gives an overview of the language, including the diversity of its application.

CLIST Programming

The CLIST Language

WHAT A CLIST IS

The CLIST language is a high-level interpreted language that also makes use of standard TSO commands. The word CLIST itself is short for *Command List,* while CLISTs are perhaps better known as foreground command procedures. The language is, however, much more extensive than either name implies. Indeed, a CLIST could be a simple list of commands and thus serve as a convenient mechanism to easily invoke and replay those commands. CLISTs, however, also serve as a resource-controlling language. In this capacity, they control the running of tasks and the use of computer resources in a way that is very similar to *Job Control Language* or JCL. Beyond that, the CLIST language also provides the same functionality as most other application-programming languages.

The rest of this chapter will expand upon the uses of CLIST programs and how they can be used by those who are involved in the program-development process. Those who do not consider themselves programmers will also see how useful the language can be in the daily use of a mainframe computer. The peculiar advantages of the CLIST language will also be discussed, but first we will examine the environment in which CLISTs operate.

THE CLIST OPERATING ENVIRONMENT

The CLIST language is available on mainframe systems that use the *Time-Sharing Option,* TSO or TSO/E (E for extensions). This would typically be on an OS type operating system. CLISTs are often used to control the foreground or interactive environment but can also be invoked in the background or batch environment using JCL. Here foreground refers to immediate, interactive access to computer resources as opposed to work that is started by the initiator function.

THE ROLE OF CLISTS IN THE COMPUTING ENVIRONMENT

In its simplest form, a CLIST could be a list of TSO commands or even a single command. The advantage to placing that command, or list of commands, in a CLIST is that one would not have to type them in again. One would merely invoke the CLIST, and the commands would be executed. The advantage increases when the commands are lengthy or difficult to remember. Invoking the commands from a CLIST not only saves time, but can help to avoid errors that might result from entering the wrong information or executing the commands out of sequence.

As a resource-controlling language, CLISTs allow the programmer to invoke programs in a foreground or real-time environment. This provides the capability of running applications immediately as well as interactively. That is to say, since the application is run as soon as it is invoked and is run directly from an individual's terminal, the application can be designed to "converse" with that individual. The application could be a supplied program product or one created by the individual. Supplied programs can be as diverse as utilities to copy data, language compilers, and fourth-generation report writers. Most compiled or assembled programs can also be run.

The CLIST language can also be used to create individual programs. It provides the functions that would be required of an application-programming language. Within the language are statements that provide for file input and output, data manipulation, selection and branching, as well as other functions that make up a typical programming language.

CLISTs can be used with the separate language, REXX, starting with version 2 of the TSO/E product. They can also be used to implement ISPF Dialog Management systems. ISPF (*Interactive System Productivity Facility*) Dialog Management is an optional program product. It can be used to supplement the CLIST language and add features that include:

full screen selection menus and data-entry panels

table data storage and access

variable data retention and access

data modification

Because they are separate, optional products, REXX and ISPF Dialog Management features will not be covered in this book. Where available, however, the two products should be investigated for the additional capability that they can supply to the CLIST language.

The distinction of different CLIST categories turns out to be somewhat arbitrary. The different types of functions can, in fact, be used together. This makes the language more powerful and allows it to be very flexible. This flexibility is our next topic.

ADVANTAGES OF THE CLIST LANGUAGE

Flexibility

One of the biggest advantages of the CLIST language is the flexibility that it provides. As just mentioned, the functions of a CLIST can readily be combined. This would allow a CLIST to be created that mixes resource-controlling statements with those that control program logic. Flexibility is further increased with the dynamic use of the resource statements, where these statements can even be conditionally executed.

Another aspect of the flexibility that a CLIST can provide is attributable to its ability to "interact" with the terminal user. This allows CLIST users to run tasks at their convenience. This also allows them to direct the CLIST and make last-minute adjustments or changes. The information they enter can then be conveyed using variables to any command or statement within the CLIST code. Those variables themselves are flexible enough to contain different data types and vastly different amounts of data without ever being declared.

Many commands provide flexibility by tolerating error conditions. This allows the CLIST code to test the disposition or success of a task and react accordingly. This might include things like reverting to a backup source of input information if the primary source is not available, or creating a new output file if one does not already exist that can be reused. CLIST input and output functions are also flexible enough to accommodate different data formats and record lengths in subsequent executions.

Assisting application development

CLISTs can be used in several ways to assist the application-development process. Both source-language compilers and the linkage-editor programs can be run using CLISTs to give better turnaround of source-code modifications. Better test turnaround of an application program can be obtained by using CLISTs to run the program in a foreground mode. This, typically, allows more tests to be run in time-sensible fashion where they can provide the most meaningful feedback of source-code changes. CLISTs are also generally used to create the execution environment prior to using most interactive debugging facilities.

Ease of development

Developing the CLIST code itself can be more expedient. Since the code does not need to be compiled, it can easily be saved and executed immediately. It is also easy to develop CLIST code in sections that can be run autonomously and later combined into larger applications. These and other features of the language (like the way variables are defined) allow periodic testing of the code under development. This, in turn, allows problems to be isolated and fixed earlier in the development process when changes are easier to effect.

ABOUT THE CHAPTERS

Chapters 2 and 3 address how to create a CLIST data set and how to invoke a CLIST, respectively. Chapter 4 is devoted to CLISTs that are composed entirely of combinations of TSO commands. Chapter 5 expands the use of those commands to provide a resource-controlling environment that will support the execution of other programs and the first of the CLIST statements are introduced.

The programmatic aspects of the CLIST language are covered in Chaps. 6 through 8. Chapter 6 moves the discussion from commands to statements. This includes facilities for variable data handling, data manipulation, and direction of logic flow. Input and output statements are discussed in Chap. 7, while Chap. 8 is reserved for special CLIST functions.

Chapter 9 contains a discussion of CLIST design considerations. This includes ways of increasing the usability of a CLIST, as well as considerations for creating the code itself. Chapter 10 includes complete CLIST examples. These examples come from all three CLIST categories and may even combine statements from the different categories within a single CLIST. Chapter 11 discusses various techniques that can be used to debug CLIST code.

Not all computer installations have the most current release of the TSO product installed. Chapters 12 and 13 contain newer features of the language that became available with a particular release. In addition, these releases represent major substantive changes to the language. The discussion of such newer features is held for later discussion so code developers can incorporate language features based upon the version of TSO/E that is available to them. This will also allow individuals who have been coding CLISTs to focus on the language's new features.

ABOUT THE EXAMPLES

The examples that are provided are not complete unless specifically stated as such. They have been kept as simple as possible to illustrate the particular statement or sequence of statements under discussion. The examples will, therefore, use the statements being discussed and may combine them with statements discussed earlier. There may well be other statements or sequences of statements that would accomplish the same end. Some of these may even be more efficient, but will not be mentioned until they are singled out for discussion.

The functions represented in the examples are heavily slanted toward utility functions that are common to most TSO users. Hopefully, this will provide a logical context which draws more attention to the CLIST statements than the application being implemented. In the next chapter, we will continue our discussion of CLISTs with how they are stored, and how their availability can be maximized.

CLIST Libraries

DATA SET CHARACTERISTICS

CLISTs are stored in and executed from sequential disk *data sets*. A sequential data set is a collection of related data records that are stored and retrieved in sequence. Each CLIST record could be considered a single line of code and must be read in the sequence that it is stored in the data set. The collection of records or lines of code is given a name known as a data set name. CLIST source statements are generally placed in the data set and modified using whatever text editor is available. The CLIST can then be invoked by referencing the data set name that contains the source statements.

The data set name of a regular sequential data set is formed using the following rules. The data set name must be:

one to forty-four characters in length (excluding quotes)

made of simple name qualifiers of one to eight characters each, where each qualifier is separated from another with periods

composed of the characters A through Z, 0 through 9, and the special characters @, $, #, and - (the use of a hyphen is not recommended, however, because of the special handling it mandates within CLIST code)

made of qualifiers that start with the characters A through Z or the special characters @, $, and #

The last qualifier of a data set name is known as the *descriptive qualifier.* Certain descriptive qualifiers have special significance in the TSO environment. One of these specially recognized descriptive qualifiers is "CLIST" which can elicit certain beneficial assumptions from the TSO program as well as certain text-editor products. It is, therefore, recommended that "CLIST" be used as the last qualifier of the data set name. A valid data set name, using the syntax rules and the recommendation above, might look like this.

```
TSO1234.SAMPLE.VALID.CLIST
```

Notice that the total data set length is less than forty-four characters. Each of the data set qualifiers is eight characters or less and, in this particular case, each qualifier starts with a letter of the alphabet.

CREATING CLIST LIBRARIES

It is highly recommended that CLISTs be stored in partitioned data sets. A *partitioned data set,* also known as a *PDS* or *library* is a special form of sequential data set storage. It groups multiple sequential data sets together and keeps track of them with what is called a directory. It is the allocation of space for the directory that is the initial difference between a PDS and a normal sequential data set.

Libraries are able to store small data sets more efficiently than regular sequential data sets. They can potentially store several data sets in the space consumed by a single sequential data set. There are other important reasons, however, for using libraries. A partitioned organization is good for grouping logically related data. This, in turn, makes the information stored in a library easier to access. CLISTs are especially suited to this type of organization because of the way they are executed. Libraries also make it easier to combine CLISTs from different sources. Individuals frequently combine their CLISTs with those provided by the computing installation they are working on, or with CLISTs provided by another individual. In either case, the data sets or libraries containing the CLISTs would be concatenated. Data set concatenation describes the process where multiple data sets are assigned to a single file. This allows multiple data sets to be processed as if there were only a single one. In the case of CLISTs, concatenation will allow multiple data sets to be searched to try to find the CLIST to be executed. Only data sets with the same data set organization can be concatenated. This means that, while multiple-partitioned data sets can be concatenated, they cannot be combined with sequential data sets. Later in this chapter we will take a look at how to determine what the system CLIST libraries are and how to concatenate other CLIST libraries to them.

Many languages have a set format that allows for little or no variance. This is not true of the characteristics that define a CLIST data set. With fixed-length records, CLIST code can be up to 255 bytes with the last eight bytes of the record used for sequence numbers. Variable-length records have four overhead bytes added to each record that are used to indicate the length of the record. With these extra four bytes, variable length CLIST code can have a record length of up to 259 bytes. Sequence numbers, if maintained in this format, are the first eight bytes of each record. It is also possible with variable length records to turn the editor-number mode off and place viable CLIST code in the first eight bytes.

In practice, the editor used to create the CLIST source code often determines the format used. An eighty-byte, fixed-length record format is recommended and has several advantages. That format is readily modified by most editors. It allows routine coding of CLIST statements beginning in the first column and would support both numbered and unnumbered statements. In this format, too, the code is compatible with the way most other source languages are stored.

Any other considerations, however, should be secondary to those of compatibility. If the CLIST library being created is to be used with other CLIST libraries, its characteristics should be compatible with those of the other libraries with which it will be concatenated. To a lesser extent, this also includes the data set blocksize. The data sets concatenated need not have identical blocksizes, but the data set with the largest blocksize should be referenced first in the concatenation. The input-buffer size will be determined by this first data set and, therefore, must be large enough to accommodate all subsequent blocksizes.

We will see in the next chapter what a profound influence the name of the CLIST data set has on the way it is invoked. For now, we will use the name "CLIST." TSO will expand this name to "prefix.CLIST", where the prefix is our assigned TSO user-ID or the high-level qualifier we have changed to using the TSO PROFILE command. The CLIST library can be created with the TSO ALLOC command or using the ISPF/PDF Data Set Utility, Option 3.2, if that is available. The following is an example of an ALLOC command which can be used to create a CLIST library.

```
ALLOC DA(CLIST) SP(5 2) TR DIR(15) RECFM(F B) LRECL(80) BLK(6160)
```

Installations may have certain requirements for the placement of individual data sets that are not handled by system defaults. In this case, UNIT and VOLUME parameters can be added as in the example below.

```
ALLOC DA(CLIST) SP(5 2) TR DIR(15) RECFM(F B) LRECL(80) BLK(6160)
UNIT(3380) VOL(TSO001)
```

Removal of the DIR or DIRECTORY keyword would cause the data set to be allocated without directory blocks. The resultant data set would, therefore, be a sequential data set rather than a PDS. While the name CLIST is one of the best for a CLIST library, it is not advisable to use it as the data set name for any sequential data set.

CONNECTING TO SYSTEM LIBRARIES

Most computing installations have CLIST libraries already in use. These often provide access to system and specialized software. In providing more convenient access to CLIST libraries, it is advisable to include system CLIST libraries. As mentioned earlier, this is effected through the concatenation of data sets. Data sets, like system CLIST libraries, are generally allocated when a user enters the TSO environment. This is typically done through JCL contained in logon procedures. The data sets that are allocated at that time stay allocated until they are freed or until the user leaves the TSO environment. A TSO command, LISTA, will list the data sets allocated to the TSO session. When the STATUS option is added to the command, the names of files that those data sets are allocated to are also listed. Part of the output from the LISTA STATUS command is listed below. Note that the file names are listed under the first data set allocated to that file name.

```
--DDNAME---DISP--
SYS1.HELP
   SYSHELP   KEEP
PUBLIC.HELP
            KEEP
SYS1.CLIST
   SYSPROC   KEEP
PUBLIC.CLIST
            KEEP
TERMFILE SYSPRINT
```

The output of the command can be used to determine what CLIST data sets are allocated by locating the SYSPROC file. This is a special system file used to attach CLIST data sets. The data sets that are allocated to the SYSPROC file are the CLIST data sets already available. The sample list above shows that data sets SYS1.CLIST and PUBLIC.CLIST are both allocated to the SYSPROC file. It is generally desirable to retain the present data sets and add the user's to them. Anything else could diminish the functionality of the user's TSO session.

Most who create their own CLIST libraries want them listed first in the concatenation. This gives the user the ability to "customize" existing system CLISTS. This is actually effected by creating CLIST members with the same member name rather than altering the system CLIST itself. That way, when a search is made for the system CLIST, the personalized version is executed because its library was searched before the system library. This also gives CLIST coders the luxury of supplying a large blocksize for their own data set. Those who add their own CLIST library as the first library of the SYSPROC file concatenation need only be sure that its blocksize is at least as large as that of any other included CLIST library. Improperly concatenated data sets may result in abends or CLISTs that cannot be located.

The SYSPROC file can be changed at almost any time. After determining what system CLIST data sets are allocated, decide where to add CLISTs relative to those that already exist. As mentioned before, it is very common to put CLIST data set(s) ahead of the system data sets. The following statement could be used to allocate a private CLIST library, TSO1234.CLIST, ahead of the system libraries that are already available.

```
ALLOC F(SYSPROC) DA('TSO1234.CLIST' 'SYS1.CLIST' 'PUBLIC.CLIST')
SHR REUSE
```

The same command could be included in a CLIST to make it easier to allocate the private CLIST library.

CLIST ALIASES

When CLISTs are stored as members of a PDS, it is possible to assign alternate names, known as aliases, to the members. Those CLISTs can then be invoked using the original member name or any of its aliases. The advantage is seen when more than one name can be used to describe a single CLIST function. For example, it might be difficult to remember whether the CLIST to invoke is called PRINTSEQ or SEQPRINT. Using an alias, both names could be used to invoke the same CLIST. The following statement shows how such an alias can be created.

```
RENAME 'TSO1234.CLIST(PRINTSEQ) (SEQPRINT) ALIAS
```

The example above uses the TSO command RENAME to assign an alias of SEQPRINT to the existing member name PRINTSEQ. The CLIST contained in that member could then be invoked using either name. In addition to assigning aliases, the RENAME command can also be used to rename a PDS member or an entire data set. In the next chapter, we will examine ways to invoke a CLIST.

3

CLIST Execution

MODES OF CLIST EXECUTION

There are four modes of CLIST execution: *explicit, modified explicit, implicit,* and *modified implicit.* CLIST execution is made possible by the TSO command EXEC. That command can also be abbreviated as EX. Because the command is explicitly stated in the first two modes, they are known as explicit modes. The implicit modes do not contain EX or EXEC as part of the command syntax. They also differ in their reliance upon a special file to identify which CLIST code to execute.

CLISTs are invoked at the TSO prompter or an interface to it. For those who have ISPF installed, this could also be OPTION 6 as well as most *Productivity Development Facility* (PDF) panels that have a command line. When a CLIST (or TSO command for that matter) is entered from a PDF panel, it should be preceded by the word TSO. This is not required from PDF Option 6 because it is designed to accept TSO commands and CLISTs.

The modes of CLIST execution will now be covered in more detail. The next few examples, used to demonstrate that execution, will assume that there is a partitioned data set, TSO1234.SAMPLE.CLIST, that contains several executable CLISTs.

Explicit mode

The first execution mode uses the TSO command EXEC followed by the complete name of the data set that contains the CLIST. That can optionally be followed by two types of parameter information that will be discussed later in this chapter. The TSO EXEC command can also be abbreviated EX and has the following syntax:

```
EXEC clist-name 'positional-parameter(s) keyword-parameter(s)'
```

Using our sample CLIST library, the explicit mode of the EXEC command followed by the CLIST name might look like the following:

```
EX 'TSO1234.SAMPLE.CLIST(HARDCOPY)'
```

This mode of execution might also be considered explicit because it pinpoints the name of the CLIST being executed. The same syntax will work for a CLIST contained in a sequential data set except, of course, that no member name is specified. It is gratifying to know that, as we progress, the syntax for CLIST execution becomes shorter.

TSO naming conventions

Before proceeding to the second execution mode, it is necessary to discuss how TSO handles data set names. When data set names are not literally specified (enclosed in single quotes), TSO will append a prefix in front of the data set name. This prefix is usually the individual's user-ID, but can be changed by any TSO user by using the TSO PROFILE command. Based upon the context in which it is used, TSO can also detect special data set types and attach an appropriate suffix. This too will only occur when the data set name is not literally specified. This suffix would become the last data set qualifier. This last qualifier (which precedes the member name, if any) is also known as the descriptive qualifier. Two such descriptive qualifiers that pertain especially to CLIST execution are .CLIST for CLIST data sets and .LOAD for load-module libraries. The former is the basis for the modified explicit-execution mode, while the latter will be discussed later with the resource controlling aspects of CLISTs. Finally, if a CLIST library is specified but the member name is omitted, TSO will assume that a member name of TEMPNAME is to be applied.

Modified explicit mode

The modified explicit mode is utilized when TSO is left to make its data set name assumptions. When the name of the CLIST data set is not quoted, TSO will append the individual's prefix to the front of the data set name. Inclusion of the data set name in an EXEC command provides the context for TSO to see the data set as a CLIST and attach the .CLIST descriptive qualifier as a suffix. The suffix .CLIST is only applied if the last qualifier of the data set name is not already the word CLIST. Our example of the explicit mode

```
EX 'TSO1234.SAMPLE.CLIST(HARDCOPY)'
```

can now be specified as

```
EX SAMPLE(HARDCOPY)
```

in the modified explicit mode. The qualifiers TSO1234 and CLIST will automatically be supplied. The most common mistake made using this format comes from specifying the word CLIST as other than the descriptive qualifier. Specifying a CLIST in the following fashion:

```
EX CLIST.SAMPLE(HARDCOPY)
```

generates the name

```
TSO1234.CLIST.SAMPLE.CLIST(HARDCOPY)
```

If this is not the intended, the likely result would be a failure to find the data set. To carry the modified explicit format to a very practical extreme, one could execute a CLIST with the name

```
TSO1234.CLIST(HARDCOPY)
```

by typing

```
EX (HARDCOPY)
```

Remember that the first qualifier, TSO1234, would be added because the data set name was not literally specified. The second qualifier, CLIST, would be added as the descriptive qualifier because the context identifies it as a CLIST data set. Below are examples of sequential data set names and the names that would result from their use in an EXEC statement.

Name Specified in EXEC	Resultant Name
'TSO1234.TEST.SEQ.CLIST'	same as specified
TEST.CLIST.SEQ	TSO1234.TEST.CLIST.SEQ.CLIST
TEST.SEQ.CLIST	TSO1234.TEST.SEQ.CLIST

```
TEST.SEQ                        TS01234.TEST.SEQ.CLIST
TEST                            TS01234.TEST.CLIST
```

When the resultant data set is determined to be a PDS, it must include a member name. If none was specified, a member name of TEMPNAME is assumed by TSO and added to the data set name. Below are examples with and without the member name specified.

Name Specified In EXEC	Resultant Name
'TS01234.TEST.LIB.CLIST(TEMPNAME)'	same as specified
'TS01234.TEST.LIB.CLIST'	TS01234.TEST.LIB.CLIST(TEMPNAME)
TEST.CLIST.LIB	TS01234.TEST.CLIST.LIB.CLIST(TEMPNAME)
TEST.LIB.CLIST	TS01234.TEST.LIB.CLIST(TEMPNAME)
TEST.LIB	TS01234.TEST.LIB.CLIST(TEMPNAME)
TEST	TS01234.TEST.CLIST(TEMPNAME)
'TS01234.TEST.LIB.CLIST(HARDCOPY)	same as specified
TEST.CLIST.LIB(HARDCOPY)	TS01234.TEST.CLIST.LIB.CLIST(HARDCOPY)
TEST.LIB.CLIST(HARDCOPY)	TS01234.TEST.LIB.CLIST(HARDCOPY)
TEST.LIB(HARDCOPY)	TS01234.TEST.LIB.CLIST(HARDCOPY)
TEST(HARDCOPY)	TS01234.TEST.CLIST(HARDCOPY)

Implicit mode

Implicit execution of a CLIST is made possible by connecting a CLIST library or libraries to the SYSPROC file. The process of allocating CLIST libraries is described in the previous chapter and learning this process is well worth the effort. Subsequent CLIST execution is very much simplified and is as easy as specifying the member name followed by any parameters. The libraries allocated to the SYSPROC file are searched in the order they were allocated until a member name matching the one specified is found. If there is no match, TSO stops and returns the message "COMMAND NOT FOUND."

Conversely, the same member name may exist in more than one CLIST library in the SYSPROC file. The contents of the like-named members could vary widely, but only the first member found with the specified name will be executed. If the CLIST code is saved and executed it in this fashion, only to end up in a totally different process, check the other CLIST libraries for a member of the same name. This problem does not occur with either of the explicit modes of execution because TSO is directed to look at a single, specific data set.

In the implicit mode of execution, CLISTs look and act just like TSO commands. When invoking a CLIST, the user might also run into like-named TSO commands. When an implicitly invoked CLIST has the same name as a TSO command, it will not execute. The like-named

TSO command will be executed instead. The next section will describe
how this problem can be circumvented, but it is advisable to avoid
using names already used by TSO commands or system-wide CLISTS.
Aside from the advantage of being able to specify a shorter name,
parameter information is easier to specify in the implicit mode.
Because our CLIST can now be found by searching the SYSPROC file,
all we would need to type to invoke that CLIST is

HARDCOPY

Modified implicit mode

This mode is only a slight variation of the implicit mode. In this mode,
the CLIST member name is prefixed by the "%" symbol, indicating the
member will come only from a search of the SYSPROC file. This
serves two useful purposes. First, it would be impossible to execute a
TSO command by mistake because only the libraries in the SYSPROC
file are searched. This would, for example, allow the user to construct
and execute a CLIST with the member name LISTDS and not invoke
the TSO command (with the same name) that lists data set attributes.
Second, this mode is a more efficient way to invoke CLISTS because
other libraries are not searched before those defined to the SYSPROC
file. To invoke the CLIST in the modified implicit mode type

%HARDCOPY

SUPPLYING INFORMATION DURING CLIST EXECUTION

A user may have occasion to execute a CLIST long before the first
attempt to write one. In fact, the way that most computing installations are set up, a user may have already invoked CLISTs without
realizing it. Many installations set up commonly needed CLISTs the
way they set up JCL cataloged procedure libraries. These are very
similar structures and either one would serve to make the task of ini-
tiating computer services easier. Our next topic will be to examine
some of the components of a CLIST that allow it to accept information
when it is invoked. At the same time, we should keep in mind how the
same components will help us to write our own CLISTs and build flexibility into them. At present, we will confine our discussion to the
parameters that are found on the CLIST PROC statement. This
includes the use of positional and keyword parameters to pass variable information to the CLIST. The discussion of additional communication components, global variables, interactive CLISTs, and file I/O
will be deferred to later chapters.

CLIST VARIABLES

A *CLIST variable* is a named area of storage used to hold data. It is called a variable because the data it contains is allowed to vary in value. Most programming languages have a similar facility, typically called a data element or field. Like some other programming languages, CLIST variables can be used virtually anywhere without having to be previously defined. Unlike most programming languages, however, CLIST variables are free to contain numeric or character data without having to commit to one or the other. CLIST variables are also dynamic in the amount of information they are able to hold. The length of a CLIST variable does not have to be defined. Our first look at variables (variables are discussed in detail in Chap. 6) will show how their values can be set as the CLIST is invoked. Those familiar with JCL will see that this is very much like the symbolic variable substitution that can occur when executing a cataloged procedure. The variables in either language give the process flexibility.

In our first CLIST example, the HARDCOPY CLIST, we will see how variables can give the CLIST user the flexibility of printing a different data set each time the CLIST is executed. This flexibility can extend to other information that may change over time, like the number of copies that are required and where the print output is to be routed. The statement that facilitates the communication of variable information in both CLISTs and JCL procedures is called the *PROC statement*. This is just the first of many similarities that will be pointed out between the two languages. In Chap. 5 we will actually translate a JCL jobstream into the CLIST language. In subsequent chapters we will see how much more versatile CLIST variables are and how they can play a key role in program flow and data management. But first, we will look at the PROC statement and its parameters in detail.

THE PROC STATEMENT

The CLIST *PROC statement* is used to establish and communicate variable information to a CLIST as it is invoked. It is also used to establish which variables are required for execution and which are optional. Required variables are defined as *positional parameters* and those that are optional are defined as *keyword parameters*. When discussing keyword parameters, we will also see how the PROC statement can be used to define defaults for optional variables.

POSITIONAL PARAMETERS

Positional parameters are, as their name implies, sensitive to the position they hold on the CLIST PROC statement. That means that these parameters must be specified in the same order that they occur on the PROC statement when the CLIST is executed. Positional parameters are provided for the CLIST writer to be able to specify information deemed critical to the CLIST execution. With that in mind, it should be noted that a CLIST will not execute until its positional parameter information has been specified. If the positional parameters are not specified when the CLIST is executed, the user will be prompted to enter these variables one at a time. The obvious advantage this holds (that of not having to remember the variables or the order in which they must be entered) is offset, however, by a missed opportunity to enter any keyword parameters. In addition, the information entered at a prompt will not be retained on the terminal to help with subsequent executions of the CLIST.

The prompt for a positional parameter is of the standard format

```
ENTER POSITIONAL PARAMETER xxxxxxxx
```

where xxxxxxxx is the variable name. The language supports positional parameter-variable names of up to 252 characters. This is a deliberate attempt to get CLIST coders to use meaningful variable names. With the standard prompt format, the only thing that distinguishes one parameter from another is the variable name.

The PROC statement is not required in a CLIST unless positional or keyword parameters are to be represented. If a PROC statement is coded, it will be the first statement in the CLIST. The first parameter of the PROC statement is a numeric value which defines how many positional parameters or variables are contained within the rest of the statement. This is the positional specification number which appears as "n" in the example below. If the CLIST contains no positional parameters, this number would be zero. If the CLIST contains any positional parameters, however, they are all specified before any keyword parameters. Remember, too, that the order of the variables is also important when the variable values are specified at execution time. The following is the syntax of the PROC statement:

```
PROC  n  positional-parameter(s)  keyword-parameter(s)
```

At this point, we will start to look at the simple application just introduced. Again, the function of the CLIST will be that of printing a data set and we will call that CLIST *HARDCOPY*. We will start by applying the PROC statement to our HARDCOPY CLIST and finish the application in Chap. 5 when we talk about the CLIST language as a resource-controlling language.

There are several pieces of information that could be useful in printing a data set. This includes the data set name, the output-print class, the number of copies, and the print destination. It is best to specify parameters in some meaningful order, even if that is only determined by the importance of the parameters. This could help the CLIST user better remember the parameters and the order in which they occur. It seems logical, for instance, to specify input related parameters before output related parameters. The following could well be the PROC statement for our HARDCOPY CLIST

```
PROC 4 A B C D
```

When executing the CLIST in the explicit mode, all parameter information must be grouped together as if it were a single entity. This is similar to supplying parm information to an executing program. To explicitly execute the HARDCOPY CLIST we might type

```
EX SAMPLE(HARDCOPY)  '''TSO1234.PRINT.TEXT'' A 2 RMT3'
```

where the inside set of two single quotes is used to designate a fully qualified data set name enclosed in single quotes. In essence, two consecutive single quotes are required to pass a single-quote value in the parameter list. The outside set of single quotes is used to group all parameter data together. During implicit execution, each parameter is a separate entity. Because of this, parameters are easier to specify in the implicit mode. When implicitly executing the same CLIST we might type

```
%HARDCOPY 'TSO1234.PRINT.TEXT' A 2 RMT3
```

The only quotes in this example are used to specify a fully qualified data set name and are retained with the data set name. If we executed the HARDCOPY CLIST in any mode without any parameters we would receive the following prompts and supply the same information

```
(prompt)      ENTER POSITIONAL PARAMETER A
(response)      'TSO1234.PRINT.TEXI'
(prompt)      ENTER POSITIONAL PARAMETER B
(response)      A
(prompt)      ENTER POSITIONAL PARAMETER C
(response)      2
(prompt)      ENTER POSITIONAL PARAMETER D
(response)      RMT3
```

Either way, the information supplied by positional parameters would be available to the CLIST in variables &A, &B, &C, and &D. In addition, any number of positional parameters could have been specified initially, with the rest picked up in a prompting mode. Notice that this last reference to variable names has them prefixed with the "&" symbol. This is how variables should always be noted in a CLIST except on the PROC statement. The ampersand is not allowed on the PROC statement, perhaps because it is understood that variables are being defined. It is not always necessary to use the ampersand to designate variables on other CLIST statements either, but it is a good practice. This practice will avoid confusing variables and literal character strings. It also makes for better-documented code and makes the variables easier to find with most text editors when changes become necessary.

Using nondescriptive variable names like &A, &B, &C, and &D is not a good idea when developing a CLIST for personal use, and even worse when the CLIST is to be used by others. A prompt to enter positional parameter A tells the CLIST user nothing about how to respond to the prompt. A more appropriate variable name might be &DSNAME because it hints that the user will have to type in a data set name. The variable name &PRINTDSNAME would be better still because it ties the function being performed (printing) to the type of information that is required. Remember that the user is allowed up to 252 characters to form a variable name that will be meaningful in a prompt to the CLIST user. Another advantage to using descriptive variable names is that the CLIST itself will be better documented and, therefore, easier to work with in the future. The revised PROC statement might be better coded

```
PROC 4 PRINTDSNAME PRINTCLASS COPIES DESTINATION
```

KEYWORD PARAMETERS

Keyword parameters must follow all positional parameters on the CLIST PROC statement. Other than that, keyword parameters can be specified in any order on the PROC statement of the CLIST, as well as when the CLIST is executed. This is because keyword values are paired with their variable names rather than relying on the order in which they are specified. Keywords are typically used to communicate noncritical or optional variable information to a CLIST. Because of this role, keyword parameters are not prompted for the way positional parameters are. Keyword parameters also differ from positional parameters in their ability to have an assigned default. The default, if any, would take effect if no value is given to the keyword as the CLIST is executed. Let us look at the PROC statement of the HARDCOPY CLIST again, after changing three of the four positional parameters into keywords. The statement would then be coded

```
PROC 1 PRINTDSNAME CLASS(A) COPIES(1) DEST(RMT0)
```

Notice that the position specification parameter has been changed from 4 to 1 to reflect the number of positional parameters now on the PROC statement. The name of the data set to be printed was retained as a positional parameter because it is the one piece of required information. It is hard to imagine a value which would be a suitable default for this parameter. Another obvious difference is the use of parentheses after the keyword-variable name. This is the standard format for keyword parameters that will be seen carried over to parameters in other CLIST statements. Think of the parentheses as a way to equate two things. In fact, if this were a JCL jobstream, one would see the COPIES variable coded as COPIES=1. Here the variable &COPIES is equated to the number one.

If the HARDCOPY CLIST containing the PROC statement above were executed specifying no parameters, the only prompt would be for PRINTDSNAME. The other variables, &CLASS, &COPIES, and &DEST, would take their values from what is coded on the PROC statement. Those values, then, constitute default values that can be overridden when the CLIST is executed. Because there is no prompting for keyword parameter information, keywords must be specified on the statement that is used to invoke the CLIST. Because all positional parameters must be specified first, the user cannot wait to go into a prompting mode if he or she wants to specify any keyword parameters.

Specifying defaults is a good coding practice when a keyword-variable value can be used that would be appropriate most of the time. For example, one might assume that most people who print a data set would only require one copy. That is why we changed the values from our original execution example. We assumed that most individuals would want one copy rather than two, and that most of the time they would want to use the main printer at RMT0 rather than the secondary printer at RMT3. These are the kinds of things that should be planned out before writing a CLIST. By setting defaults that can be used most of the time, a CLIST will be created that is much easier to use.

It might be noticed that in changing the positional parameters to keyword parameters we also changed the variable names. We would still like to use meaningful names, but the CLIST user will no longer see the variable name in a prompt for information. The user will now have to type in the variable name to equate it to a particular value. It would probably be wise to reach a compromise, then, between variable names that are easily understood and those that will not require an excessive amount of typing. The language, in fact, only supports keyword variable names up to thirty-one characters.

If that were not enough to think about, any parameter name, positional or keyword, should be planned around installation standards and conventions. For example, if all CLISTs use DEST as the destination of print output, it is easier for CLIST users to recognize that variable and know what to do with it. Conventions that exist in CLIST and other languages help to influence the choice of variable names. The variable name DEST is a prime example. DEST not only shows up as a different type of parameter on two different TSO commands, but it is also a parameter used in JCL. In all of these uses, it controls the routing of print output. That means that people familiar with either language will have a head start on recognizing and understanding the use of the variable.

What if we wanted to execute the HARDCOPY CLIST and send three copies of the data set to print class T? To execute the CLIST we would type:

```
%HARDCOPY 'TSO1234.PRINT.TEXT' COPIES(3) CLASS(T)
```

Notice that the DEST keyword was not coded. This indicates that we are willing to accept the default. Remember that keyword parameters that we supply can be specified in any order.

When the CLIST is executed in the explicit mode, all keyword and positional parameters would be grouped together in single quotes. Using the same example, this would be coded in the following manner:

```
EX HARDCOPY '''TSO1234.PRINT.TEXT'' COPIES(3) CLASS(T)'
```

Keyword parameters can also be used as an efficient means of initializing variables that were not meant to be modified by the CLIST user. By adding any number of variables as keywords to the PROC statement, the CLIST coder can supply them with an initial value. The need to support certain functions with initial variable values is the same in CLISTs as in most other programming languages. These variables might take the form of numeric counters, switches, or message literals. Using this method not only reduces the number of CLIST statements required, but also makes the CLIST more efficient to run.

MODIFIED KEYWORD PARAMETERS

A more restrictive use can be made of keywords that are specified on the PROC statement without a value. When used in this fashion, the keyword is only able to pass the name of the variable itself or a value of spaces. This sort of on-or-off condition is well-suited to the way most switches are used in programs. A classic example would be to use such a variable with a name like TRACE or DEBUG to determine whether or not debugging functions are to be turned on within the CLIST. Let us expand our PROC statement to include the variable &TRACE. The statement might then be coded

```
PROC 1 PRINTDSNAME CLASS(A) COPIES(1) DEST(RMTO) TRACE
```

The position of the keyword TRACE among other keyword parameters is not important. It is important, however, that it does not have parentheses like the other keyword parameters. This keeps the variable from accepting other values and also means that the only possible default would be a value of spaces. If the following statement

```
%HARDCOPY 'TSO1234.PRINT.TEXT' COPIES(3) CLASS(T) TRACE
```

is used to invoke the CLIST, the variable &TRACE will contain the value "TRACE." The CLIST logic could then test the variable &TRACE, turning the list function on if its value was "TRACE." If the word TRACE had not been typed on the statement that invokes the HARDCOPY CLIST, the variable &TRACE would have contained spaces. (See the chapter on debugging for a more detailed explanation of the use of modified keywords in controlling debugging options within a CLIST.)

DATA-DRIVEN PARAMETERS

As a final consideration for which type of parameter to use, we will look at the kind of data each will accept. Positional parameters will accept all data, including quotes. The quotes are treated as part of the data as it is conveyed to the variable. The ability to tolerate parentheses and retain quotes makes positional parameters ideally suited to convey data set names. Positional parameters have problems, however, accepting data that contains embedded spaces or commas, since they both serve as delimiters to separate parameters.

Keyword parameters are not well-suited to convey values that contain parentheses. This is because parentheses are normally used to set off the parameter value. They can handle embedded spaces, commas, and special characters (including parentheses) when they are enclosed in quotes. The quotes serve to define the parameter value literally. In so doing, they are stripped away as the value is passed to the CLIST.

The following code illustrates how keywords can be used to pass values that contain both spaces and commas. Coding

```
MESSAGE('DATA SET NOT FOUND, PLEASE TRY AGAIN.')
```

would pass the value

```
DATA SET NOT FOUND. PLEASE TRY AGAIN.
```

to the variable &MESSAGE. Notice that the quotes were stripped off of the parameter value. Keyword parameters can contain fully qualified data set names. The following code

```
DSN('''TSO1234.CLIST(HARDCOPY)''')
```

would pass the data set name

```
'TSO1234.CLIST(HARDCOPY)'
```

to the variable &DSN. Here it is necessary to code three consecutive quotes to have one retained in the parameter value.

HALTING CLIST EXECUTION

Once a CLIST has started executing, the user may have occasion to want to stop it before its normal end. There are many reasons for wanting to do this. One of the most common is having executed the wrong CLIST or having supplied the wrong parameter information. Maybe the user wants to stop the CLIST from flooding the screen with information or looping uncontrollably. Before taking action to stop an executing CLIST, however, the user should consider the consequences. While most CLISTS can be safely stopped, there are some which contain processing that should not be. These almost exclusively fall into the category of CLISTs that write over existing information. That might be an important output-data set that is used elsewhere or a data set that is itself rewritten. An example of this is the compression of a partitioned data set. Because such a process typically writes over the original PDS, it should never be interrupted. When writing a CLIST for use by others that falls into this category, it is important that a message be written to the screen warning the user not to interrupt the CLIST execution be written.

There are three keys on the keyboard that can be used to interrupt a CLIST. These keys are PA1, ATTN, and SYS REQ and should be used in that order. That is to say, once the user has decided to interrupt the CLIST, he or she should first try the Program Access 1 key. If this fails to stop the CLIST, try the attention key. The last attempt to stop the CLIST should be the system request key, since it will physically disconnect the TSO session and allow the user to logoff.

Version 2 enhancements

With version 2 of TSO/E, the EXEC command has parameters for identifying the type of code to be executed. The parameters are CLIST and EXEC, which identify CLIST and REXX EXEC code respectively. CLIST is a default when no value is specified and need not be used to execute a CLIST. There is, therefore, no need to alter the procedures detailed earlier in this chapter.

Another enhancement available with version 2 is the addition of the ALTLIB command. This command can be used to add two additional levels of libraries to the SYSPROC file search for implicitly invoked CLISTs. User and application levels can be added (in that order) in front of system-level libraries. The ALTLIB command works in conjunction with an ALLOCATE command to activate any of the three levels.

With all three levels active, the user level is searched first. This would be all libraries allocated to the file name SYSUPROC. Where multiple libraries are concatenated to the file, they are searched in the order that they were specified on the ALLOCATE command. The application-level libraries are searched next. That level can be paired with any file name. The system-level libraries are still paired with the file name of SYSPROC and they are the last in the search sequence.

Application-level libraries can also be specified from the ALTLIB command using a DATASET keyword. The command below

```
ALTLIB ACTIVATE APPLICATION(CLIST) DA(FINANCE.CLIST)
```

activates the application level with a single CLIST library, prefix.FINANCE.CLIST.

The ALTLIB command can also be used to display the search order or deactivate any of the three library levels. Below is an example of all three ALTLIB command functions:

```
ALLOC F(SYSUPROC) DA(TEST.CLIST)   SHR   REUSE
ALTLIB ACTIVATE USER(CLIST)
ALTLIB DISPLAY
.

.
ALTLIB DEACTIVATE USER(CLIST)
```

Before the user-library level is activated, its file name SYSUPROC is paired with a CLIST library using the ALLOCATE command. The next command actually activates the user-level search. The third statement uses the ALTLIB command to display the search order, and at the end of processing, the user level is deactivated.

The information we have seen in this chapter can be used to execute existing CLISTs, and should be used 'to increase the usability of CLISTs as they are constructed. In Chap. 6 we will see how the PROC statement fits into other CLIST code and how the variable information it conveys can be utilized. We will turn our attention next, however, to creating simple CLISTs that are a combination of TSO commands.

CLISTs as a Combination of Commands

One of the simplest functions a CLIST can perform is to replay a TSO command or commands. This can have several advantages and represent a substantial savings in time and effort. Placing commands in a CLIST has the obvious benefit in reduced typing. Where a command sequence will have to be repeated, it can be placed in a CLIST and invoked with several keystrokes. The code typed into a CLIST data set is not lost like native TSO commands, which means that it can be reinvoked many times over its useful life. In addition, the code can be changed to meet new requirements or can serve as a model upon which to base similar code. The storage of TSO commands in CLIST data sets can also help in efforts to create and modify the command syntax until it executes properly.

A very simple example of such a CLIST is one that includes the TSO EDIT command with some of its subcommands. Such a CLIST follows below:

```
EDIT 'TSO1234.JCL(PRINTJOB)' OLD CNTL NONUM
C * 99 'USERIDS' 'TSO1234' ALL
SUBMIT
END NOSAVE
```

This CLIST changes every instance of the character string USERIDS to the value TSO1234 in the data set TSO1234.JCL(PRINTJOB). The data in that data set is then submitted to execute as a background job, and the edit session is ended without saving the changed data.

Another very simple example of such a CLIST is one that deletes several data sets before a job is reexecuted. This command can be issued each time the job must be executed, leaving the job free to create those data sets again. Aside from saving time, the CLIST would help to insure that the user did not forget to delete one or more of the data sets, creating data management problems. If one or more of the data sets cannot be deleted, a high return code is issued and a message is written to the terminal. The CLIST execution will continue to try to delete the subsequent data sets. The following is an example of what this simple CLIST might look like when coded to delete seven data sets:

```
DELETE 'TSO1234.TEST.STEP1.BACKUP.DATA'
DELETE 'TSO1234.TEST.STEP1.MESSAGE.OUTPUT'
DELETE 'TSO1234.TEST.STEP2.MASTER.DATA'
DELETE 'TSO1234.TEST.STEP2.TRANSACT.DATA'
DELETE 'TSO1234.TEST.STEP2.HISTORY.DATA'
DELETE 'TSO1234.TEST.STEP2.TRANSACT.REPORT'
DELETE 'TSO1234.TEST.STEP3.BALANCE.REPORT'
```

Another advantage to placing commands in a CLIST is that it can free the user from having to remember complex command parameters or command sequences. Even when the command being executed is one of the user's own CLISTs, it can be invoked from another CLIST. The HARDCOPY CLIST from the previous chapter is a perfect example. Assuming that a given data set will have to be printed out periodically, we can code the following simple CLIST and call it HC1.

```
HARDCOPY 'TSO1234.TEST.STEP3.BALANCE.REPORT' CLASS(A) +
COPIES(3) FCB(PRT4)
```

The CLIST above prints a balance-report data set. That CLIST can be invoked repeatedly by merely typing HC1. Not only does this expedite the task, but it also frees the CLIST user from having to remember the parameter syntax.

USING THE HELP FUNCTION

The TSO HELP command can be used to determine what TSO commands are available, including many that an individual may want to include in his or her CLISTs. The command issued with no other parameters will list the available commands. Some installations have wisely added documentation on commands and CLISTs that were developed in-house. For more detailed help with any particular command or CLIST, the user can typically enter the HELP command followed by the name of the command or CLIST. The HELP command can be abbreviated using the letter H. This shortened form of the command should be used in an ISPF environment to distinguish it from the ISPF help function. The HELP command is a good source of information for functions that could be included in CLISTs and to determine the required syntax.

The CLIST example below uses TSO commands in a logical sequence that is very familiar to those who use VSAM (*Virtual Storage Access Method*) data sets. The three TSO commands used are DELETE, DEFINE, and REPRO. The first command, DELETE, is used to remove the existing VSAM data set components. The next command, DEFINE, is used to re-allocate those components and provide their characteristics. The last command, REPRO, is used to load data into the newly created VSAM data set. Upon successful execution of the CLIST, a viable VSAM data set exists which can be used by many other applications. Following is the code for that CLIST. It includes a plus sign at the end of certain lines of code that allow the command to be continued on the next line without regard for leading spaces. A minus sign can also be used to continue a command, although it retains leading spaces on the next line:

```
DELETE 'TSO1234.VSAM'
DEFINE CLUSTER(    NAME('TSO1234.VSAM') +
                   VOLUME(TSO001) KEYS(22,0) +
                   RECORDSIZE(80,80) RECORDS(200,50) +
                   CONTROLINTERVALSIZE(3024) SHAREOPTIONS(1,3)) +
         DATA( NAME('TSO1234.VSAM.DATA') +
               CONTROLINTERVALSIZE(4096))
         INDEX( NAME('TSO1234.VSAM.INDEX') +
               CONTROLINTERVALSIZE(4096))
REPRO INDATASET('TSO1234.LOAD.VSAMDATA') +
               OUTDATASET('TSO1234.VSAM) REUSE
```

Not only would it be terribly inconvenient to type these three commands out each time it was necessary to recreate the data set, but the chance of typing that much information without making a mistake is not good. Adding just a single alternate index to the VSAM data set could more than double the amount of code required, as in the example below:

```
DELETE 'TSO1234.VSAM'
DEFINE CLUSTER(   NAME('TSO1234.VSAM') +
                  VOLUME(TSO001) KEYS(22,0) +
                  RECORDSIZE(80,80) RECORDS(200,50) +
                  CONTROLINTERVALSIZE(3024) SHAREOPTIONS(1,3)) +
          DATA( NAME('TSO1234.VSAM.DATA') +
                  CONTROLINTERVALSIZE(4096))
        INDEX( NAME('TSO1234.VSAM.INDEX') +
                  CONTROLINTERVALSIZE(4096))
REPRO INDATASET('TSO1234.LOAD.VSAMDATA') +
                  OUTDATASET('TSO1234.VSAM) REUSE
DEFINE ALTERNATEINDEX ( NAME('TSO1234.VSAM.ALTINDEX') +
                  VOLUME(TSO001) KEYS(8,7) +
                  RECORDSIZE(3024,3024) TRACKS(4,4) +
                  CONTROLINTERVALSIZE(3024) SHAREOPTIONS(1,3) +
                  RELATE('TSO1234.VSAM') +
                  UNIQUE NONUNIQUEKEY))
        DATA( NAME('TSO1234.VSAM.ALTINDEX.DATA')) +
      INDEX( NAME('TSO1234.VSAM.ALTINDEX.INDEX')) +
BLDINDEX INDATASET('TSO1234.VSAM') +
                  OUTDATASET('TSO1234.VSAM.ALTINDEX')
DEFINE PATH (NAME('TSO1234.VSAM.PATH') +
                  PATHENTRY('TSO1234.VSAM.ALTINDEX'))
```

The functions that create and link the VSAM data set components are logically related. Stored in a CLIST, they become easy to invoke. In addition, there would not be the worry each time about balancing the parentheses and other syntax difficulties. Nor would there be any difficulty remembering which data set component links to another component.

COMMON TSO COMMANDS

Below is a list of common TSO commands. Following each command is a brief summary of the command function. These commands can be included in replay-type CLISTs as well as resource-controlling and programmatic CLISTs. Some of these commands will be discussed in later chapters as they relate to the other two CLIST types. There are also certain, optionally available, compiled and assembled language-related commands that are not listed here.

ALLOCATE   This command is used to create space for new data sets or connect to existing data sets. This command will be covered in detail in the next chapter. ALLOC is an acceptable abbreviation for this command.

ALTLIB   This command is first available with version 2 of TSO/E. The command can be used to add two additional levels of libraries to the SYSPROC file search for implicity involved CLISTs.

ATTRIB   This command can be used to define data set characteristics. Those characteristics can then be used with the ALLOCATE command when creating or referencing data sets. ATTR is an acceptable abbreviation for this command.

CALL   This command is used to execute a program by pointing to a particular load library and member. It will be discussed further in Chap. 5.

CANCEL   This command is used to cancel jobs that are executing or are waiting to execute in a background mode. When the PURGE option is used it will also delete job sysout.

COPY   This is an optional command and may not be installed on all systems. The command is used to copy partitioned or sequential data sets. If the "TO" data set does not exist, the copy command will create it.

DEFINE   This command is used to create entries in the system catalog for data sets and VSAM objects. DEF is an acceptable abbreviation for this command.

DELETE   This command is used to delete data sets. This includes removing entries from the disk VTOC or system catalog for the specified data set(s). When the NOSCRATCH option is used, the data set is only uncataloged. DEL is an acceptable abbreviation for this command.

EDIT   This command provides a way to create data. The EDIT command also allows existing data to be modified. There is an extensive set of subcommands, and *E* is an acceptable abbreviation for this command.

END   This command can be used to terminate a command procedure. It will be discussed further in Chap. 5.

EXEC   This command allows CLIST code to be executed. As mentioned in the previous chapter, this could be done implicitly or explicitly. EX is an acceptable abbreviation for this command. With version 2 of TSO/E, REXX EXEC code also can be executed.

FORMAT   This is an optional command and may not be installed on all systems. The command is used to format data to provide text characteristics for printing. This includes control of page characteristics and headings. FORM is an acceptable abbreviation for this command.

FREE   This command deallocates resources that are provided at
            logon time or added with the ALLOCATE and ATTRIBUTE
            commands. This command will be discussed further in the
            next chapter and can also be invoked using the name UNAL-
            LOC.

HELP   This command displays text explanations of the various TSO
            commands and their subcommands. *H* is an acceptable abbre-
            viation for this command.

LINK   This command invokes the linkage-editor program to convert
            compiler output (object code) into executable load code. It can
            also be used to create nonexecutable load modules and to
            incorporate these load modules in an executable format.

LIST   This is an optional command and may not be installed on all
            systems. The command is used to display the contents of a
            data set at the terminal. *L* is an acceptable abbreviation for
            this command.

LISTALC   This command lists the resources that are allocated to the
            TSO session. LISTA is an acceptable abbreviation for this
            command.

LISTBC   This command lists the current broadcast message.
            Installations will typically leave messages in a broadcast data
            set that are of interest to all or most TSO users. LISTBC will
            access that data set and write the messages that it contains to
            the terminal. LISTB is an acceptable abbreviation for this
            command.

LISTCAT   This command lists information from the system catalog, par-
            ticularly information used to locate data sets. LISTC is an
            acceptable abbreviation for this command.

LISTDS   This command is used to list data set characteristics. LISTD is
            an acceptable abbreviation for this command.

LOADGO   This command can be used to convert compiler output (object
            code) into executable code and then execute it. The executable
            code is not permanently retained. LOAD is an acceptable
            abbreviation for this command.

LOGOFF   This command is used to terminate the TSO session.

MERGE   This is an optional command and may not be installed on all
            systems. The command is used to merge one data set into
            another. M is an acceptable abbreviation for this command.

OUTDES   This command was added with version 2 of TSO/E. It is used
            to define the characteristics of a SYSOUT data set. It is used
            like the ATTRIB command, and like that command, can be
            referenced on both ALLOCATE and FREE commands.

OUTPUT   This command can be used to print held sysout or turn it into a conventional disk data set. OUT is an acceptable abbreviation for this command.

PRINT   This command is used to print VSAM data sets. It is able to print parts of the data based on key value.

PROFILE   This command is used to change certain TSO session characteristics for an individual. PROF is an acceptable abbreviation for this command.

PROTECT   This command can be used to create or change a data set password. PROT is an acceptable abbreviation for this command.

RENAME   This command is used to change the name of a data set or a member of a data set. As demonstrated in Chap. 2, it can also be used to create an alias for a PDS member. REN is an acceptable abbreviation for this command.

REPRO   This command is used to copy data sets. As part of the copy process, REPRO is able to load and unload VSAM data sets.

RUN   This command can be used to compile load and execute the source code of selected languages. R is an acceptable abbreviation for this command.

SEND   This command is used to send messages to terminal users. SE is an acceptable abbreviation for this command.

STATUS   This command is used to check on the status of jobs running in the background.

SUBMIT   This command is used to read jobstreams into the system for background execution. SUB is an acceptable abbreviation for this command.

TERMINAL   This command is used to change terminal characteristics. TERM is an acceptable abbreviation for this command.

TEST   This command can be used to test a program and contains an extensive set of subcommands.

TIME   This command will display time and date information as well as CPU time, connect time, and service units used by the current TSO session.

VERIFY   This command is used to reconcile catalog information with actual VSAM data set information. VFY is an acceptable abbreviation for this command.

WHEN   This command can be used to conditionally execute functions based upon the return code of a program that immediately precedes it.

In the chapters that follow, we will look at more complex uses for a CLIST. TSO commands will play a large part in those CLISTs as well, and will become even more useful when they incorporate symbolic variable substitution (discussed in Chap. 6). In particular, the next chapter will make use of selected TSO commands to establish an environment that will support program execution.

5

Resource-Controlling Statements and Program Execution

A second category of CLIST involves using *commands* to control system resources. The function of such a CLIST is to establish the environment for foreground program execution. In this capacity, CLISTs can provide for foreground execution what JCL does for background execution, and the two languages become very much alike. Part of this similarity even extends into the language syntax itself. Part of the chapter will be devoted to translating JCL code into the CLIST language. In subsequent chapters we will see how other aspects of the language can give CLISTs much more versatility than JCL, even in regard to how it functions as a resource-controlling language.

Either mode of program execution, foreground or background, requires some knowledge of what the program needs in order to properly execute (see Program Considerations in Chap. 9). The primary resources to be dealt with in such a CLIST, or for that matter in JCL, are those required by the program's various files. In JCL, these resources are obtained using DD statements. In CLISTs, the equivalent statement is the ALLOCATE command which is the basis of a resource-controlling CLIST. With either DD statement or ALLOCATE command output data can readily be switched from one media to another or, in some cases, even eliminated. Before we look more closely at resource allocation, let us take a moment to examine the rules of statement formatting. These rules will help us build the statements used here and in subsequent chapters.

STATEMENT FORMATTING

CLIST statement and command parameters can be separated by spaces, commas, or both. Whether spaces or commas are used as the delimiter, the spacing between parameters of a CLIST statement is not important. A free format exists between parameters and also between subparameters. This gives the CLIST coder a great deal of flexibility in the appearance of the actual code. This flexibility should be put to good advantage to format the code in a structured format. The term structured format, here, refers to the alignment of related or conditional code to improve its readability. We will see more of this in Chap. 6, but one example includes starting all unconditionally executed statements in the same column while indenting those that are contingent upon a previous condition test. Another common practice is to indent all lines that represent a continuation of another line of code.

Just as with the use of TSO commands, there are two characters that allow a CLIST statement to be continued on the next line. These two characters are the arithmetic symbols + and −. The difference between the two characters is that the plus sign will remove leading blanks from the continuation line that follows, while the minus sign will cause leading spaces on the continued line to be retained. The removal of those leading blanks can be especially helpful when continuing a literal string on to a subsequent line. It is good coding practice to only break lines of a CLIST statement between parameters. The readability of a CLIST can also be enhanced by using blank lines within the CLIST code. This has the effect of making the lines of code between any two blank lines appear to be grouped together, but has no effect upon CLIST execution. Caution should be used, however, to not interrupt continued statements with blank lines. This would result in a syntax error.

The concept of positional and keyword parameters discussed in Chap. 3 for invoking CLISTs also applies to the CLIST code itself. Wherever a parameter and its value(s) are specified, they are specified in keyword format. As discussed previously, the keyword parameter is followed immediately by its value or values. As shown in the example below, these values are listed within parentheses with delimiters used only to separate multiple values.

```
keyword(value1 value2 ...)
```

Depending on the particular keyword parameter, multiple values may in turn be positional within the keyword. They are known as *positional subparameters*. One of the parameters discussed in this chapter is the SPACE keyword. This keyword accepts one or two numeric values. The first value specified always becomes the primary space value because the subparameters are positional. True positional parameters also exist, as in the OPENFILE statement. In that statement, the first string that follows the word OPENFILE is always interpreted as the file name. As we saw in Chap. 3, positional parameters are used to convey required information. In the case of the OPENFILE statement, the file name is required to determine what file should be opened. The access mode, if specified, is the second positional parameter. In general, any optional parameters would have to follow all positional parameters. We will now return to the subject of resource allocation and look at the fundamental ALLOCATE command and its many parameters.

FILE ALLOCATION

A *file* is a collection of information. Specifically, when used with computer programs, files can be thought of as the mechanism linking data with program execution. The data may take many forms and formats, but is always linked to a given program through a particular file name. File allocation is the process of allocating or assigning a particular data resource, whether it be disk, tape, or spooled data, to a given file. This must be done before the program can execute. To do otherwise would likely result in the abnormal end (ABEND) of the program. The ALLOCATE command is used to effect this connection. The command can also be abbreviated ALLOC and can be used in CLISTs or as a native TSO command.

CLISTs can also be coded to function as programs themselves, and as such, may also require file allocations to link to data resources for other CLIST services. As with JCL, superfluous files properly allocated will not harm program execution. This latter fact allows the ALLOCATE command to be used for data set maintenance even when the data maintained is not directly related to the execution of the program.

A subfunction of file allocation is the data set allocation process. This describes the actual creation of the data set itself, and may accompany the pairing of the data set to a specific file. In the case of a disk-resident data set, the data set creation process could set aside room for the data, define the characteristics of the data set, and give the data a name and volume to reside on.

ALLOCATION PARAMETERS

There are many *allocation parameters* available. All ALLOCATE command parameters are keywords, but not all must have a keyword value. All of the parameters are optional, although some parameters must be used in conjunction with other parameters. As with JCL, there are a few allocation parameters that are used fairly often. There are also parameters that will seldom be used. The following discussion of ALLOCATE command parameters will feature those that are used most often. These basic parameters will be mentioned first. The discussion of occasionally used parameters will follow in less detail.

File name

One of the most basic parameters is the *file name*. The FILE parameter is used to link data resources to programs that need the resource. The resource might be input information that the program will process, or a printer that the program will write to. The value for the FILE keyword is the name of the file within the program that the data resources are being paired with. This name is one to eight characters in length and is not arbitrary if it is used for program execution. When used for program execution, it must match what was coded in the program or CLIST. The following example uses a common utility file name, SYSUT2:

```
ALLOCATE FILE(SYSUT2)
```

The DDNAME keyword is an equivalent parameter. It merely provides the same mechanism for specifying the file name under a differently named keyword. The name itself is undoubtedly derived from the JCL parameter of the same name. The statement below is equivalent to the last example.

```
ALLOCATE DDNAME(SYSUT2)
```

Most CLIST coders seem to prefer the FILE keyword, and so it will be used in all subsequent examples. Neither statement above is yet complete, however. They will, instead, serve as the basis for building several complete ALLOCATE command examples. Each parameter will be added as it is discussed until we have built complete commands to allocate new and existing data sets.

The file-name parameter need not be coded if the ALLOCATE command is being used only to create a data set. This is also true when the ALLOCATE command is coded merely to effect some other form of data management (data deletion, cataloging or uncataloging). In this particular situation any file name or none can be used.

Data set name

Another frequently used parameter is DATASET or DSNAME. Both forms of the parameter are equivalent and are used to provide the name of a data set that is being created, maintained, or connected to a file for use in a program or CLIST. Below is our previous example with the DATASET keyword added.

```
ALLOCATE FILE(SYSUT2) DATASET('TSO1234.SEQ.DATA')
```

As mentioned earlier, if a data set name is enclosed in single quotes, it is taken literally. Another way to have specified this particular data set name would be to omit the quotes, and begin with the second data set qualifier SEQ. In this latter instance, TSO would append the user-ID TSO1234 to derive the full name. The reader might want to refer to Chap. 2 for syntax rules that must be followed in creating a data set name.

The ability to specify a temporary data set name does not exist here as it does with JCL. It is possible, however, to write to a disk file that has no data set name. In this case, a system-temporary data set name is generated just as it would be in background processing. The data set is not permanently saved either, but it is not deleted until the file it is allocated to is freed. Because the CLIST did not supply the temporary data set name, subsequent data set name reference is not possible in a CLIST the way it is in JCL. Any such backward reference would have to be done, instead, using the file name. The effect of a temporary data set can also be obtained by using a permanent data set name and deleting the data set from within the CLIST when it is no longer required.

An asterisk in place of the data set name has a special significance. This indicates that data is transferred to or from the terminal rather than to or from a data set. This alternative will be discussed in more detail later with the discussion of instream data.

The data set name keyword is also capable of accepting a value that is a list of data sets. The process of assigning multiple data sets to a single file is know as data set *concatenation*. The process was discussed earlier when it was suggested that multiple CLIST libraries could be concatenated to the special system file SYSPROC. That example looked like this:

```
ALLOC F(SYSPROC) DA('TOS1234.CLIST' 'SYS1.CLIST' 'PUBLIC.CLIST') +
```

SHR REUSE

It is only possible, and in fact only logical, to concatenate input data sets. These data sets must have the same data set organization (all sequential or all partitioned) and compatible characteristics (like record length). When sequential data sets are concatenated, all such data sets are read in turn. End-of-file is not detected until after the last record of the last listed data set. When partitioned data sets are concatenated, a member search would involve all listed libraries, in order, until the member is found or all directories are exhausted and the member cannot be found. In the above example, three libraries become eligible for an automatic search to locate a given CLIST member being implicitly invoked.

Data set dispositions

There are two parameters in the above example that we have not yet discussed. One of those is the *disposition parameter*. This parameter describes what to do with the data set. There are two types of disposition for a data resource. These are the current data set disposition and the ending disposition. The dispositions are similar to those in JCL and also carry many of the same defaults. If no disposition is specified for a data set, the default is NEW and to CATALOG the data set. This means that the data set is being created, and an entry will be made in the system catalog to keep track of the volume residence of the data set.

The disposition in the last example (for allocating CLIST libraries) is SHR. This shared disposition allows concurrent use of existing data set(s) by multiple tasks and is therefore appropriate for a read-only mode. Other tasks that also allocate the resource with a disposition of SHR would be able to read the data at the same time. Other dispositions that indicate the current status and handling of the data set are:

NEW   This indicates that the data set does not yet exist but is to be created. When the disposition is NEW, additional data-set characteristics may have to be specified in the ALLOC command. When NEW is specified as the current disposition, the default ending disposition is CATALOG.

OLD   This indicates that the data set already exists and should have an exclusive enqueue placed upon it. With this disposition giving exclusive use of the data set, the data set can be opened for either input or output. If the program or CLIST opens the corresponding data set for output, the current data set content is completely written over with new data. A disposition of OLD should be avoided when the intent is merely to read the data. This will prevent unnecessary contention problems which cause other users or jobs to wait before they can read the same data set. When OLD is specified as the current disposition, the default ending disposition is KEEP.

MOD   This indicates that a sequential data set already exists and will have data appended to the end of the data that already exists. MOD can be used to extend a sequential data set, but cannot be used to extend an existing PDS member. If the data set does not yet exist, it can be created with MOD, as if a disposition of NEW had been specified. When MOD is specified as the current disposition, the default ending disposition is CATALOG for a new data set and KEEP for an existing data set.

Other dispositions can be specified that indicate the final disposition or handling of the data set. Some of these dispositions have been mentioned as defaults that may result from the use of a particular current disposition. The dispositions that determine the final status of a data set are listed below:

CATALOG   This indicates that the data set should be retained and its unit and volume information recorded in the system catalog. The system catalog keeps track of where data sets reside and makes data set retrieval much easier. It is, therefore, advisable to catalog all permanent data sets. This is the default when a starting disposition of NEW is specified.

KEEP   This indicates that the data set should be retained. This is used where the data set is already cataloged or no catalog entry is desired. KEEP is the default when a starting disposition of OLD is specified.

DELETE   This indicates that the data set should be deleted. When a data set is deleted, entries are removed from the disk VTOC (*Volume Table of Contents*) and the system catalog.

UNCATALOG   This indicates that the data set exists and should be retained but removed from the system catalog.

Unit-residence parameters

There are two ALLOCATE command parameters, *UNIT* and *VOLUME,* that deal with unit residence. These parameters can determine the volume placement of newly created data sets, or help to retrieve existing data sets. The use of these two parameters is minimized by the convenience provided by the system catalog and the fact that most installations have established acceptable defaults for where new data sets are allocated. The parameters are very useful, however, when a data set must, for some reason, be placed on a specific volume.

There may be valid reasons for maintaining uncataloged data sets, like the need to maintain multiple versions of the same data set, since only one data set with a particular data set name can be cataloged at a given time. The UNIT and VOLUME parameters can be used to point to the specific volume or volumes that contain an uncataloged data set. The following illustrates the parameters used to point to an existing data set on a 3380 disk with the volume serial number SYSTM4.

```
ALLOC F(ISPLLIB) DA('SYS1.LINKLIB') SHR UNIT(3380) VOLUME(SYSTM4)
```

The UNIT parameter above uses a specific device type to provide unit-residence information. Many installations have defined generic or esoteric unit names that can be helpful when creating data sets. These generic names usually refer to a number of eligible volumes. This is particularly helpful when a data set must be placed on a disk volume with certain characteristics, but the particular volume used is not important. In a case such as this, the VOLUME parameter can be omitted and an appropriate volume is automatically selected. When the VOLUME parameter is utilized, it references the name of one or more disk or tape volumes. When multiple volumes are specified, they are separated by spaces or commas.

```
VOLUME(SYSTM4 SYSTM7)
```

FILE-CHARACTERISTIC PARAMETERS

ALLOCATE command parameters are also used to define the characteristics of a data set. Many of these seem to have evolved from their JCL counterparts. Like their JCL counterparts, these parameters need only be specified when a new data set is being created. The characteristics of an existing disk data set need not be specified since they can be read from the data set label contained in the volume table of contents or VTOC. On a standard label tape, such information can be read from the header labels that precede the data. Three of the these file characteristic parameters take on increased importance when a data set is created. They are the record format, record length, and blocksize parameters. Their importance is based, in part, upon the fundamental nature of the characteristics they define.

Record format

The first of the three basic parameters is *RECFM,* or the *record format parameter.* This parameter defines the type of data set record as fixed, variable, or undefined. It can also define whether the data set is blocked or spanned, and whether the records contain printer carriage-control information. Below is a list of the values that can be included with the RECFM keyword. Each is a single letter that can be used in combination with other letter codes. When multiple codes are specified, they can be specified in any order, but must be separated from all other codes using spaces or commas:

F   indicates fixed-length records. Every record in the data set is the same length as every other record in that same data set.

V   indicates variable length records. Each record in the data set could be a different length up to a specified maximum.

U   indicates undefined. Each record in the data set can vary in length and is the same length as the blocksize.

B   indicates that the records are blocked with more than one logical record per physical record (also known as a block).

S   indicates that records can span from one block into the next.

A   indicates that the first byte of the data set is used for ASCII carriage-control characters.

M   indicates that the first byte of the data set is used for machine carriage-control characters.

Below we see the result of adding the RECFM keyword to a previous example. The statement is directed toward creating a new data set and associating it with a file named SYSUT2.

```
ALLOCATE FILE(SYSUT2) DATASET('TSO1234.SEQ.DATA') NEW CATALOG +
UNIT(3380) VOLUME(SYSTM4) RECFM(F B A)
```

The values coded in the RECFM parameter indicate that all records are of a single fixed length, that there are multiple records per block, and that the records contain printer carriage-control information. Notice that each of the letter codes used is separated by spaces. Separation by space or comma delimiters is required for values of this particular parameter. Even with the addition of the RECFM (and disposition parameters NEW and CATALOG), the command is still incomplete.

Record length

The *LRECL* parameter is another fundamental parameter which describes file characteristics. This parameter is coded with a numeric value that indicates the length of records in a data set. Again, this parameter is typically only needed when a new data set is being created. There are even circumstances where data set characteristics need not be specified for data sets being created. This is true when a program is executed that is able to supply this information. Many programs already specify this information through file-control sections, data descriptions, or open statements. Many utility programs create default characteristics or pass on the characteristics read from other data sets.

For fixed-length records, the LRECL parameter indicates the number of bytes or columns of data contained in each record. For variable length records, the LRECL parameter indicates the maximum length that any single record can attain. The record length used for a data set with variable length records is four bytes more than the maximum data length. These four bytes are used to hold the *Record Descriptor Word* (RDW). The RDW is unique to variable-length records and indicates the length of each individual record. In most applications, these four bytes are stripped off the front of each record and never seen by the application. Room for the RDW must, however, be accounted for in the record length. Below is our ALLOCATE command example with the record-length keyword added:

```
ALLOCATE FILE(SYSUT2) DATASET('TSO1234.SEQ.DATA') NEW CATALOG +
UNIT(3380) VOLUME(SYSTM4) RECFM(F B A) LRECL(133)
```

Blocksize

The last of the basic file characteristic parameters is the *blocksize* parameter. This parameter is coded BLKSIZE(xxxxx) where xxxxx is the numeric value of the blocksize. The blocksize is actually the input or output buffer set aside for file-data transfer. In the case of fixed-length records, the blocksize must be a multiple of the record length (LRECL). This is not true for variable-length records since each record could well be a different length. The blocksize for variable-length records should, however, be at least four bytes greater than the record length. Just as four bytes are added to each record to indicate the record length, four bytes are added to each block to indicate the block length. These four bytes are the *Block Descriptor Word* or BDW. The minimum variable blocksize, then, should allow for at least one data record of maximum length plus four bytes for the RDW and another four bytes for the BDW.

The blocksize determines how much data is transferred in a physical I/O operation. The larger the blocksize, the more logical records it will contain and fewer physical input and output operations will have to be performed. This makes the data-transfer process more efficient. Another reason to use large blocksizes is that they store large amounts of data more efficiently.

```
ALLOCATE FILE(SYSUT2) DATASET('TSO1234.SEQ.DATA') NEW CATALOG +
UNIT(3380) VOLUME(SYSTM4) RECFM(F B A) LRECL(133) BLKSIZE(23408)
```

Notice in the example above that a large blocksize is used and that the blocksize is an even multiple of the record length because the records are fixed in length.

DISK-SPACE PARAMETERS

There are several parameters that pertain to obtaining *space* on a disk volume. Before we discuss these parameters, we will cover basic information about disk data sets in general. Each disk data set must have space reserved for it on at least one volume. The space for a data set on a particular volume can be fragmented in up to sixteen pieces or *extents*. These extents are defined as some number of blocks, tracks, or cylinders which are also called *allocation units* and describe some portion of a disk volume.

Each disk data set can have both primary and secondary space allocated to it. Primary space is obtained when the data set is first defined. Secondary space is added if and when it is needed, until all sixteen data set extents are used up, or there is no more space available on the disk volume. The amount of total space a data set may consume on a single disk volume depends on the type of allocation units (blocks, tracks, or cylinders), the number of primary and secondary units specified, and the number of units or extents consumed to obtain the primary space amount. For example, if a data set takes three extents to obtain its primary space, it would have only thirteen secondary extents that could be used for later expansion. If, however, the primary space was obtained in a single extent, the data set would still have fifteen secondary extents with which to expand.

A data set can have directory blocks allocated to it when it is defined. The addition of directory blocks creates a special type of data set mentioned before and known as a *Partitioned Data Set* (PDS) or library. To simplify matters, we will assume at this point that a data set created without directory blocks is a sequential data set. A PDS is actually a collection of multiple sequential data sets indexed by a directory, and it can have several advantages over regular sequential data sets. We have already discussed the advantage it may have in the search for executable code. This was demonstrated with multiple CLIST libraries concatenated to the SYSPROC system file. Some types of data, like executable programs, must be stored in a PDS. A PDS is usually able to store small data sets more efficiently, and is also an excellent way to group related data together. We will see how this information translates into actual ALLOCATE command parameters.

Allocation units

As mentioned earlier, there are three *allocation units* that can be used as the basis for defining how much disk space a data set can consume. The allocation units, BLOCKS, TRACKS, and CYLINDERS, all describe some portion of a disk volume. For example, there are typically some number of blocks in each track, some number of tracks in each cylinder, and some number of cylinders on each addressable volume. The relation of one allocation unit to another differs depending upon the blocksize used and the disk-device type. For example, on a standard 3380 disk device, using a blocksize of 6,233 bytes, there would be seven blocks per track. That will also affect how much data can be stored on the disk's fifteen tracks per cylinder and 885 cylinders. Other disk-device types may have a different number of cylinders or tracks per cylinder.

When the allocation units are specified in blocks, the word BLOCK is coded with the actual size of a block enclosed in parentheses. When the BLKSIZE parameter is also coded, the value of each parameter should agree, since they both represent the size of a block of data. Below is our previous example with the BLOCK parameter added.

```
ALLOCATE FILE(SYSUT2) DATASET('TSO1234.SEQ.DATA') NEW CATALOG +
   UNIT(3380) VOLUME(SYSTM4) RECFM(F B A) LRECL(133) BLKSIZE(23408) +
   BLOCK(23408)
```

The BLOCK parameter is the only one of the three allocation unit parameters that contains a value. That is because there is a lot of flexibility in what blocksize is used. When TRACK or CYLINDER is specified, they have no value because the size of either is fixed by the unit-device type. Each allocation-unit type has its own advantages. Allocation in blocks is most flexible over different device types and makes calculating space requirements very simple. The basic or minimum allocation unit, however, is a track. Allocation in tracks makes the monitoring of space consumption easier and gives greater flexibility in the release of unused space than does allocation in cylinders.

Allocation in cylinders carries with it a certain efficiency in the I/O transfer of data in large data sets because multiple tracks are aligned on a cylinder boundary and therefore would minimize the need to reposition the disk read/write heads.

Primary and secondary space

The amount of space available to a disk data set is determined by both *primary* and *secondary space amounts*. These are specified using the SPACE keyword. Within the keyword, the two values are positional with the primary space amount coded first. When the SPACE parameter is used, a primary space value must always be coded. The secondary space value is optional. Secondary space need only be specified if subsequent data set expansion is a requirement, but should probably be routinely included on most data sets to avoid running out of space. The SPACE parameter works in conjunction with the allocation units parameters. We saw that the allocation units could be BLOCKS, TRACKS, or CYLINDERS. The SPACE parameter requests some number of these units. Let us add the SPACE parameter to the ALLO-CATE command we are developing and examine it in further detail.

```
ALLOCATE FILE(SYSUT2) DATASET('TSO1234.SEQ.DATA') NEW CATALOG +
UNIT(3380) VOLUME(SYSTM4) RECFM(F B A) LRECL(133) BLKSIZE(23408) +
BLOCK(23408) SPACE(15 5)
```

Notice that the values for primary and secondary space are separated by a space. A comma could also have been used to separate the two values. The primary space value of 15 indicates that fifteen blocks will be obtained when the data set is first defined. Each of these blocks will be 23,408 bytes in size as indicated by both the BLOCK and BLK-SIZE parameters. If the allocation units had been TRACKS, then fifteen tracks would have been obtained. If the allocation units had been CYLINDERS, fifteen cylinders or 255 tracks would be reserved for the data set on this type of disk device. This is because each cylinder on a 3380 disk device has fifteen tracks. Getting back to the coded example above, the request for fifteen blocks would provide an initial allocation of eight tracks. On a 3380 disk device, each track could accommodate two blocks each with a blocksize of 23,408. This would translate to seven and a half tracks, except that a complete track is the minimum allocation unit. The space obtained is, therefore, rounded up to the next complete track.

Our example has secondary space coded to allow the data set to expand. If more than the initial eight tracks are needed when writing to the data set, secondary extents can automatically be added as needed. The secondary space parameter above requests five blocks. That would cause three tracks to be added every time a secondary extent was required. Again, the space obtained is actually more than was requested because the minimum allocatable unit is a complete track. Five blocks of 23,408 bytes each would have otherwise been two and a half tracks since two 23,408 byte blocks will fit on a track. The secondary space allocation can be added up to fifteen times. This would result in a maximum data set size of fifty-three tracks. This value is derived by multiplying the number of tracks in each secondary extent, in this case three, by the number of extents that can be obtained, fifteen. That result, forty-five, is then added to the space that was obtained in the primary space allocation, eight, to arrive at the maximum of fifty-three tracks.

Almost all data sets should be allocated with secondary space. If this flexibility is not built in to a data set, the probability of encountering an *abend* (*Abnormal End* or termination of program processing) becomes very significant. The data set would then typically have to be reallocated with more space before processing could be restarted. On the other hand, data sets that are used a lot should not be left fragmented in many secondary extents. Because secondary extents are only obtained when they are actually needed, they are not likely to be physically located near other extents for the same data set. This could significantly reduce the efficiency of input and output processing. Such data sets should also be reallocated periodically even if they have not run out of space yet. The goal here is to make the primary space amount at least large enough to accommodate all of the current data. Making the data space contiguous in this way would make input and output processing more efficient and free secondary extents that could again allow for future expansion of the data set.

The ALLOCATE command that we have been building is now complete and would serve to create a sequential data set and associate it with a file named SYSUT2. This statement does not use all of the ALLOCATE command parameters that could be applied to a sequential data set, but would still be sufficient in virtually all instances where it was necessary to create a sequential disk data set. Later in this chapter, we will see how certain circumstances will allow some of these parameters to be removed.

Before we proceed to other ALLOCATE command parameters, let us briefly review the meaning of the parameters below in the order they are coded.

```
ALLOCATE FILE(SYSUT2) DATASET('TSO1234.SEQ.DATA') NEW CATALOG +
   UNIT(3380) VOLUME(SYSTM4) RECFM(F B A) LRECL(133) BLKSIZE(23408) +
   BLOCK(23408) SPACE(15 5)
```

The first line of code identifies the statement as an ALLOCATE command with parameters that name the file that resources are allocated to, identifies the resource as a data set and supplies its name and indicates that the data set will be created and also entered into the system catalog. Line two requests that the data set be placed on a 3380 disk device that has a volume serial number of SYSTM4. It also defines the characteristics of the data set records as being fixed in length with multiple logical records per physical record or block. It also indicates that the first byte of the record is used to contain printer carriage-control information. The last line of the ALLOCATE command example defines the allocation unit size as blocks that are each 23,408 bytes. It also requests fifteen of the blocks from the disk volume immediately with five more blocks of space up to fifteen times later as the space is needed.

Disk space release

There are instances when a data set should be allocated with the minimum amount of disk space possible. This is especially true of many sequential data sets, and especially where subsequent expansion is not anticipated. Many data sets are written once and have no need for subsequent growth. In this case, the *RELEASE parameter* should be added to the ALLOCATE command as in the example below:

```
ALLOCATE FILE(SYSUT2) DATASET('TSO1234.SEQ.DATA') NEW CATALOG +
   UNIT(3380) VOLUME(SYSTM4) RECFM(F B A) LRECL(133) BLKSIZE(23408) +
   BLOCK(23408) SPACE(15 5) RELEASE
```

This would cause any unused space to be released when the data set is deallocated. That is true whether the space is primary or secondary. Including secondary space and allowing unused space to be released from the same ALLOCATE command is not really incongruent. Secondary space builds flexibility into a data set, and can even be utilized after unused space is released. It should be noted that only totally unused units can be released. The units here refer to either tracks or cylinders and relate back to the allocation units parameter. If the data set was allocated with either TRACKS or BLOCKS, then only completely unused tracks can be released (remember that the minimum allocation actually occurs in tracks, not blocks). If the data set was allocated in CYLINDERS, then only completely unused cylinders can be released. If disk space is at a premium, and it always seems to be, then consider allocating space in tracks to maximize what can be released.

Another ALLOCATE command parameter, *ROUND*, can be used

with larger data sets allocated in tracks. This parameter would cause the tracks obtained to be aligned on cylinder boundaries. This retains the advantage of space release at the track level while it adds the I/O efficiency benefits of obtaining space at the cylinder level. When data is read or written from tracks on a cylinder boundary, no movement of the read/write heads is required, and so the data-transfer process is more efficient.

Directory space

With a single parameter, we can change our ALLOCATE command to create a PDS rather than a sequential data set. The DIRECTORY parameter *DIR* reserves the specified number of directory blocks from the space obtained using the SPACE parameter. It is these directory blocks that distinguish a PDS from a regular sequential data set. Note in the example below, the DIRECTORY parameter has been added to the end of the ALLOCATE command to request fifteen directory blocks.

```
ALLOCATE FILE(SYSPROC) DATASET('TSO1234.CLIST') NEW CATALOG +
    UNIT(3380) VOLUME(SYSTM4) RECFM(F B) LRECL(80) BLKSIZE(6240) +
    TRACKS SPACE(3 1) DIRECTORY(15)
```

Each of these directory blocks is 256-bytes long. Directory entries vary somewhat for different types of data sets and how the data was written to the data set. The number of directory entries that each block can hold will vary depending on how much information each entry contains. As a minimum, however, each directory entry will contain the name of a member and a pointer to where that member resides in the data space. A member is essentially a sequential data set of its own. Those with like characteristics can be grouped together in a PDS to save space and make related data easier to locate.

Other characteristics have been changed in the example above to highlight the preferred use of a PDS. The example, in fact, is the familiar example of creating a CLIST library and connecting it to the SYSPROC file to allow implicit invocation of CLIST code. A PDS is more efficient at storing numerous smaller data sets. To accommodate this fact, the space request has been reduced and the RELEASE parameter has been removed. The data set characteristics were changed to be more appropriate for a CLIST library, and the data set and file names were changed.

As we mentioned before, the SYSPROC file is a special system file used to connect CLIST libraries. As such it was probably already allocated to the TSO session at LOGON. Files normally have to be freed before they can be allocated again. By merely adding an additional parameter to our last ALLOCATE command example, we can bypass that process. That parameter is *REUSE*. It allows a previously allocated file to be reused without first being freed.

```
ALLOCATE FILE(SYSPROC) DATASET('TSO1234.CLIST') NEW CATALOG +
   UNIT(3380) VOLUME(SYSTM4) RECFM(F B) LRECL(80) BLKSIZE(6240) +
   TRACKS SPACE(3 1) DIR(15) REUSE
```

We will discuss the process used to free files and other resources later in this chapter. The REUSE parameter, however, should routinely be included in any ALLOCATE command. This would avoid problems with files that are already allocated even if just because the same ALLOCATE command had been previously executed.

THE ATTRIBUTE LIST PARAMETER

An alternative to specifying the file characteristics on the ALLOC command is to include them in a named *attribute list* that is created using the ATTRIB command. The attribute list would then be referenced by name by one or more ALLOC commands to make use of its defined characteristics. The ALLOC command parameter used to make the reference is the USING keyword. The value of the keyword is, of course, the name (much like a file name) given to the attribute list. This is an archaic process that is not recommended because the CLIST code is better documented when file characteristics are included on the ALLOC command itself. Another drawback is that attribute lists often need to be freed like files or data sets. Below is an example of how the ATTRIB command can be used.

```
CONTROL NOMSG
FREE ATTR(DCB1)
CONTROL MSG
ATTR DCB1 RECFM(F B) LRECL(80) BLKSIZE(6240) DSORG(PO)
ALLOC DA(NEW.PDS1) USING(DCB1) SP(1 1) TR DIR(3)
ALLOC DA(NEW.PDS2) USING(DCB1) SP(1 1) TR DIR(3) BLKSIZE(23440)
CONTROL NOMSG
FREE ATTR(DCB1)
```

In the example above, an attribute list is created using the ATTRIB command (abbreviated ATTR). The attribute list name DCB1 is freed at the beginning and end of the process to ensure its availability (the FREE command and surrounding CONTROL statements are discussed later in this chapter). It is given specific record format, record length, block size, and data set organization information. The attribute list is then referenced by two ALLOCATE commands that create new partitioned data sets. The second of those commands overrides one of the specified characteristics, the block size, by including its new value.

REQUIRED PARAMETERS

Knowing what the system defaults are can make coding the ALLOCATE command much easier. These defaults can be determined quite easily with a little experimentation. For example, try removing the UNIT and VOLUME parameters and see where the system places the data set. If the placement is acceptable, those two parameters can be removed, reducing the amount of information needed to be coded and, at the same time, making the code more flexible. The code is more flexible because it is less susceptible to changes. Such changes might include the volume being taken off-line, removed, renamed, or just running out of free space. Below is the example presented earlier for creating a sequential data set. The code that can be removed when default data set placement is acceptable is included but not highlighted.

```
ALLOCATE FILE(SYSUT2) DATASET('TSO1234.SEQ.DATA') NEW CATALOG +
   UNIT(3380) VOLUME(SYSTM4) RECFM(F B A) LRECL(133) BLKSIZE(23408) +
   BLOCK(23408) SPACE(15 5) RELEASE REUSE
```

Another default that would be acceptable in this particular case is the data set disposition. When no disposition is specified, the defaults are NEW and CATALOG for the initial and ending dispositions respectively. In this case, it is the interaction of other parameters that create the default values. The default value of NEW for the initial disposition is mandated by the request for disk space. The default value of CATALOG for the ending disposition would result from having coded a data set name. Again, the ALLOCATE command example is shown below. The UNIT and VOLUME parameters have been removed, and the disposition parameters that can be removed are no longer highlighted.

```
ALLOCATE FILE(SYSUT2) DATASET('TSO1234.SEQ.DATA') NEW CATALOG +
   RECFM(F B A) LRECL(133) BLKSIZE(23408) BLOCK(23408) SPACE(15 5) +
   RELEASE REUSE
```

Again, executing the code above without the parameters NEW and CATALOG will provide immediate feedback on the acceptability of the defaults.

The characteristics that describe a data set can come from three different sources. We have discussed the three most common attributes, RECFM, LRECL, and BLKSIZE. Bringing these and other attributes together is sometimes referred to as the *DSCB merge*. The order of the merge includes information obtained from the executing program, the resource language, and finally, from the data set label. The data set label in the case of a disk data set is the DSCB. It is only a potential source of information if the data set already exists. That is not the case here, because the ALLOCATE command we have coded is designed to create a new data set. Depending on the executing program, however, this information may be provided for us. Let us look at two examples. In the first example, we wish to invoke the standard system utility to copy an existing sequential data set to the one being created in the ALLOCATE command example. The program we would execute is IEBGENER. This program is fairly flexible and is able to obtain the characteristics of the data set being copied and supply them to the data set being created.

If the data set were being written to by an application program written in COBOL, the information could be obtained from the FILE CONTROL SECTION and the DATA DIVISION of the program. This information, in turn, could be supplied to the data set being created and would not need to be specified. These are two examples of how programs can supply the data set attribute information. In cases such as these, the information need not be included in the ALLOCATE command. Below, the disposition parameters have been removed from the example, and the DSCB parameters that can be removed are no longer highlighted.

```
ALLOCATE FILE(SYSUT2) DATASET('TS01234.SEQ.DATA') RECFM(F B A) +
LRECL(133) BLKSIZE(23408) BLOCK(23408) SPACE(15 5) +
RELEASE REUSE
```

Under the conditions just described, the resultant command need only account for the file name, the data set name, and the space request.

```
ALLOCATE FILE(SYSUT2) DATASET('TS01234.SEQ.DATA') BLOCK(23408) +
SPACE(15 5) RELEASE REUSE
```

The RELEASE and REUSE parameters are optional, but represent good coding practice and so are retained in the example. Remember, the best way to determine the minimum information required is to remove a particular parameter and execute the statement. If the desired result is still obtained, then the parameter is not really required.

ALLOCATING PRINT RESOURCES

The ALLOCATE comand is also used to connect to print resources. This is done using the SYSOUT parameter rather than a current disposition. *SYSOUT* is short for *System Output,* and causes data written to the associated file to be spooled to the job entry subsystem (JES). From there, the data waits until selected by an output device. The following statement would allow data associated with the file, SYSUT2, to be written to output class *A.* It is all that is needed to direct print output.

```
ALLOCATE FILE(SYSUT2) SYSOUT(A)
```

The first parameter of the statement should look very familiar by now. It associates whatever else follows with a particular file name. The SYSOUT parameter indicates that a system output data set will be written to the output class of *A.* The output class value need not be coded, if the system assigned default is acceptable.

```
ALLOCATE FILE(SYSUT2) SYSOUT
```

Output classes are typically defined around certain characteristics. These characteristics vary by installation. Some of the characteristics that might be considered in defining these output classes include amount of output, requirements for special forms, special distribution requirements, special breakdown or trimming requirements, whether or not the output is from a production job, and sensitivity or special security that might be attached to the printed output. Using these and other factors, an installation is able to define output classes that give them better control over what prints where, how, and when. Control is achieved when a printer is started by an operator and directed to print a certain class or classes of output. The user's print data waits until it is selected by a printer designated to print that particular output class. After printing, the system output data set is deleted.

Other parameters can be added to this basic statement to change various characteristics of the print output. Several of these parameters (COPIES, FCB, DEST, AND HOLD) have been added to the ALLOCATE command below:

```
ALLOCATE FILE(SYSUT2) SYSOUT(A) COPIES(3) FCB(PRT1) +
DEST(RMT5) HOLD REUSE
```

(Note that the COPIES and FCB parameters are first available with release 1.3 of the TSO/E product.)

The COPIES keyword can be used to specify multiple copies of the same print output. The parameter is only valid in conjunction with the SYSOUT parameter. The default is one copy, and if only one copy were needed there would be no need to include the parameter. Some installations may have set limits as to how many copies can be obtained.

The second added parameter is the FCB keyword. It can be used to load a different *Forms Control Buffer* (FCB) into a particular printer. This in turn invokes certain print characteristics. For impact printers, this may only determine the number of lines per inch or invoke a carriage-control format that is defined with special channel skips. For laser printers, this might add other characteristics like print size, style, and orientation. The values that can be specified for this keyword are installation-specific.

The DEST keyword was also added to the ALLOCATE command example. It can be used to specify special routing of print output causing it to print somewhere other than the default location. In some installations, this might even be in a remote location many miles away. The DEST keyword could even be used to select a printer with more desirable print characteristics. For example, RMT5 might be the remote number of a laser printer that is better able to handle print needs than the default impact printer that would otherwise be used.

The HOLD parameter was added to cause the output data to be ineligible to print until a JES command is issued to release it. This might be used for several reasons. This could, for example, give an individual a chance to verify some aspect of the output data before allowing it to print. It might also be used to give the operator a chance to obtain any special forms or paper that it needed to print on. When that is taken care of, the operator could then load the special form, and then release the output.

We mentioned before that the REUSE parameter could and probably should be included on every ALLOCATE command. It prevents problems that arise when a file is already in use from activity earlier in a TSO session. This is also true when file output is directed to a print device.

NULLIFYING I/O TRANSFER

There are some times that the data that is output through a particular file is not required. This may be the case, for example, when a particular program was designed to produce several reports each time it is executed. One or more of those reports may not be required on a given instance. Some installations have defined special output classes that are not assigned to any device. By using this special class in a

SYSOUT parameter I/O transfer still takes place, but no output is actually produced.

Two other parameters exist for this purpose as well. When they are used, no output is produced and no I/O transfer takes place. This can make the program run more efficiently. The first such parameter, DUMMY, could be coded in the following fashion.

```
ALLOCATE FILE(SYSUT2) DUMMY
```

The other parameter is actually a special value for the DATASET keyword. That value is the word NULLFILE. That statement might look like the following.

```
ALLOCATE FILE(SYSUT2) DATASET(NULLFILE)
```

The DUMMY and NULLFILE parameters will also work to prevent I/O transfer of data from input files. In this case, however, it should first be determined that a given program can run to successful completion without the data. Stopping input-data transfer is sometimes used to test programs early in the development process.

Depending on the circumstances, either DUMMY or NULLFILE might require the addition of DCB information to complete the DSCB merge process. If the file characteristics are not sufficiently defined, the result could be a system 013 abend.

OTHER ALLOCATE COMMAND PARAMETERS

We have presented the ALLOCATE command parameters that are used most often. There are additional parameters that are not used as frequently. These parameters will be presented now with a brief description of how they are used.

INPUT   This parameter indicates that the data set referenced in the ALLOCATE command is used for input only. This may be of use when certain programs (like those written in FORTRAN) are invoked that would otherwise routinely open the data set for output.

OUTPUT   This parameter indicates that the data set referenced in the ALLOCATE command is used for output only. This parameter and the INPUT parameter are similar to those functions available with the JCL LABEL parameter.

DSORG   This parameter specifies the data set access method. It is generally not needed when creating sequential data sets and partitioned data sets. These can easily be determined by the presence or absence of directory blocks. The parameter would be required, however, when creating a BDAM, or direct access data set. This particular access method allows certain programs to get at each record directly and should not be confused with the term direct-access data set that merely refers to any readily accessible disk-resident data set. The values for this keyword parameter are:

> PS (Physical Sequential)
>
> PO (Partitioned Organization)
>
> DA (Direct Access)

BUFNO   This parameter specifies the number of buffers to be used in the I/O transfer process. The system default is generally acceptable for this keyword, but up to 255 buffers can be specified in an effort to affect data-transfer efficiency.

OPTCD   This keyword parameter has many possible uses, all of which apply to some aspect of data transfer. Perhaps the most common of these seldom-used functions translates between ASCII and EBCDIC data codes.

PARAMETER ABBREVIATION

ALLOCATE command parameters can be abbreviated. There is a general rule for abbreviating these and the parameters used in other CLIST statements. Parameters may be truncated to the extent that the leading characters remain unique. This rule for abbreviation applies only to the command parameters, and not to the command name itself. Command names have a prescribed set of acceptable abbreviations. Below is an example using three different parameters.

DATASET		
DATASE		
DATAS	DUMMY	
DATA	DUMM	FILE
DAT	DUM	FIL
DA	DU	FI
		F

Any of the above representations of the three parameters is acceptable. The DATASET and DUMMY parameters can both be truncated to as few as two characters. This is possible because no other ALLOCATE command parameters start with DA or DU. Neither parameter, however, could be reduced to a single letter the way the FILE parameter can, because they would no longer be unique. No other parameter starts with the letter *F*, and so the FILE parameter remains unique even when represented by only a single letter.

Below is the ALLOCATE command that we used to create a PDS. It is followed by the same command with the parameters abbreviated.

```
ALLOCATE FILE(SYSPROC) DATASET('TSO1234.CLIST') NEW CATALOG +
UNIT(3380) VOLUME(SYSTM4) RECFM(F B) LRECL(80) BLKSIZE(6240) +
TRACKS SPACE(3 1) DIR(15) REUSE

ALLOC F(SYSPROC) DA('TSO1234.CLIST') NE CA +
UNI(3380) VO(SYSTM4) REC(F B) LR(80) BLK(6240) +
TR SP(3 1) DI(15) REU
```

Parameters should not be shortened so much that they become cryptic. A compromise should be made to arrive at parameter names that are easy to code but are still easily recognized. Convention also dictates how a parameter appears. DA is the shortest abbreviation for the DATASET parameter, but it is also very widely used. This alone increases its readability.

PROGRAM EXECUTION

The execution of a program from within a CLIST is effected using the *CALL* command. All files required for use by the program should be allocated before the CALL command is used unless those files are dynamically allocated by the program. The CALL command will cause a program to be loaded and executed. That program should already be fully resolved using the linkage-editor program and stored as a member of a partitioned data set. The following CALL command

```
CALL 'TSO1234.TEST.LOAD(PAYROLL)'
```

invokes a program called PAYROLL within a data set named TSO1234.TEST.LOAD. The same program can also be executed with the following version of the command.

```
CALL TEST(PAYROLL)
```

This is an equivalent statement because the quotes are omitted from the data set name. As we saw before, certain data set assumptions are made in the TSO environment when the data set name is not fully qualified and contained within quotes. The presence of the data set name within a CALL command provides a special context. Within this context, TSO will look for a last qualifier of LOAD or will add that qualifier. Specifying a different low-level qualifier requires the use of fully qualified data set name like 'TSO1234.PAYROLL.PGMLIB'. Assumptions are even made about the member name when it is omitted from the CALL command. When omitted, a member name of TEMPNAME is assumed.

The CALL command can pass up to 100 bytes of information to the executing program. This information is often called *parm* or *parameter data* and is restricted by the program's ability to receive such information. The amount of data and the format in which the data should be entered will differ according to the program that accepts the data. Some sophisticated programs, like the linkage editor, can accept free-form data. This means that the program will parse the data into meaningful information. In this case, the information is used to specify various options that are to apply as the linkage-editor program converts compiler-output data into a load module. Below is the CALL command used to execute the linkage-editor program and pass it twenty-eight bytes of parm information.

```
CALL 'SYS1.LINKLIB(IEWL)' 'XREF,CALL,AMODE=31,RMODE=ANY'
```

The parm information above contains pieces of information that are separated by commas. That information requests that the linkage editor produce a cross-reference listing and resolve external references. In addition, two other parameters set the addressing and residence modes. The pieces of information could have been specified in any order because the linkage editor program was written to accept it that way. It is looking for a finite set of predefined parameters and their values. Less-sophisticated programs would probably have stricter requirements. If users were to code their own COBOL program to receive parm information, for example, they would probably code it to look for specific information starting in prescribed positions. Below is a CALL command that was used earlier. Parm information has been added to it.

```
CALL 'TSO1234.TEST.LOAD(PAYROLL)' 'NORMAL CYCLE    03/28/92'
```

The parm information that was added identifies the type of run and a check-issue date. The date information would always be coded to start in position 18 of the parm data. To do otherwise would require a program "smart" enough to find the information it needs.

RETURN CODES

A *return code* is a device by which a program can communicate back to the resource-controlling language that invoked it. This could take place, for example, between a program and a CLIST as the program finishes executing and passes control back to the CLIST. The return codes are set within the program and are therefore peculiar to the program that is running. The program, in fact, need not set any such code. Return codes are often numeric, and some of these numeric codes have taken on special meaning. The meaning of these codes has been determined by convention, but they only have meaning when issued by a program known to follow those conventions. Those code values and their typical meanings are:

0   normal completion or no-code value set

4   warning or informational messages have been issued

8   conditional errors exist (where under certain conditions an error might occur)

12   severe error(s) have occurred

16   indicates the presence of fatal errors

These codes are typically tied to the severity level of problems within the program. The higher the code, the more severe the problem. Remember though, just because this convention exists, it does not mean that every program follows it. In fact, a return code in the thousands may signal the successful completion of some programs. Many programs issue no codes at all. In such cases, the return code passed back to the CLIST is zero. Other programs, like the utility sort, return much higher code values that relate to specific error or warning messages. In the case of the utility sort, the return codes also correspond to published message-identification numbers.

In addition to the codes passed back from programs, return codes resulting from the execution of other CLIST statements or TSO commands can also be used. The CLIST can test the return codes passed back from programs or CLIST statements to conditionally execute other code. The mechanism for doing this will be demonstrated in the next chapter. There are two system variables that contain return codes. The variable &LASTCC contains the return-code value from the last previous statement executed. This is true whether the statement was a CALL to a program or another CLIST statement. For example, the variable &LASTCC could be tested immediately after an ALLOCATE command to determine the success of that statement.

The variable &MAXCC contains the highest return code issued during the CLIST execution. This would be the maximum value attained by variable &LASTCC. This variable can also be updated by the CLIST code. It might be desirable, for example, to set a high value after sensing an error. Conversely, if previously encountered errors had been corrected or determined to be of little consequence, it might be desirable to reset &MAXCC to zero. That way, the value of variable &MAXCC would only reflect the return codes of subsequently executed statements. In the next chapter, we will look at variables in more detail and see how to set them.

FREEING RESOURCES

There are several reasons for wanting to free resources. What we mean by *resources,* in this particular instance, are files, data sets, and attribute lists. These resources tend to accumulate throughout a TSO session with each ALLOCATE command that is used. If they are not freed, they remain allocated until the session is ended. This can present several problems. Perhaps the biggest problem is data set contention. This describes the situation where multiple sessions or jobs need the same data set, but one session or job has the other(s) locked out of the data set. This is called an *exclusive enqueue* and is tied to the disposition used to open a data set. An exclusive enqueue is generally placed on a data set when it is opened for update. This ensures the integrity of the data which could otherwise be compromised if more than one task at a time were changing the data.

The command used to free resources is the FREE command. Any of the three resource types, files, data sets, and attribute lists, can be specified just as they are in the ALLOCATE command. Remember that DATASET or DSNAME, FILE or DDNAME, and ATTRLIST were all keyword parameters in the ALLOCATE command. Remember, too, that the parameter names can be abbreviated to as few characters as uniquely identify the parameter. Below is an example of a FREE command used to free a particular data set.

```
FREE DATASET('TSO1234.SEQ.DATA')
```

When a file or data set resource is freed, the corresponding data set or file is also freed. In the above example, if data set TSO1234.SEQ.DATA were the sole data set allocated to file SYSUT2, then that file would also be freed at the same time. Conversely, the following statement

```
FREE FILE(SYSUT2)
```

would have accomplished the same result. If more than one data set is allocated to a single file (known as data set concatenation), no single data set can be freed separately from the file. In the case of concatenated data sets, it would be necessary to execute the FREE command using the file name. This would disconnect all of the data sets for the specified file. The file could then be reallocated with whatever data sets should remain connected.

Another reason for freeing resources is to allow them to be reused in a given TSO session. Before the REUSE ALLOCATE parameter became common it was customary for a CLIST to free its resources, allocate them, invoke a program, and free the resources again. The reason for freeing the resources at both the beginning and end of such a CLIST is that the program may not always run to completion. In such a case, the resources would be freed in the beginning of the CLIST when it is rerun. This problem is easy to avoid using the REUSE parameter in all ALLOCATE commands, but resources should still be freed by a CLIST when they are no longer required.

Still another reason for freeing resources is to avoid installation limits that may exist for how many resources can be obtained during a TSO session. It is not common to reach this limit; but if reached, it would not allow the user to allocate any additional resources until some had been freed.

The FREE command can also make data available for output processing. Specifically, where data has been directed to a SYSOUT data set, it can be freed, and is then eligible for printing. When freeing a SYSOUT data set, it is possible to change the output class, the destination, or to delete the output entirely.

```
FREE F(PRINTOUT) DEST(RMT5) SYSOUT(T)
```

The data written to file PRINTOUT would not print until the file is freed. The above example makes the output directed to file PRINT-OUT immediately available to the printer that has been designated as RMT5. At the same time, the output class is changed (from whatever had been specified on the ALLOCATE command for file, PRINTOUT) to class T.

It is also possible to free multiple resources with a single FREE command, whether it is the same resource type

```
FREE F(SYSPRINT SYSIN SYSUT1 SYSUT2)
```

or a mixture of resource types.

```
FREE F(SYSPRINT SYSIN) DA (INPUT.DATA) ATTR (DCB1 DCB2)
```

EXITING THE CLIST

A CLIST can be halted using the *END* command. This command is not required, since a CLIST will also stop when it runs out of statements. The END command, however, can appear anywhere within the

CLIST code and thereby give flexibility to when the CLIST is terminated. In the next chapter, for example, we will see how conditional tests can be applied to sense circumstances under which a CLIST should be terminated. Those circumstances might reflect the normal end of processing or might reflect an error situation from which there is no recovery.

A third method of ending CLIST execution is with the *EXIT* statement. The EXIT statement is similar to the END command, but it provides an extra feature. The EXIT statement can be used to set a return code. This is particularly useful when the CLIST being terminated was invoked by another CLIST. The return code can be passed back to that CLIST as an indicator of the processing status of the terminating CLIST. Below is an EXIT statement that would terminate a CLIST and return a condition code of 12.

```
EXIT CODE(12)
```

The code value can be any numeric expression. It is also not necessary to adhere to conventional code values discussed earlier of 0, 4, 8, 12, and 16. In fact, the maximum code value is 16,777,215. It is more important that whatever values used are coordinated with the function that will sense those values.

We have covered the basic statements that will allow us to construct a simple CLIST. We will use the HARDCOPY CLIST that was discussed in Chap. 3. The function of that CLIST is to print a data set. For now, we will construct the CLIST to always print a particular data set to a given output class. We will learn how to make the CLIST more flexible in the next chapter.

The program that we will use to print the data set is the standard utility *IEBGENER*. This utility merely takes sequential data from file SYSUT1 and puts it to file SYSUT2. That means that the data set to be printed, TSO1234.SEQ.DATA, will have to be allocated to the SYSUT1 file.

```
ALLOC FILE(SYSUT1) DATASET('TSO1234.SEQ.DATA') SHR REUSE
```

The SYSUT2 file will be allocated to SYSOUT rather than a data set.

```
ALLOC FILE(SYSUT2) SYSOUT(T) REUSE
```

Other required files must also be allocated before the program can be invoked. This includes the SYSPRINT file for utility program-message output and the SYSIN file for control-card input.

```
ALLOC FILE(SYSPRINT) SYSOUT(U) REUSE
ALLOC FILE(SYSIN) DUMMY REUSE
```

Because there is no control card input, the DUMMY parameter is used to negate any I/O transfer to the SYSIN file. The same parameter could have been used on the SYSPRINT file to suppress printing of the utility messages. After all the required files are allocated, the program is invoked.

```
CALL 'SYS1.LINKLIB(IEBGENER)'
```

Finally, after control is returned to the CLIST from the program, the files that were allocated are freed.

```
FREE FILE(SYSUT1 SYSUT2 SYSPRINT SYSIN)
```

When the statements above are brought together, the CLIST looks like the following.

```
ALLOC FILE(SYSUT1) DATASET('TSO1234.SEQ.DATA') SHR REUSE
ALLOC FILE(SYSUT2) SYSOUT(T) REUSE
ALLOC FILE(SYSPRINT) SYSOUT(U) REUSE
ALLOC FILE(SYSIN) DUMMY REUSE
CALL 'SYS1.LINKLIB(IEBGENER)'
FREE FILE(SYSUT1 SYSUT2 SYSPRINT SYSIN)
```

The SYSOUT classes will, of course, vary by installation. So might the name of the data set containing the utility program. If the program is not in the library specified, the CLIST execution will terminate, issuing a condition code of 12. The related message would indicate that the member could not be found in the data set.

Now let us try another example. In this example a FORTRAN program, FORMAT, is executed from our private load library TSO1234.FORT.LOAD. The program reads input data from an existing data set into file 5 and outputs 200-byte records to file 7. File 6 will be made available for normal message output which will be sent to the screen.

```
ALLOC F(FT05F001) DA(SEQ.DATA) SHR INPUT REUSE
ALLOC F(FT07F001) DA(NEW.OUTPUT) CAT SP(1 1) TRACK UNIT(SYSDA) +
   RECFM(F B) LRECL(200) BLKSIZE(23400) REUSE
ALLOC F(FT06F001) DA(*) REUSE
CALL FORT(FORMAT)
FREE F(FT05F001 FT06F001 FT07F001)
```

Note in the example above that the common abbreviations, *F* for FILE and *DA* for DATASET, are used. Notice too that the short form for all data set names is used. TSO will supply the user-ID in all such instances. In addition, TSO will supply the qualifier LOAD in the CALL statement to arrive at the full data set name of TSO1234.FORT.LOAD(FORMAT).

CONTROLLING THE EXECUTION ENVIRONMENT

There are several aspects of CLIST execution that can be controlled. This includes messages and prompts that are issued during CLIST execution as well as what the CLIST does when it encounters an error. These, and other aspects discussed in subsequent chapters, are set with the *CONTROL* statement.

Perhaps the most useful of the CONTROL-statement parameters allows the CLIST to continue executing after an error is encountered. The default is for all remaining CLIST statements to be flushed. To prevent this, the statement

```
CONTROL NOFLUSH
```

can be included anywhere within the CLIST. It is most typical for this to be one of the first CLIST statements, however, since the feature does not become effective until the statement is actually executed. One should be very careful about using the NOFLUSH parameter. It should only be used when error conditions can be handled by the CLIST or can be determined to be inconsequential. In our previous example, for instance, it would not be appropriate to continue execution if any of the files could not be allocated. The possible exception in that example would be file FT06F001. By adding CONTROL statements on either side of that ALLOCATE command,

```
ALLOC F(FT05F001) DA(SEQ.DATA) SHR INPUT REUSE
ALLOC F(FT07F001) DA(NEW.OUTPUT) CAT SP(1 1) TRACK UNIT(SYSDA) +
   RECFM(F B) LRECL(200) BLKSIZE(23400) REUSE
CONTROL NOFLUSH
ALLOC F(FT06F001) DA(*) REUSE
CONTROL FLUSH
CALL FORT(FORMAT)
FREE F(FT05F001 FT06F001 FT07F001)
```

we could turn the NOFLUSH option on for that statement only. This would allow the CLIST to continue executing even if there was a prob-

lem allocating file FT06F001. Including the statement CONTROL
FLUSH sets that option back to the default. Since FLUSH is the
default, it is only needed to reverse a prior NOFLUSH parameter.

Another useful CONTROL statement function determines whether
or not messages are written to the terminal. The content of any message depends on the statement being executed. Some commands, like
the TSO DELETE command, issue messages every time they are executed. A different message is issued when the data set is successfully
deleted than when a problem arises. Most commands, however, issue
messages only when there is a problem. The messages might describe
error conditions or may just be informational in nature. Messages
issued from the execution of an ALLOCATE command, for example,
generally describe some sort of error. When an FREE command issues
error or warning messages, however, they are usually of little consequence. They typically result from trying to free resources that were
not allocated in the first place. It may be advisable, then, to suppress
those particular messages.

```
ALLOC F(FT05F001) DA(SEQ.DATA) SHR INPUT REUSE
ALLOC F(FT07F001) DA(NEW.OUTPUT) CAT SP(1 1) TRACK UNIT(SYSDA) +
  RECFM(F B) LRECL(200) BLKSIZE(23400) REUSE
CONTROL NOFLUSH
ALLOC F(FT06F001) DA(*) REUSE
CONTROL FLUSH
CALL FORT(FORMAT)
CONTROL NOMSG
FREE F(FT05F001 FT06F001 FT07F001)
```

As with the previous CONTROL statement parameter, it is possible
to turn the messages on and off anywhere within the CLIST. In the
example above, the messages are turned off just before the FREE
command is executed. With the end of the CLIST reached, execution
stops and there is no reason to turn the messages back on. This might
be desirable, however, if there were more statements to execute.

The CONTROL statement parameters PROMPT/NOPROMPT control whether or not an executed command can issue a prompt. This
refers to commands that are interactive and should not be confused
with the prompts discussed in Chap. 3. Those prompts are always
issued when a CLIST is invoked without all positional parameters
specified. They are not subject to control.

INSTREAM DATA

There are several ways to handle instream data. The term *instream
data* refers to any type of data that is imbedded among the source lan-

guage statements. For a CLIST this could be anything from utility control statements to raw application-program data.

Perhaps the best way to handle instream data is to convert it into a normal data set. In this instance, the data is really no longer instream. The file that would have accepted the data can instead reference the data set name. This would be no different than any other ALLOCATE command we have seen which pairs a file with an input data set. The main advantage to putting the data in a separate data set is that the data would not have to be retyped each time the CLIST is executed.

Another alternative for including instream data provides much more flexibility. It involves allocating the instream data file to the terminal. The data is then entered manually as the file in question is opened. Because the data must be entered each time the CLIST is executed, this alternative is usually used only with small amounts of data. The ALLOCATE command used to obtain data from the terminal is very simple. It uses the DATASET keyword with the special character "*" to represent the terminal.

```
ALLOCATE F(SYSIN) DA(*)
```

With this statement, all input for the file SYSIN will be entered from the terminal. When the program being invoked by the CLIST issues a read from that file, the terminal display will stop. The first data record can then be typed and read using the ENTER key. The operator-information area at the bottom of the terminal will indicate when input data can be entered. This is indicated when the terminal is no longer input-inhibited (sometimes referred to as "on the clock"). If and when the next read is issued against that file, the terminal will again "unlock." This sequence can be repeated until all input data is entered. The characters "/*" can be entered in positions one and two of the next data record to indicate the end of the data file. This signals an end-of-file situation to the program being executed. Many of those who create CLISTs that require instream data will use the CLIST or the program that is invoked to write to the screen to signal that instream data is required.

The same type of ALLOCATE command can be used to direct output to the terminal.

```
ALLOCATE F(SYSPRINT) DA(*)
```

Caution should also be used in deciding what is directed to the screen. It would not be wise to overwhelm terminal users with more output than they could reasonably handle. Such users might also get irate at having to hit the enter key hundreds or thousands of times to page through voluminous output. Such output is better directed to a data set or hardcopy file.

There is a seldom-used but very useful technique that is a variation of the previous method of handling instream data. That involves using the CLIST or the executing program to write out sample data that the terminal user can use as the basis for new information. Many terminal users do not even know that much of the information that is written to a terminal can be reused as terminal input. This technique can prove to be extremely useful, for example, with complicated utility-control statements. Terminal users can use a sample control statement written to the screen as a guide in typing their own. When the same or less information is required, terminal users can even move the cursor up to the sample and change it to fit their own needs. They would also want to erase any extraneous information on the same line, but when they press the ENTER key, that display line will be read in as new input data. Below is an example of both ways of entering data. The example presents a sample sort control statement which would be read as input data to the utility sort program.

```
ENTER THE SORT CONTROL FIELDS BELOW OR USE
THE SAMPLE STATEMENT PROVIDED BELOW.
  SORT FIELDS=(S1,L1,F1,D1,S2,L2,F2,D2,S3,L3,F3,D3)
WHERE S=STARTING POSITION, L=LENGTH, F=FORMAT, AND D=DIRECTION
_
```

Users can then enter their own sort control statement based upon the example and description

```
SORT FIELDS=(1,12,CH,A,35,5,CH,D)
/*_
```

or they can move the cursor to and retype the next-to-last line. The remainder of the line is erased, and the modified line becomes input to the sort program.

```
ENTER THE SORT CONTROL FIELDS BELOW OR USE
THE SAMPLE STATEMENT PROVIDED BELOW.
  SORT FIELDS=(1,12,CH,A,35,5,CH,D)_
WHERE S=STARTING POSITION, L=LENGTH, F=FORMAT, AND D=DIRECTION
/*
```

In both cases, the characters "/*" are entered in positions one and two to signal the end of the instream data. This is done on a new line when the terminal again "unlocks."

Another way to include instream data is with the DATA and END-DATA statements. This particular function, however, is limited to the use of TSO commands and subcommands. Together, the DATA and ENDDATA statements form a group or sequence of statements that are considered together, and where symbolic substitution is allowed to take place. This allows the inclusion of instream data that would otherwise not be considered as a valid CLIST statement. Conversely, instream data might unintentionally be confused for a CLIST statement. The following illustrates just such a case.

```
    .
    .
DATA
    EDIT 'TS01234.SAMPLE.JCL' OLD CNTL NONUM
    C  *  999  '$'  ' '  ALL
    END SAVE
ENDDATA
    .
    .
```

The three lines between DATA and ENDDATA are treated as data. The word *END* in the above example is an EDIT subcommand. Without the DATA-ENDDATA sequence, however, it is misinterpreted and causes a syntax error.

Yet another method exists for those installations that have the ISPF Dialog Manager product installed. This method involves a process that is known as *file tailoring*. File tailoring is a fairly extensive topic itself and will not be discussed in detail here. Briefly, the process involves modifying skeleton or archetype data through special ISPF commands. The basic modification process includes substitution of variable information as well as the conditional inclusion of data. The resolved data could then be made available in place of instream data.

CLISTS AS A TRANSLATION OF JCL

Mention has been made of the similarities between JCL and the CLIST language. Most of the functions available using JCL are also part of the CLIST language. Below we have included the JCL that would be used to sort a data set in-place. Following that is a line by line translation of the JCL into CLIST code.

```
//TS01234A JOB TS01234,'SORT PROGRAM',
// CLASS=A,MSGCLASS=A
//SORTSTEP EXEC PGM=SORT
```

```
//STEPLIB  DD   DSN=SYS1.SORTLIB,DISP=SHR
//SYSOUT   DD   SYSOUT=T
//SORTWK1  DD   SPACE=(CYL,(1,1)),UNIT=SYSDA
//SORTWK2  DD   SPACE=(CYL,(1,1)),UNIT=SYSDA
//SORTWK3  DD   SPACE=(CYL,(1,1)),UNIT=SYSDA
//SORTIN   DD   DSN=TSO1234.SEQ.DATA,DISP=SHR
//SORTOUT  DD   DSN=TSO1234.SEQ.DATA,DISP=OLD
//SYSIN    DD   *
    SORT FIELDS=(5,12,CH,A)
```

The first two statements

```
//TSO1234A JOB TSO1234,'SORT PROGRAM',
//CLASS=A,MSGCLASS=A
```

comprise the job statement. The equivalent information is obtained at
logon time and maintained throughout the TSO session. This information need not be included in CLIST code. The next two statements
together identify the complete load module name.

```
//SORTSTEP EXEC PGM=SORT
//STEPLIB DD DSN=SYS1.SORTLIB,DISP=SHR
```

These statements would be combined into the single CLIST CALL
statement

```
CALL 'SYS1.SORTLIB(SORT)'
```

A search of multiple-program libraries is supported using JCL but
not within a CLIST. When converting from background to foreground execution, an examination of the load libraries should be
made to determine which library contains the program version to be
executed. For example, the following JCL STEPLIB statement lists
three libraries to be searched for the PAYROLL program mentioned
earlier.

```
//STEP1    EXEC PGM=PAYROLL,PARM='NORMAL CYCLE    03/28/92'
//STEPLIB  DD   DSN=TSO1234.TEST.LOAD,DISP=SHR
//         DD   DSN=PAYROLL.TEST.LOADLIB,DISP=SHR
//         DD   DSN=PAYROLL.PROD.LOAD,DISP=SHR
```

The first of the libraries to contain the member PAYROLL contains
the version being executed. It is this data set name that would be
included on the CALL command.

```
CALL 'TSO1234.TEST.LOAD(PAYROLL)' 'NORMAL CYCLE    03/28/92'
```

Notice that the information that was used to form the CALL command comes from three different JCL keyword parameters on two different statements. These parameters are PGM=, PARM=, and DSN=. Another significant difference between the two languages is that file-allocation statements follow the relevant program name in JCL but they must precede it in CLIST code. When we bring all of the CLIST code together, we will see the CALL statement placed at the bottom of the CLIST following the required ALLOCATE commands. Below are the normal file allocation statements with the CLIST equivalent in bold print.

```
//SYSOUT    DD    SYSOUT=T
ALLOCATE F(SYSOUT) SYSOUT(T)


//SORTWK1  DD    SPACE=(CYL,(1,1)),UNIT=SYSDA
ALLOCATE F(SORTWK1) SP(1 1) CYL UNIT(SYSDA)


//SORTWK2  DD    SPACE=(CYL,(1,1)),UNIT=SYSDA
ALLOCATE F(SORTWK2) SP(1 1) CYL UNIT(SYSDA)


//SORTWK3  DD    SPACE=(CYL,(1,1)),UNIT=SYSDA
ALLOCATE F(SORTWK3) SP(1 1) CYL UNIT(SYSDA)


//SORTIN   DD    DSN=TSO1234.SEQ.DATA,DISP=SHR
ALLOCATE F(SORTIN) DA(SEQ.DATA) SHR


//SORTOUT  DD    DSN=TSO1234.SEQ.DATA,DISP=OLD
ALLOCATE F(SORTOUT) DA(SEQ.DATA) OLD


//SYSIN    DD    *
  SORT FIELDS=(5,12,CH,A)
ALLOCATE F(SYSIN) DA(CNTL(CNTLCARD)) SHR
```

With this last pair of JCL statements, we have placed the sort control statement in the data set TSO1234.CNTL(CNTLCARD). The SYSIN file then references that data set. This is one of the alternatives discussed for handling instream data. We would want to add the REUSE parameter to all of the ALLOCATE commands. When we bring all the CLIST statements together and add a FREE command at the end, the CLIST looks like the following:

```
ALLOCATE F(SYSOUT) SYSOUT(T) REUSE
```

```
ALLOCATE F(SORTWK1) SP(1 1) CYL UNIT(SYSDA) REUSE
ALLOCATE F(SORTWK2) SP(1 1) CYL UNIT(SYSDA) REUSE
ALLOCATE F(SORTWK3) SP(1 1) CYL UNIT(SYSDA) REUSE
ALLOCATE F(SORTIN) DA(SEQ.DATA) SHR REUSE
ALLOCATE F(SORTOUT) DA(SEQ.DATA) OLD REUSE
ALLOCATE F(SYSIN) DA(CNTL(CNTLCARD)) SHR REUSE
CALL 'SYS1.SORTLIB(SORT)'
FREE F(SYSOUT SORTWK1 SORTWK2 SORTWK3 SORTIN SORTOUT SYSIN)
```

This ends our discussion of the CLIST language used to control system resources. The statements covered in this chapter, however, will play a large part in making use of the functions that we will see in subsequent chapters. In the next chapter, we will look into the programmatic aspects of a CLIST. These CLIST functions give the language logic and data-manipulation capabilities.

6

Programmatic Statements

We now turn our attention to the programmatic aspects of the CLIST language. We will start with the structures that facilitate the manipulation of data, *condition testing, branching,* and *iteration.* These structures, along with others introduced in the next chapter, allow the CLIST language to go beyond a simple resource-controlling language and act like many high-level compiled languages.

VARIABLES

One of the most important functions in a programmatic CLIST is the ability to symbolically represent information. By this we mean that a constant symbol or name is used to represent information that is allowed to vary. The symbol used to represent this information is called a *variable* and is similar to what other languages typically call a *field* or *data element.* The variable is the basis for giving a CLIST flexibility. It allows constantly changing data to be stored under fixed, known names. First we will look at how a variable is defined and how its contents are set and changed. Following that, we will see how variables fit into other CLIST statements.

Many programming languages have strict rules for when and how data elements or variables are defined. This is not true of CLISTs. A CLIST variable can be defined at virtually any point in a CLIST. In addition, a CLIST variable need not be defined or declared before its first use or reference in the CLIST. To increase flexibility even further, it is also not necessary or even possible to describe the characteristics of a given variable. Many languages require that the type of data a variable will contain (like numeric data as opposed to character data) and the length of the data be defined. This is not possible in a CLIST variable which automatically accommodates any type or length of data. The variable contents can also readily be changed without regard for the data type or length.

A variable name can be from one to 252 characters in length. It is made up of alphabetic characters, numbers, and the special symbols @, #, $, and _. It must begin with an alphabetic character or the special symbols @, #, $, or _. The name devised for a variable should be preceded by the special character "&". Using these rules, acceptable variable names might look like &CLASS, &HOMEADDRESS#2, or &INPUT_DATASET_NAME. In the last variable name, the underscore character is used to increase the readability of the variable name and is not required for any limitation on the number of contiguous characters. Variable names are sometimes recognized by the context of their use. In many such instances, the leading "&" is not required. It is advisable to use it, however, to provide better readability to the CLIST. This also makes the variables easier to find using most text editors.

VARIABLE SETTING AND REPLACEMENT

A variable can be assigned a value using the CLIST *SET statement.* The SET statement pairs a variable with a literal or expression. Below are examples of simple SET statements using numeric and character data.

```
SET &COPIES = 3
SET &MSG1 = INVALID DATA SET NAME. PLEASE REENTER.
```

The format of the SET statement includes the variable name on the left side of the equal sign, and a literal or expression on the right side. Variables can be included on the right side of the equation, and those variables can contain either numeric or character data. The SET statement can, therefore, be used to combine information

```
SET &MESSAGE = &READ_COUNTER RECORDS HAVE BEEN READ
```

or to extend variable values.

```
SET &MESSAGE = &MESSAGE BEFORE REACHING END OF FILE.
```

If the last two SET statements were executed, and the variable &READ_COUNTER contained a value of 256, the variable &MES-SAGE would contain the character string.

```
256 RECORDS HAVE BEEN READ
```

after the first SET statement, and the character string,

```
256 RECORDS HAVE BEEN READ BEFORE REACHING END OF FILE.
```

after the second. Notice that the second SET statement sets &MES-SAGE equal to itself plus additional text.

A period can be used to separate a variable from a literal value. This is only required when a variable is immediately followed by a literal without an intervening delimiter. Below is a series of SET statements and the result of setting a new variable. Assume that the variable &USERID has a value of TSO1234, and that it is the only variable that has an initial value.

Statement	Value
SET &JOBNAME = &USERIDA	
SET &JOBNAME = &USERID.A	TSO1234A
SET &DSN = &USERID.COMPILE.LIST	TSO1234ACOMPILE.LIST
SET &DSN = &USERID..COMPILE.LIST	TSO1234A.COMPILE.LIST

The first SET statement leaves the variable &JOBNAME with a null value. That is because &USERID followed by the letter *A* becomes a new variable name, &USERIDA. As a new variable, it would not have an initial value. The second SET statement separates the variable name from the letter *A* with a period. The result after substitution is the variable value TSO1234 plus the letter *A*. The third SET statement uses a similar process in trying to build a data set name. The period following &USERID properly serves to delimit the literal from the variable name. The result, however, is probably not what was expected because it is not a valid data set name. The fourth SET statement uses two consecutive periods after &USERID. The first period serves as a delimiter, while the second period is retained after variable substitution to create what would be a valid data set name.

As mentioned before, the variables that are being set do not have to be defined before the SET statement is used to "move" data into them. These variables and the data they contain are placed into a function pool that is available throughout the CLIST execution. The value of a variable can be reset just as easily as it was set using another SET statement. Later, we will see other CLIST statements that can be used to establish variable values.

When setting the value of a CLIST variable, there are some peculiarities that should be noted. Variables containing character data will not normally retain spaces that are not embedded. This means that leading or trailing spaces will be lost. Only those spaces that exist between nonblank characters will be retained. Leading zeros are also removed from numeric data during normal variable assignment. We will soon see how to treat numeric and character data literally to avoid losing both spaces and leading zeroes.

VARIABLES IN ARITHMETIC EXPRESSIONS

The expression portion of the SET statement can also be a regular arithmetic expression. The expression can use the standard arithmetic operators +, −, *, /, and **; variables; and numeric literals. Substitution occurs for the variables on the right side of the equal sign. The expression is then evaluated and the result is placed into the named variable. The following examples set the variables &RATE and &SUM.

```
SET &RATE = &BASE * 12
SET &SUM = &VALUE1 + &VALUE2 + &VALUE3
```

The order of performed operations is exponentiation, division and multiplication, and addition and subtraction. Expressions are evaluated from left to right, although the order of evaluation can also be changed using parentheses. In the next example, the substituted value of &BASE is multiplied by twelve. The substituted value of &ADJUST is then added to that product before being placed in variable, &RATE.

```
SET &RATE = &BASE * 12 + &ADJUST
```

The use of parentheses in the next example, however, causes the addition to occur first. Except where &ADJUST is less than one, this will result in a larger number being placed in the variable, &RATE.

```
SET &RATE = &BASE * (12 + &ADJUST)
```

A variable can also be used as a counter. This is accomplished by setting the variable to itself plus some increment value. Some CLIST coders first initialize the variable to zero before using it as a counter. This is not required unless the variable already contains a value that is inappropriate or must be reset. Within an iteratively executed portion of the CLIST code, for example, we could include the following statement.

```
SET &COUNTER = &COUNTER + 1
```

This would serve to increment the counter by one each time the SET statement was executed.

A significant limitation of the CLIST language is that only integer arithmetic is supported. The following statements, however, take advantage of this fact to calculate the optimum block size on a 3380 disk device for whatever record length (less than or equal to 23,476) is contained in the variable &LRECL.

```
SET &BLKFACTOR = 23476 / &LRECL
SET &BLKSIZE = &BLKFACTOR * &LRECL
```

The variable &BLKSIZE is not equal to 23,476 unless &LRECL is, because the remainder was dropped in deriving the value for &BLKFACTOR. While true decimal values are not supported within CLIST code, this limitation can be overcome by multiplying numbers by a factor of ten for each significant digit that is to be retained. For example, if we wanted to divide &VALUE1 by &VALUE2 and retain two decimal places, we would first multiply &VALUE1 by 100.

```
SET &RESULT = &VALUE1 * 100 / &VALUE2
```

If &VALUE1 contained the number 25 and &VALUE2 contained the number 4, the result would be 625. You could then place the decimal point two places into the result (to obtain the value 6.25) using the data manipulation functions that we will discuss later. As in other languages, division by zero is not possible. To avoid this potential problem, the divisor can be checked for a value greater than zero before the SET statement is allowed to execute.

The CLIST language also contains a remainder function that is designated by a double forward slash character. It provides what is left after the integer result of division is obtained. When 25 is divided by 4, for example, the remainder is 1. The following statement shows the basis for using the remainder function to test for leap years.

```
SET &TEST = &YEAR // 4
```

In the above example, &TEST is a new variable that will contain the remainder after dividing the variable &YEAR by 4. If the variable

&YEAR contains a two- or four-digit year value, then &TEST will be 0 when testing against a leap year since they are evenly divisible by four. The variable &TEST could then be tested and used as the basis for directing other logic.

DATA MANIPULATION FUNCTIONS

Several built-in functions are available for handling variable and literal information. This includes a function to make sure that an expression is not evaluated as well as one that makes sure that it is. Another makes sure that variables are not resolved. Other functions supply information about data length and type or allow for the extraction of data. We will start the discussion of these functions with the &STR function.

The &STR function

The *&STR system function* is similar to a literal function. It allows the treatment of data literally the way it is entered. The only difference is that substitution of variable values will still occur. Perhaps the main value of the &STR function is to prevent further evaluation of data during variable assignment. This is especially helpful when the data contains normal arithmetic operators. These operators would otherwise prompt the evaluation of the data as an arithmetic expression. For example, the second SET statement below

```
SET &VALUE1 = 1
SET &ANSWER = 3 + &VALUE1
```

would provide the result 4, and place it in variable &ANSWER. The following SET statement, however, produces a different result because evaluation is limited to the resolution of variable values.

```
SET &VALUE1 = 1
SET &ANSWER = &STR(3 + &VALUE1)
```

The result of this last SET statement is the value "3 + 1." The value 1 is substituted for the variable &VALUE1, but because of the &STR function, that value is not added to the literal number "3." Prohibiting the evaluation of the expression also would allow us to retain variable values with leading zeros or nonembedded spaces. The statement

```
SET &ANSWER = 000003
```

would result in the number 3 being stored in the variable &ANSWER. The same statement containing the &STR function

```
SET &ANSWER = &STR(000003)
```

would cause the value "000003" to be stored in the variable &ANSWER. The following examples demonstrate the effect that the &STR function has when used with character data.

Statement				Value
SET &ANS =	MESSAGE A			"MESSAGE A"
SET &ANS =	&STR(MESSAGE	A	)	" MESSAGE A "
SET &ANS =	WARNING - I/O ERROR			**Would cause an error!**
SET &ANS =	&STR(WARNING - I/O ERROR		)	" WARNING - I/O ERROR "

Notice the difference between the first two examples. The &STR function allows leading and trailing blanks to be retained. The same is true of the third and fourth examples. In this case, however, the third example would cause an error. The error would result from trying to perform arithmetic on character values. When the &STR function is used, no evaluation takes place, and the error is avoided. Character variable values, used within the string function, are substituted just like numeric values.

The &NRSTR function

The *&NRSTR system function* is similar to the &STR literal function. It can be used in similar fashion with the added feature that no substitution of included variable values occurs when a double leading ampersand (&&) is used. Other substitution is limited to one level, and arithmetic expressions are not evaluated.

The &SUBSTR function

The *&SUBSTR function* can be used to extract information from a variable or character string. It does this using parameters that define the start and end positions within the variable value or character string. The statement,

```
SET &STRING1 = &SUBSTR(3:6,INFORMATION)
```

would place the value "FORM" in the variable &STRING1. This is the result of extracting the characters from position three through position six, inclusive. The start and end column numbers are separated from each other by a colon. The two numbers are then separated from the character string by a comma. If only a single number is used, the colon is omitted. The effect of including only a single value is to extract only a single byte of data from the variable or character string. The start and end column specifiers could themselves be expressed using variables or expressions.

```
SET &START = 3
SET &STRING1 = &SUBSTR(&START:&START + 4,INFORMATION)
```

If the variable &STRING2 contains the value "JANUARY 1992," the statements

```
SET &STRING3 = &SUBSTR(1:3,&STRING2)
SET &STRING3 = &STRING3&SUBSTR(9:12,&STRING2)
```

would result in the string "JAN 1992" being placed in the variable &STRING3.

The &LENGTH function

The *&LENGTH function* can be used to determine the length of a character string or of the contents of a variable. This is extremely important because, as we saw earlier, variable values are readily able to change lengths since they have no predefined constraints. The &LENGTH function is often used with the &SUBSTR function. In this context, it can be used to show the last available position, and help to insure that no attempt is made to reference data beyond that point. The value contained in &STRING2 from our previous example would vary in length depending on the value of the month that it contained. Using the &LENGTH function,

```
SET &LEN = &LENGTH(&STRING2)
```

we can place the length of the string in &STRING2 (in this case the value 12) in the variable &LEN. This can be used to avoid an error by trying to access beyond the last available position of the variable. It would also make it easy to extract the last four positions and store the value of the year into the variable &YEAR.

```
SET &LEN = &LENGTH(&STRING2)
SET &YEAR = &SUBSTR(&LEN-3:&LEN,&STRING2)
```

This code is flexible enough to extract the year whether the string value is "JANUARY 1992" or "MAY 2001." The first set statement obtains the length of the data in variable &STRING2. The second statement uses that variable to define the last position of the data. By subtracting three from this value it is also possible to derive the starting position of the four-character year.

Let us take a look at another practical application of these data-manipulation functions. If one knew that a variable, &DSN, contained a fully qualified data set name in quotes (like 'TSO1234.SEQ.DATA'), the &SET, &SUBSTR, and &LENGTH functions could be used to remove the quotes.

```
SET &LEN = &LENGTH(&DSN)
SET &LEN = &LEN - 1
SET &DSN = &SUBSTR(2:&LEN,&DSN)
```

The same thing could be accomplished with two lines of code.

```
SET &LEN = &LENGTH(&DSN)
SET &DSN = &SUBSTR(2:&LEN-1,&DSN)
```

or

```
SET &LEN = &LENGTH(&DSN) -1
SET &DSN = &SUBSTR(2:&LEN,&DSN)
```

The &DATATYPE function

The *&DATATYPE function* can be used to determine if an expression is numeric or not. If an expression is entirely numeric, including numbers and valid arithmetic operators, a value of "NUM" is returned. When this is not true of the expression, the value "CHAR" is returned.

```
SET &TYPE_OF_DATA = &DATATYPE(&YEAR_TOTAL)
```

The value of the new variable, &TYPE_OF_DATA, could then be checked before the variable &YEAR_TOTAL was used in a calculation.

The &EVAL function

The last data manipulation function to be discussed in this section is *&EVAL*. It is used to force the evaluation of an expression. This built-in function is not often needed since expressions are generally evaluated by default. Certain circumstances, however, preclude such evaluation. The most common of these is when the expression is used within a WRITE statement. The WRITE statement is used to write information to be displayed at the terminal. We will be using it to display the results of some of the subsequent examples, and it will be further discussed in the next chapter. The WRITE statement allows symbolic substitution of variable values to take place, but is more oriented toward literal data than to arithmetic expressions. For example, with variable values of 252 and fifty-seven respectively, the following WRITE statement.

```
WRITE AMOUNT DUE IS &PREV_BAL - &PAYMENT
```

would display as

```
AMOUNT DUE IS 252 - 57
```

Substitution of variable values has occurred, but the statement is not further evaluated. To display the difference between the two variable values, it would be necessary to force the evaluation of the expression. To that end, the &EVAL function is used in the same WRITE statement below.

```
WRITE AMOUNT DUE IS &EVAL(&PREV_BAL - &PAYMENT)
```

With the same variable values, the display from the execution of this statement would be

```
AMOUNT DUE IS 195
```

Another situation that could mandate the use of &EVAL is when variables are used that appear to be "character" in nature. Perhaps this characteristic was placed on the variable by using it earlier with the &STR function. In addition to using the &EVAL function, this latter problem can also be circumvented by using the SET statement to equate a new variable to the old one, and using the new variable name for arithmetic operations.

CONDITION TESTING

As in many other languages, the IF-THEN-ELSE statement is available for *condition testing*. In its simplest form, a single expression is compared with another. Each expression can contain literals, variables, arithmetic operators, and built-in functions. A single imperative is allowed in either the true or false path. The false path is implemented using the ELSE clause. It is not required, but when coded, ELSE pairs itself with the last previously unmatched IF statement.

The following symbols and letters can be used for comparison in an IF statement.

=	or	EQ	¬=	or	NE
<	or	LT	¬<	or	NL
<=	or	LE	>=	or	GE
>	or	GT	¬>	or	NG

The following IF statement tests a variable, &STATE, against a character literal, CALIFORNIA.

```
IF &STATE = CALIFORNIA  THEN  SET &REGION = WEST
```

The statement is true when the variable &STATE contains the value CALIFORNIA. When the statement is true, the variable &REGION is set to the value WEST. The following statement shows the comparison of two arithmetic expressions.

```
IF &PREV_BAL + &CURR_CHARGE >  &PAYMENT + &ALLOWANCE THEN +
SET &AMOUNT_DUE = &CURR_CHARGE + &PREV_BAL - &PAYMENT
```

When the expressions are evaluated, and the first expression is found to be greater than the second, another variable, &AMOUNT_DUE, is set. Notice that the first line of this IF statement is continued. Not only is the IF statement normally restricted to a single imperative, it is also expected on the same line. By using a continuation character after THEN, we are able to continue the true path of the statement on the next line. The ELSE portion of the statement, if included, can also be continued. We can also use the condition test to avoid problems that would result from trying to divide by zero.

```
IF &VALUE1 > 0 THEN SET &RESULT = &VALUE2 / &VALUE1
```

This is easily accomplished by using the IF statement to insure that the divisor is greater than zero before attempting to divide. If the above statement is true, then variable &RESULT is set to the result of dividing variable &VALUE2 by variable &VALUE1. If the above statement was evaluated and found to be false, the SET statement is not executed. In either case, execution would fall through to the next sequential instruction. An ELSE or false-path imperative could also have been specified. Just as with the true condition, only a single imperative can be specified for the false path. That is illustrated in the following statements.

```
IF &VALUE1 > 0 THEN SET &RESULT = &VALUE2 / &VALUE1
ELSE SET &RESULT = 0
```

In the false path, where the divisor is not greater than zero, we have chosen to set the variable &RESULT to zero. The following IF statement helps to avoid another error, that of referencing beyond the length of a variable value or string. With the statement, we can insure that the value of variable &OLDSTRING is at least nine characters before we try to extract information through the ninth position.

```
      .
      .
      .
IF &LENGTH(&OLDSTRING) GE 9 THEN +
  SET &NEWSTRING = &SUBSTR(3:9,&OLDSTRING)
```

Earlier mention is made of code used to simulate decimal arithmetic. We can combine several statements that we have discussed in this chapter to effect such a solution. The simple example below provides code that will allow the result of division to display with four decimal places.

```
      .
      .
      .
SET &NUM1 = &NUM1 * 10000
SET &ANS = &NUM1 / &NUM2
SET &LEN = &LENGTH(&ANS)
IF &LEN > 4 THEN +
  SET &ANS = &SUBSTR(1:&LEN - 4,&ANS).&SUBSTR(&LEN - 3:&LEN,&ANS)
ELSE SET &ANS = .&ANS
WRITE &ANS
```

We saw earlier that we could multiply a number by a factor of 10 for each decimal place that we would like to retain. To that code, we have added logic that places a period four places in from the end of the result. An IF statement first tests to see that the result is greater than four bytes in length; if not, the period is placed in front of the result. The example above only handles results that are at least .1. See the example in Chap. 10 for an expanded version of this code and a more detailed explanation.

The IF statement can also be useful for testing return codes. The following is an example of testing the return code issued from an ALLOCATE command.

```
CONTROL NOFLUSH
ALLOCATE FILE(SYSUT2) DA('TSO1234.SEQ.DATA') OLD
IF &LASTCC > 0 THEN ALLOCATE FILE(SYSUT2) DA('TSO1234.SEQ.DATA') +
  CATALOG SPACE(1 1)
  TRACK UNIT(SYSDA)
```

An attempt is made to allocate an existing data set with a disposition of OLD. This, of course, means that the data set must already exist and would allow the data set to be overwritten in subsequent processing. If the data set does indeed exist, the resultant return code will be zero. If, on the other hand, the data set does not currently exist, a nonzero return code is passed. The IF statement tests for a return code that is greater than zero. When it is, an ALLOCATE command is executed to create the data set. This accounts for either situation that is likely to result from the allocation of an output data set. The CONTROL statement specifying NOFLUSH should be used prior to the ALLOCATE command to insure that the CLIST will not terminate before it gets to the IF statement.

It should also be noted that the IF-statement test immediately follows the statement whose return code is being tested. If there are any intervening statements, they will store their own return codes in the variable &LASTCC and therefore change its value. To delay the test of a particular return code, or use it more than once in a CLIST, the value of &LASTCC must be saved. The time to do this is, of course, immediately after the statement whose return code is to be utilized. Below is the example of a utility sort CLIST from the previous chapter. The highlighted statements have been added to test for a few anticipated return codes. In addition, a CONTROL statement has been added with the NOFLUSH parameter to insure that the CLIST does not terminate before the return code can be tested.

```
ALLOCATE F(SYSOUT) SYSOUT(T) REUSE
ALLOCATE F(SORTWK1) SP(1 1) CYL UNIT(SYSDA) REUSE
ALLOCATE F(SORTWK2) SP(1 1) CYL UNIT(SYSDA) REUSE
ALLOCATE F(SORTWK3) SP(1 1) CYL UNIT(SYSDA) REUSE
ALLOCATE F(SORTIN) DA(SEQ.DATA) SHR RFUSF
ALLOCATE F(SORTOUT) DA(SEQ.DATA) OLD REUSE
ALLOCATE F(SYSIN) DA(CNTL(CNTLCARD)) SHR REUSE
CONTROL NOFLUSH
CALL 'SYS1.SORTLIB(SORT)'
SET &RETCODE = &LASTCC
FREE F(SYSOUT SORTWK1 SORTWK2 SORTWK3 SORTIN SORTOUT SYSIN)
IF &RETCODE LE 4 THEN +
  WRITE SORT PROGRAM COMPLETED SUCCESSFULLY
```

```
ELSE IF &RETCODE = U0007 THEN +
  WRITE SORT FAILURE. CONTROL STATEMENT SYNTAX ERROR
ELSE IF &RETCODE = U0010 THEN +
  WRITE SORT FAILURE. SORT CONTROL STATEMENT MISSING
ELSE IF &RETCODE = U0005 THEN +
  WRITE SORT FAILURE. INVALID STATEMENT IDENTIFIER
ELSE WRITE SORT FAILURE. SORT USER ABEND CODE IS &RETCODE
```

The sort program would have set a return code to reflect the success of its operations. This code is then available to the CLIST. Notice that the value of &LASTCC is saved immediately after the CALL to the sort program. Stored in variable &RETCODE, the value of the return code can be tested as often as desired. In the example above, some common return code values are tested. The meaning of the code, when known, is written to the screen to help the CLIST user determine what problems were encountered. The IF statement tests are written in order of highest to lowest expected frequency. This, and the fact that all condition tests are tied together using ELSE, makes that section of code more efficient. The message written in the last ELSE condition is different because, at that point of the logic, the particular error encountered was not anticipated. In this latter case, the return code itself is displayed so the user can look it up in the available sort-message documentation.

COMPOUND IF STATEMENT TESTS

Conditions tested by the IF statement can be combined with *AND* and *OR*. When AND is used with two or more conditions, all of those conditions must be met for the test to be true. When OR is used, any single condition which satisfies the test makes it a true condition. The following IF statement tests the value of two different variables. For the SET statement to be executed, both conditions must be true.

```
IF &STATE = CALIFORNIA AND &AMOUNT_DUE > 0 THEN +
  SET &CA_COUNT = &CA_COUNT + 1
```

The next IF statement tests for multiple values from the same variable. The SET statement will be executed if any of the conditions are met.

```
IF &STATE = CALIFORNIA +
  OR &STATE = WASHINGTON +
  OR &STATE = OREGON THEN +
  SET &REGION = WEST
```

Notice in the example above that the variable &STATE is coded three times. Even though it is the only variable being tested, the name must be repeated to maintain the subject/operator/object sequence. On a related note, the use of multiple negative OR should be avoided. In some cases, it will create a logical incongruity and produce the opposite result. Take for example a simple test of two state codes.

```
IF &STATE_CODE NE 23 +
   OR &STATE_CODE NE 32 THEN +
   SET &RATE = 12
```

The intended purpose of the above statement is to place the number 12 in the variable &RATE for every state code except 23 or 32. It should be obvious, however, that &RATE will be set to 12 no matter what the state code is. Even when the value of &STATE_CODE is 23, any other value tested for (including 32) will cause the statement to be true. Since it is true that 23 is not equal to 32, the variable &RATE would still be set to 12. It is better to use positive OR logic as in the following example.

```
IF &STATE_CODE EQ 23 +
   OR &STATE_CODE EQ 32 THEN
ELSE SET &RATE = 12
```

The above example also shows that when there is an ELSE condition, it is possible to have a null true condition. Quite simply, this is an IF statement with no imperative for the true condition.

DO GROUPS

The previously mentioned limitation of the IF statement to execute only a single imperative in the true or false path can be easily overcome. This is done by grouping statements together. The group of statements is then treated as a single entity and can be included in either path of an IF statement. Below is an example of a *DO group* used in the true path of an IF statement that tests to see if a variable value starts with a single quote.

```
   .
   .
   .
IF &SUBSTR(1:1,&DSNAME) = ' THEN +
   DO
     SET &LEN = &LENGTH(&DSN)
```

```
      SET &LEN = &LEN - 1
      SET &DSN = &SUBSTR(2:&LEN,&DSN)
    END
```

This is a way to conditionally execute some of the data-manipulation functions that we discussed earlier. Notice that the group of statements starts with DO and ends with END. All statements between will be executed if the first character of the data in variable &DSNAME is a single quote.

The END statement that is used to delimit a group of statements looks just like the END command used to end a CLIST. An END statement matches with the previously unmatched DO statement, just like an ELSE statement matches up with the last previously unmatched IF statement. This is true despite the alignment or starting position of the statements. In our examples, we have aligned statements to show the other statements that they are paired with or depend on. Careless pairing of DO and END statements could, then, cause the CLIST to end prematurely. An effective way of avoiding this potential problem is to change the string that is used to mark the end of a DO group.

```
CONTROL END(ENDO)
```

A CONTROL statement like the one above, placed early in the CLIST, would allow the user to end every subsequent DO group with the string ENDO rather than END. This can make the code less confusing and easier to read. Below is a section of CLIST code that includes both the END command (to terminate the CLIST) and END statement (to terminate a DO group).

```
CONTROL END(ENDO)
  .
  .
  .
IF &DSNAME =   THEN END
IF &SUBSTR(1:1,&DSNAME) = ' THEN +
    DO
      SET &LEN = &LENGTH(&DSN)
      SET &LEN = &LEN - 1
      SET &DSN = &SUBSTR(2:&LEN,&DSN)
    ENDO
```

NESTED IF STATEMENTS

As an alternative to compound condition testing, IF statements can be *nested*. This would entail including additional IF statement tests in the true or false logic paths. Below is a compound IF statement and imperative that was presented earlier.

```
IF &STATE = CALIFORNIA AND &AMOUNT_DUE > 0 THEN +
  SET &CA_COUNT = &CA_COUNT + 1
```

The same functionality could also be given by the following statements.

```
IF &STATE = CALIFORNIA THEN +
  IF &AMOUNT_DUE > 0 THEN +
    SET &CA_COUNT = &CA_COUNT + 1
```

The condition test for &AMOUNT_DUE > 0 is nested under the previous test. As such, it is not even considered unless the first test produces a true condition. The example above, however, has no advantage over a compound IF statement. The advantage is seen when each portion of a compound test may have multiple consequences.

```
IF &STATE = CALIFORNIA THEN +
DO
  IF &AMOUNT_DUE > 0 THEN +
    SET &CA_COUNT = &CA_COUNT + 1
  ELSE IF &AMOUNT_DUE < 0 THEN +
    SET &CA_COUNT = &CA_COUNT - 1
  ELSE GOTO SKIPBILL
END
```

Used properly, nested IF-statement tests can minimize the number of times it is necessary to test for a particular condition. The use of DO groups, as in the above, helps to contain the code under a given true or false path.

LABELS AND BRANCHING

A *label* is a one- to thirty-one-character name that can be used for *branching* within a CLIST. When used, it is the first element on a line and is immediately followed by a colon. The label is then followed by some other CLIST element or a continuation character which would allow any additional code to start on the next line.

```
REALLOC: ALLOCATE FILE(SYSPROC) DATASET(CLIST) SHR REUSE
```

or

```
REALLOC: +
ALLOCATE FILE(SYSPROC) DATASET(CLIST) SHR REUSE
```

The CLIST GOTO statement uses labels to direct the flow of execution in other than a straight fall-through fashion. The only parameter that is used on a GOTO statement is the name of a label that is coded somewhere else in the CLIST.

```
GOTO REALLOC
```

The above statement will unconditionally cause execution to branch to the statement containing the label *REALLOC*. It does not matter whether that labeled statement is above or below the current statement. Execution will then continue sequentially from that point. Branching can be made conditional by simply combining it with IF statement tests. Below, a variable that contains a location-code value is tested for each possible value. A paired GOTO statement then causes a branch to the corresponding label where location-dependent code could be executed.

```
READ &LOC_CODE
IF &LOC_CODE = 1 THEN GOTO SECT1
ELSE IF &LOC_CODE = 2 THEN GOTO SECT2
ELSE IF &LOC_CODE = 3 THEN GOTO SECT3
  .
  .
  .
SECT1: +
  .
  .
  .
SECT2: +
  .
  .
  .
SECT3: +
  .
  .
  .
```

The code under each label is not included here, but might also include yet another GOTO statement. That GOTO would typically redirect execution to what is sometimes referred to as a *common collector*. The common collector, quite simply, would be a labeled statement that, in this case, could be branched to from any location-dependent code. This would bring processing back to a single point and avoid falling through to CLIST code (relevant to a different location) that should not be executed.

It is also possible to branch to multiple labels with a single GOTO statement. This is sometimes referred to as a *variable GOTO*. In this format, at least part of the label name is a variable. In the following example,

```
READ &LOC_CODE
GOTO SECT&LOC_CODE
.
.
.
SECT1: +
.
.
SECT2: +
.
.
SECT3: +
.
.
```

branching still occurs based upon a value read into the CLIST. The IF-statement tests are not required because the label name in the GOTO statement contains the variable &LOC_CODE. When the variable &LOC_CODE is resolved, its value will combine with the literal portion of the label name to cause branching to SECT1, SECT2, or SECT3. Again, the code under each label is not included here but would typically include a GOTO to a common labeled statement.

LOOPING AND DO WHILE

The GOTO statement can also be used to create an iterative structure or *loop*. Iterative processing is fundamental to programming in most languages, and allows the program to process a single unit of information before cycling back to work with the next unit. Below is an example of a simple loop that displays powers of 2 from 2 to 67,108,864. The loop is created with the IF statement by branching back to the label START until the counter is equal to 25. When the variable &COUNTER is equal to 25, the condition test will fail and the next sequential instruction, if any, will be executed, ending the loop.

```
SET &COUNT = 0
SET &ANSWER = 2
WRITE &ANSWER
START: +
SET &COUNT = &COUNT + 1
SET &ANSWER = &ANSWER * 2
WRITE &ANSWER
IF &COUNT < 25 THEN GOTO START
```

The same logic can be implemented with a *DO WHILE* structure. DO WHILE constitutes a DO group that can be iteratively executed. Like any other DO group, its end is designated with the END statement. The DO WHILE group is repeated as long as the condition is true at the top of the loop. Note that, depending upon the conditions set, the loop need not be executed at all.

```
SET &COUNT = 0
SET &ANSWER = 2
WRITE &ANSWER
DO WHILE &COUNT < 25
  SET &COUNT = &COUNT + 1
  SET &ANSWER = &ANSWER * 2
  WRITE &ANSWER
END
```

In the example above, the loop is established with the DO WHILE statement, which becomes the condition test. While the test is true, the statements between the DO WHILE statement and the END statement are executed. The END statement delimits the statements within the DO WHILE group. It is possible that this same code will never be executed. This is true if the conditional test proves to be false initially. In the above example, this would be when the value of variable &COUNT was 25 or greater.

Let us bring several of this chapter's topics together in a section of CLIST code. The statements below convert an eight-character numeric date of the format mm/dd/yy into a five-digit Julian date of the format yyddd. The initial date value is assumed to already be in a CLIST variable called &DATE. The date conversion is effected by calculating how many days are in each month, and adding this value to the total number of days each time the loop counter is less than the numeric month value.

```
  .
  .
SET &MM = &SUBSTR(1:2,&DATE)
SET &DD = &SUBSTR(4:5,&DATE)
SET &YY = &SUBSTR(7:8,&DATE)
IF (&YY // 4) EQ 0 THEN SET &DAYS = &STR(313232332323)
ELSE SET &DAYS = &STR(303232332323)
SET &I = 1
LOOP: IF &I LT &MM THEN +
```

```
DO
    SET &DD = &DD + 28 + &EVAL(&SUBSTR(&I,&DAYS))
    SET &I = &I + 1
    GOTO LOOP
END
IF &LENGTH(&STR(&DD)) = 2 THEN SET &DD = &STR(0&DD)
WRITE JULIAN DATE IS &YY.&DD
```

Initially, the numeric values for month, day, and year are extracted from the variable &DATE using the &SUBSTR function. Two separate strings are maintained to designate the number of days each month contains that is greater than 28 because the number of days in a month (for February) differs between leap years and other years. The remainder function is used to test for two-digit year values that are evenly divisible by 4. When this is true (indicated by a remainder of 0) the leap-year string is used to indicate the number of days that each month contains.

Both strings provide a way to handle the number of days in a month during loop processing. The strings are used as if they were a one-by-twelve element table representing the twelve months. Each digit is the number of days that can be added to 28 to arrive at the total number of days in the month. This is a way to make all months look more alike for iterative processing. The loop counter is used to test against the month value. It is also used within the loop to extract a single digit for the month in question. This is accomplished by using the loop counter in the &SUBSTR function. The &EVAL function is required here to force the evaluation of the expression because the variable &DAYS is seen as containing character data. The digit obtained is then added to 28 to provide the number of days in the month. The sum is added to the existing total of days. When the loop terminates, the variable &DD will contain the sum of added days and will become the day portion of the Julian date.

Notice that before the date is displayed, the length of variable &DD is tested. The variable starts as a two-digit numeric variable. It may later be involved in calculations or its value could simply be carried forward. The result, therefore, could be either two or three digits. If the variable contains a two-digit day value, a leading zero is added to maintain a consistent three digits. The &STR function is included in the length test because leading zeroes are otherwise not considered in a numeric value.

This code can easily be converted to use a DO WHILE structure. The code below shows the IF statement test and GOTO removed and replaced with DO WHILE/END.

```
.
.
SET &MM = &SUBSTR(1:2,&DATE)
SET &DD = &SUBSTR(4:5,&DATE)
SET &YY = &SUBSTR(7:8,&DATE)
IF (&YY // 4) EQ 0 THEN  SET &DAYS = &STR(313232332323)
ELSE SET &DAYS = &STR(303232332323)
SET &I = 1
DO WHILE &I LT &MM
  SET &DD = &DD + 28 + &EVAL(&SUBSTR(&I,&DAYS))
  SET &I = &I + 1
END
IF &LENGTH(&STR(&DD)) = 2  THEN SET &DD = &STR(0&DD)
WRITE JULIAN DATE IS &YY.&DD
```

The code within the DO WHILE group is only executed as long as the loop counter, &I is less than the extracted month variable &MM. If the date value 07/04/92 is entered, the loop would be executed six times. After the sixth execution, the loop counter &I and the month variable &MM would be equal. This would cause execution to fall through to the next sequential instruction, which happens to be the IF-statement test, which conditionally adds a leading zero to the &DD variable before the resultant date is written to the screen.

NESTED LOOP STRUCTURES

Either type of loop structure, whether it is implemented with the GOTO statement or DO WHILE, can be nested within other loops. This would allow multiple independent variables to be systematically controlled. Application needs may require, for example, that a loop control a variable representing the month. That iterative structure could then be included within another that controlled a variable representing the year.

```
SET &YEAR = 90
DO WHILE &YEAR < 92
  SET &MONTH = 1
  DO WHILE &MONTH < 13
    WRITE &YEAR &MONTH
    SET &MONTH = &MONTH + 1
  END
  SET &YEAR = &YEAR + 1
END
```

Notice that the variable that varies most often, the month, is addressed in the inner loop. When the CLIST above is executed, it writes to the terminal the values 90 1 through 90 12 and 91 1 through 91 12. Embedded loop structures are not restricted to two levels either. The user could decide to include day and month loops within one that accounted for the year. The limit to how many levels are nested are, of course, dictated by the application solution being provided, but one should keep in mind the maintainability of the resultant code.

SYSTEM VARIABLES

There are a number of special variables available within the CLIST language. These variables are used to convey information about the environment, and unless noted, are not user-modifiable. The variables are listed below with a brief description of the information they convey.

&SYSUID   This variable contains the user-ID of an individual as logged-on to TSO. This can be helpful in constructing data set names that contain the CLIST user's user-ID or determining special users from others who use a given CLIST.

```
SET &DSNAME - '&SYSUID.OUTPUT.DATA'
IF &SYSUID   - TSO1234 THEN SET &AUTH - 1
```

&SYSPREF   This variable reflects the value that has been set for the default data set high-level qualifier. Its value may be the same as &SYSUID and can be set using the TSO PROFILE command. The value of &SYSPREF is used by the system in constructing complete data set names from those that are partially qualified.

&SYSPROC   This variable contains the name of the procedure used at time of logon to gain access to TSO. The logon procedure typically allocates the data sets that would be used in a basic TSO session.

&SYSICMD   This variable contains the name used to invoke the current CLIST if the CLIST was invoked implicitly. If the CLIST was explicitly invoked, this variable will be blank. This can provide valuable information about how the CLIST was invoked. That in turn may have relevance to whether other CLISTs are also available implicitly. The &SYSICMD variable can also be used to determine which command or alias name was used and logic can be directed accordingly.

&SYSPCMD   This variable contains the name of the TSO command that the CLIST last executed. If no such commands are executed, the variable value will reflect how the CLIST was initially invoked. This would be the value EXEC, for example, when invoked using the EXEC command implicitly and EXEC or EX when it is invoked explicitly.

&SYSSCMD   This variable contains the name of the TSO subcommand that the CLIST last executed.

&SYSSCAN   This variable can be modified. It contains the number of times symbolic substitution can occur to resolve the variables in a line of CLIST code. The default value for this type of substitution is 16, but may be changed by the CLIST from a value of zero to a value of 2,147,483,648. When the value zero is used, no substitution occurs before the statement is executed.

&SYSNEST   This variable contains a yes or no value indicating whether the current CLIST was invoked directly or through another CLIST. Invocation is considered to be nested when the current CLIST is invoked by another CLIST. In this instance, the variable &SYSNEST contains a value of YES. If the currently executing CLIST was invoked directly by the terminal user, the variable value is NO.

Date and time variables

&SYSDATE   This variable contains the current date in eight characters in the format mm/dd/yy.

&SYSTIME   This variable contains the system time in eight characters in the format hh:mm:ss representing hours, minutes, and seconds. The time is that set for the computer's time-of-day clock with the hour value represented in twenty-four–hour format.

COMMUNICATION BETWEEN CLISTs

It is possible for one CLIST to execute another CLIST. In fact each secondary CLIST could, in turn, execute yet another CLIST. This sort of CLIST nesting can be repeated where each subsequently invoked CLIST is a new copy of that CLIST code. As mentioned previously in this chapter, the variable &SYSNEST can be tested to determine whether or not the currently executing CLIST was invoked by another CLIST. When that is true, the variable &SYSNEST will contain the value YES.

There are several reasons to have one CLIST execute another. One such reason is to simplify the execution of the second CLIST. This might entail including a series of positional and keyword values in one CLIST that often need to be supplied to the second CLIST. The first CLIST can even be designed to check these values before passing them to the second CLIST.

Secondary CLISTs can also be used as subroutines. This is especially beneficial when the secondary CLIST code can be executed from many different CLISTs or from multiple places from within a given CLIST. Either way, the amount of code in the invoking CLIST is reduced and typically simplified. Maintenance of the secondary code is often made easier as well since it would only need to be changed in a single place.

Before we look at CLIST-to-CLIST communication, let us review the communication between the EXEC function and a CLIST. In Chap. 3 we discussed how variable data can be passed to a CLIST when it is executed. This included positional-parameter data for required information, and keyword-parameter data for optional information. Both parameter types are specified when the CLIST is explicitly or implicitly invoked, and both are supported by the PROC statement.

Let us take a closer look at the PROC statement within a CLIST. The CLIST below is from the previous chapter. That CLIST was designed to always print the same data set. The code has been altered here to provide flexibility with regard to the data set that is printed, and the print characteristics used. Only changed or added code is highlighted.

```
PROC 1 PRINTDSNAME CLASS(A) COPIES(1) DEST(RMTO)
ALLOC FILE(SYSUT1) DATASET(&PRINTDSNAME) SHR REUSE
    ALLOC FILE(SYSUT2) SYSOUT(&CLASS) COPIES(&COPIES) DEST(&DEST) +
    REUSE
ALLOC FILE(SYSPRINT) SYSOUT(&CLASS) REUSE
ALLOC FILE(SYSIN) DUMMY REUSE
CALL 'SYS1.LINKLIB(IEBGENER)'
FREE FILE(SYSUT1 SYSUT2 SYSPRINT SYSIN)
```

The PROC statement that has been added contains one positional parameter and three keywords. When a PROC statement is included, it must be the first executable CLIST statement. This particular PROC statement was used in Chap. 3 to convey information about the print data set name, the output class to be used, the number of copies to be printed, and the printer destination. We can see now how the variables might be applied in the rest of the CLIST.

The rationale for using a positional parameter to specify the name of the data set to be printed is that it is required information. The CLIST could not be executed without the data set name. All other variable information communicated through the PROC statement is optional. In the previous example, these keyword parameters are also given suitable default values. When the following is used to invoke the modified CLIST,

```
%HARDCOPY 'TS01234.PRINT.TEXT' COPIES(3) CLASS(T)
```

variable information is passed to three of the four PROC-statement variables. The fourth variable, &DEST, will assume the default value RMTO. All variable values are then applied to the subsequent CLIST statements.

The same form of communication—positional and keyword parameters—can be used between one CLIST and another. Just as in the previous example, the flow of that variable information is in one direction only. The secondary CLIST can, however, set and pass back a return-code value by way of the system variable &LASTCC. The following example is from a traditional update application. Before the files are brought together, it is necessary to be sure that they are sorted in the same sequence. A separate CLIST, SORT, is used to resequence each file before further CLIST processing. Below is the sort CLIST from Chap. 5. Changes that were made to adapt it to this particular use are highlighted.

```
PROC 2 DSN CNTLCARD PRIM(5) SEC(1)
ALLOCATE F(SYSOUT) SYSOUT(T) REUSE
ALLOCATE F(SORTWK1) SP(&PRIM &SEC) CYL UNIT(SYSDA) REUSE
ALLOCATE F(SORTWK2) SP(&PRIM &SEC) CYL UNIT(SYSDA) REUSE
ALLOCATE F(SORTWK3) SP(&PRIM &SEC) CYL UNIT(SYSDA) REUSE
ALLOCATE F(SORTIN) DA(&DSN) SHR REUSE
ALLOCATE F(SORTOUT) DA(&DSN) OLD REUSE
ALLOCATE F(SYSIN) DA(&CNTLCARD) SHR REUSE
CALL 'SYS1.SORTLIB(SORT)'
SET &RET_CODE = &LASTCC
FREE F(SYSOUT SORTWK1 SORTWK2 SORTWK3 SORTIN SORTOUT SYSIN)
EXIT CODE(&RET_CODE)
```

The changes in the above CLIST are to make the CLIST more flexible. Positional parameters allow the specification of both the data set to be sorted, and the data set from which the sort control statements are to be read. Keyword parameters allow the primary and secondary sort workspace to be adjusted while they supply defaults when values are not supplied. It should be possible to invoke the CLIST directly or from another CLIST as in the following:

```
CONTROL END(ENDO)
%SORT MASTER.DATA CNTL(SORTCRD1) PRIM(15)
IF &LASTCC > 4 THEN +
  DO
    WRITE ERROR SORTING MASTER FILE
    END
  ENDO
%SORT TRANSACT.DATA CNTL(SORTCRD2)
IF &LASTCC > 4 THEN +
  DO
    WRITE ERROR SORTING TRANSACTION FILE
    END
  ENDO
ALLOC F(TRANS) DA(TRANSACT.DATA) SHR REUSE
ALLOC F(MASTER) DA(MASTER.DATA) OLD REUSE
CALL (UPDATE)
FREE F(TRANS MASTER)
```

The return code in &LASTCC is tested after each return from the SORT CLIST. If the return code is greater than 4, a problem is indicated and execution is terminated. Otherwise, the sorted data sets are allocated for use by the UPDATE application program.

Global variables

Global variables can be established to facilitate the communication of variable information between CLISTs. Using global variables, the passed information updated in secondary CLISTs is available upon return to the invoking CLIST. Global variables are established using the GLOBAL statement in both the primary CLIST and the CLIST that it executes. A section of code from a main CLIST is shown below.

```
.
GLOBAL &NUM_DATE &JUL_DATE
SET &NUM_DATE = &STR(&SYSDATE)
DATECONV
SET &CURR_DATE = &JUL_DATE
SET &NUM_DATE = &STR(&DUE_DATE)
DATECONV
IF &JUL_DATE < &CURR_DATE THEN GOTO DELINQUENT
.
.
.
```

Notice that a GLOBAL statement is used to define two variables, &NUM_DATE and &JUL_DATE. These variables are used to communicate date values to and from a second CLIST, DATECONV. DATE-CONV is executed twice to convert a different date each time from numeric to Julian format. Having been established as global variables, the variables are not included as parameters when DATECONV is implicitly executed. Upon returning from DATECONV the second time, the main CLIST is then able to directly compare the converted date values.

Below is the secondary CLIST. Notice that it, too, has a GLOBAL statement. That statement references the same two variable names as the main CLIST. This is not a requirement with global variables, however, since the linkage between the variables is established by position and not by name.

```
GLOBAL &NUM_DATE &JUL_DATE
SET &MM = &SUBSTR(1:2,&NUM_DATE)
SET &DD = &SUBSTR(4:5,&NUM_DATE)
SET &YY = &SUBSTR(7:8,&NUM_DATE)
IF (&YY // 4) EQ 0 THEN SET &DAYS = &STR(313232332323)
ELSE SET &DAYS = &STR(303232332323)
SET &I = 1
DO WHILE &I LT &MM
  SET &DD = &DD + 28 + &EVAL(&SUBSTR(&I,&DAYS))
  SET &I ;EQ &I + 1
END
IF &LENGTH(&STR(&DD)) = 2 THEN SET &DD = &STR(0&DD)
SET &JUL_DATE = &YY.&DD
EXIT
```

The code above is terminated with an EXIT statement. The EXIT statement is not required here because it is located at the physical end of the CLIST. At this point, control would have returned to the invoking CLIST anyway. The EXIT statement is useful for terminating the secondary CLIST at other than the physical end, and for setting a return code that is passed back to the invoking CLIST. Another parameter that is useful in terminating a secondary CLIST is the *QUIT* parameter.

```
EXIT QUIT
```

That parameter causes secondary CLIST code to be flushed, and control to return to a higher level CLIST that is protected. That protection is derived from the CONTROL statement parameters MAIN and NOFLUSH. If higher-level code is not protected in this fashion, all CLIST processing will stop, and control will return to TSO.

GLOBAL variables can be communicated to lower-level nested CLISTs as well. The highest-level CLIST that uses any of the global variables should define all subsequently used global variables. This is true even if that CLIST does not use some of those variables. This is important in maintaining the identity of the variables, since that identity is established by position rather than by name.

7

Input and Output Controlling Statements

TERMINAL INPUT AND OUTPUT

Terminal *input* and *output* is effected quite easily within the CLIST language. Information is written to the terminal with the WRITE statement. We have used the WRITE statement in previous examples as a simple way of displaying our processing results. This statement can be used to write literal or variable data and is often used to interact with the terminal user. Information written to the screen can be any combination of literal and variable data strung together. This includes leading and embedded blanks. Symbolic substitution of variable values occurs before the information is written to the screen. No attempt is made, however, to further evaluate the information. Information too lengthy to display on a single line will wrap to subsequent lines. The following statement,

```
WRITE   PLEASE ENTER THE NAME OF THE DATA SET TO BE PRINTED.
```

could be used, for example, in our hardcopy CLIST to better prompt the terminal user for the information that should be entered. That statement could then be followed with a *READ* statement to capture the response.

```
READ &PRINTDSNAME
```

The READ statement would cause the CLIST execution to halt until the terminal user enters a response. In this case, the user's response would be placed in the variable &PRINTDSNAME. That variable could then be used throughout the rest of the CLIST. To be sure that a nonblank value was entered, it might be desirable to test the response in variable &PRINTDSNAME. If the enter key was pressed without any information being typed, the positive path of the IF statement will branch back ahead of the WRITE statement. This will cause the request to be displayed again at the terminal and give the user another chance to enter the print data set name.

```
RETRY: +
WRITE    PLEASE ENTER THE NAME OF THE DATA SET TO BE PRINTED.
READ &PRINTDSNAME
IF &PRINTDSNAME = THEN GOTO RETRY
ALLOCATE F(SYSUT1) DA(&PRINTDSNAME) SHR REUSE
```

If data were entered, execution would instead fall through to the ALLOCATE command. This would allocate the data set to the input file name SYSUT1.

The READ statement above was used to set the value of a single variable. By supplying additional variables, the added variables can also be set in the same statement.

```
WRITE PLEASE ENTER THE FOLLOWING INFORMATION IN THE ORDER SPECIFIED
WRITE PRINT DATA SET    OUTPUT CLASS   NUMBER OF COPIES
READ &PRINTDSNAME &CLASS &COPIES
```

The example above has been changed to accept three variables at the same time. The prompt created by the *WRITE* statement is important because it tells the user what information is to be entered, and in what order. The order in which the data is entered is important to supplying the right data to the right variable. Normal space and comma delimiters, used to input data, define separate readable entities. Each piece of data is read into a separate variable. If there are more data entities than there are variables in the READ statement, the excess data is lost. It would be better to have the obverse condition, where after the READ is executed, the extra variables could be tested for blank values.

It is also possible to read information into a CLIST without using a specific variable name. When a READ statement appears without a variable name, the information is automatically read into the variable &SYSDVAL. Generally, it is better to use one's own variable names, rather than using &SYSDVAL and moving the information to another variable later on. The variable &SYSDVAL is helpful, however, in reading data that contains embedded delimiters but should be treated as a single data entity. The following text,

```
PLEASE ENTER THE FOLLOWING INFORMATION
```

when read using the following statement,

```
READ &VARIABLE1 &VARIABLE2 &VARIABLE3 &VARIABLE4
```

would cause each word of the text to be placed in a different variable. Because spaces serve as delimiters, the data entered appears to be five separate pieces of data. Since there were five pieces of data entered and only four variables, the last word, INFORMATION, would be lost. The same data read into variable &SYSDVAL, whether it is explicitly coded on the READ statement or not, would retain its integrity as a single string of data containing five words. &SYSDVAL can also be used to insure that single quotes or parenthesis surrounding a value read-in from the terminal are not stripped-off. This is especially helpful when the information read from the terminal is meant to represent a fully qualified data set name.

The system variable &SYSDVAL is perhaps most useful when it is used with the READDVAL statement to parse information into multiple variables. The value to be parsed is placed into the variable &SYSDVAL, either through a READ statement or using the SET statement. The READDVAL statement is then used with multiple variables to separate the information contained in &SYSDVAL. Each delimited string is placed in a new variable, with any left-over strings being lost. In that sense, it is just like the READ statement with more data items than variables.

```
SET &SYSDVAL = PLEASE ENTER THE FOLLOWING INFORMATION
READDVAL &VAR1 &VAR2 &VAR3 &VAR4 &VAR5
```

The result of these two statements is the variables below, each containing a separate portion of the information contained in the variable &SYSDVAL.

```
&VAR1        PLEASE
&VAR2        ENTER
&VAR3        THE
&VAR4        FOLLOWING
&VAR5        INFORMATION
```

With fewer variables, for example,

```
SET &SYSDVAL = PLEASE ENTER THE FOLLOWING INFORMATION
READDVAL &VAR1 &VAR2 &VAR3
```

the result would be

```
&VAR1          PLEASE
&VAR2          ENTER
&VAR3          THE
```

and the loss of some data.

Information written to the terminal can be formatted using the WRITE statement as well as a second version that leaves the cursor positioned after the information that is written to the screen. This statement is illustrated below.

```
WRITENR   ENTER INPUT CLASS ====>
```

This statement would leave the cursor positioned immediately after the special characters placed there to look like an arrow. In that way, the CLIST user could input the information right after the prompt that requests it. Some installations also have a command or program (often called *CLEAR*) that will clear the screen. If such a function is available, it can be used before formatted prompts to remove distracting information from the terminal and help direct the terminal user's attention to the prompts.

FILE INPUT AND OUTPUT

Another form of input and output that is available using CLIST statements is that which is directed to a particular file. It does not matter if that file is allocated to a disk data set, a spool data set for hardcopy, or even the terminal. That can, in fact, be readily changed using the ALLOCATE command. There are several steps involved in reading from a file or writing to one. First, the file must be allocated to the desired resource. Again, this can be a data set, sysout, or the terminal. The statement used to make this connection is the ALLOCATE command. We even saw, in Chap. 5, how the ALLOCATE command could be coded to negate file I/O transfer. The other statements used to effect file input and output will be discussed subsequently. They include opening the file, reading from or writing to the file, and closing the file.

The OPENFILE statement

The *OPENFILE statement* is used to open a file and describe how the file will be processed. It is coded after the relevant ALLOCATE command and before anything is read from or written to the file. The only required information is the file name. This file name must match that of a previously allocated file. The file could have been allocated by a previously executed ALLOCATE command or by the TSO procedure at logon time. An optional parameter may be used to specify the processing mode that will be used with the file. Values for this parameter include INPUT, OUTPUT, and UPDATE. INPUT indicates that the file will be opened in a read-only mode. In this mode, nothing can be written to that file. INPUT is the default and, therefore, need not be specified. OUTPUT indicates that a file will be written to with nothing read from the file. UPDATE indicates the possibility of both reading from and writing to the same file. In this mode, a write operation would replace the last record read, and therefore constitute an update in place process.

```
OPENFILE HISTORY OUTPUT
```

The above OPENFILE statement prepares the file named *HISTORY* for output processing. The file HISTORY must have been previously allocated, and opened in this fashion, can only be written to.

The GETFILE statement

The *GETFILE statement* reads from a previously opened file. The file can be allocated to a data set or to the terminal, and the file must have been opened in read or update mode. The only parameter included on the GETFILE statement is the file name. This file name should match that of a previously executed OPENFILE statement. Only sequential reading of records is possible, which means that each record must be read in turn from the beginning of the data set. With each GETFILE statement, a record is returned from the external data set. The content of the record is placed in the variable that corresponds to the file name in the corresponding ALLOCATE and OPENFILE commands. The following GETFILE statement would perform a read from the resource allocated to file TRANSACT. After the statement is executed, the data read from the file is stored in variable &TRANSACT.

```
GETFILE TRANSACT
```

A CLIST application could use the *GETFILE* statement to obtain a specific number of records, or using iterative logic, could obtain all the records in the data set. In the latter case, special consideration should be given to the way an end-of-file condition is handled. Within a CLIST, reading past the last record in the data set is considered an error, and will normally cause the immediate termination of the CLIST. Later in this chapter we will discuss different alternatives for handling the end-of-file condition.

The PUTFILE statement

The *PUTFILE statement* writes data to an external file. That file could have been allocated to a disk data set, a hardcopy spool file, or the terminal. The file name written to should have been previously opened for output or update. Again, the file name serves as a link between PUTFILE and OPENFILE statements and the ALLOCATE command. Whatever has been placed in the file name variable, if anything, is written to the file. In the case of a file opened for update, the last record obtained using GETFILE is replaced with PUTFILE. When the file is opened for output, the PUTFILE output replaces or extends the data set. The disposition used to allocate a data set determines how the data is written. Remember that a data set allocated with a disposition of OLD is completely rewritten. A data set allocated with a disposition of MOD, however, has new records appended after existing records.

```
SET &HISTORY = &SYSUID &ACCTNUM START OF TSO SESSION &SYSTIME
PUTFILE HISTORY
```

The above statements illustrate how a combination of literal and variable data can be written to a file. The first statement stores the information in the variable &HISTORY. That variable is then used in the PUTFILE statement to write the same information out to the pre-allocated file HISTORY.

It is often necessary to write variable-length information out in specific output columns. The example below shows how certain variable values can be made to conform to fixed lengths so that when they are strung together, they can be written in column format.

```
    .
    .
SET &SPACES = &STR(                    )
SET &LASTNAME = &SUBSTR(1:20,&LASTNAME&SPACES)
SET &FIRSTNAME = &SUBSTR(1:15,&FIRSTNAME&SPACES)
SET &MIDDLENAME = &SUBSTR(1:15,&MIDDLENAME&SPACES)
```

```
SET &OUTFILE = &STR(&LASTNAME &FIRSTNAME &MIDDLENAME)
PUTFILE OUTFILE
  .
  .
```

The code above insures that each of three variables &LASTNAME, &FIRSTNAME, and &MIDDLENAME, achieve a particular length before they are placed in the output variable and written-out. This is accomplished by stringing a second variable (that contains spaces) behind each of the other variables and extracting a fixed number of bytes from the combined variables. To illustrate how the length of a variable can be fixed, two values of the variable &LASTNAME are displayed below. The bold print shows the result of joining variables &LASTNAME and &SPACES. The boxed area is the portion of the combined value that is actually used after the &SUBSTR function is executed.

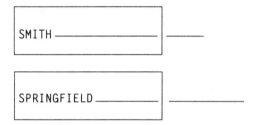

In the following example, some of the concepts just discussed are brought together. In the example, records are read-in from a file called TRANSACT. They are then added to the end of an existing data set after the system date is added to the data that was read-in. The data is output through the file name of HISTORY.

```
ALLOCATE FILE(TRANSACT) DATASET('TS01234.INPUT.DATA') SHR REUSE
ALLOCATE FILE(HISTORY) DATASET('TS01234.OUTPUT.DATA') MOD REUSE
OPENFILE TRANSACT
OPENFILE HISTORY OUTPUT
READREC: +
GETFILE TRANSACT
SET &HISTORY = &STR(&SYSDATE &TRANSACT)
PUTFILE HISTORY
GOTO READREC
```

The loop coded above, and in fact, the entire CLIST will stop executing when an attempt is made to read past the end of the input file.

After we examine the CLOSFILE statement, we will discuss methods for handling end-of-file conditions.

The CLOSFILE statement

When input or output processing is finished for a given file, the file should be closed. The *CLOSFILE statement* performs this function. Its only parameter, like many of the related statements, is the file name. In many cases, a data set left opened cannot be used in other TSO functions. All data sets are closed as a result of logging off of TSO, but it is best to close and free resources (using the FREE command) as soon as they are no longer needed. It is also possible to close and reopen files to reprocess the data they contain. In doing so, processing starts from the beginning of the data set (with dispositions of SHR or OLD).

```
CLOSFILE TRANSACT
```

The above statement closes the file TRANSACT. The file could then be opened again, or the file name freed to complete the release of resources.

End-of-file considerations

There are several ways that end-of-file conditions can be handled. The last complete example showed how a CLIST can be left to terminate as a result of a GETFILE error. The CLIST was coded to take care of any processing immediately. It reset the record value and wrote the output record before obtaining another record. That way, an abrupt termination does not cause a problem.

A CLIST may also have a predetermined number of reads to execute. This could be because there is always a set number of records to be input, or it could have been determined by a priming read. In the former case, the amount of information to be brought into the CLIST is known and is included in the CLIST. It could well be determined beforehand, for instance, that three eighty-byte records would have to be read by a certain CLIST. This could easily be incorporated in the CLIST code that controls iterative processing. In the latter case, the number of input records is known to vary. The data is designed so that the first record read-in contains a value indicating the number of subsequent reads required to obtain all data records. That information could then be used to control the read loop, and thus avoid reading past end-of-file. Below is an example of that code based upon the previous example. The GOTO-based loop has been replaced with a DO WHILE structure.

```
ALLOCATE FILE(TRANSACT) DATASET('TS01234.INPUT.DATA') SHR REUSE
ALLOCATE FILE(HISTORY) DATASET('TS01234.OUTPUT.DATA') MOD REUSE
OPENFILE TRANSACT
GETFILE TRANSACT
SET &RECORDS = &TRANSACT
OPENFILE HISTORY OUTPUT
DO WHILE &COUNT < &RECORDS
  GETFILE TRANSACT
  SET &HISTORY = &STR(&SYSDATE &TRANSACT)
  PUTFILE HISTORY
  SET &COUNT = &COUNT + 1
END
CLOSFILE TRANSACT
CLOSFILE HISTORY
FREE F(TRANSACT HISTORY)
```

The key to this process is the first data record. It was created to indicate how many actual data records exist in the data set. An example of such a data set is shown below.

```
2068
data record 1...
data record 2...
data record 3...
  .
  .
  .
data record 2068...
```

The first data record indicates that 2068 data records follow. An initial READ statement is added to the CLIST code outside and before the normal loop. This statement reads in the numeric value that specifies the number of remaining records. That value is placed in a variable that is used to control iterative DO WHILE processing. A CLOSFILE statement and a FREE command have been added to the example to clean up the environment. This code will be executed, since this process avoids the immediate termination that can accompany reading past the end of the file.

Another way to avoid end-of-file–read errors may also entail making changes to the data. In some cases, the last data record may contain a value which could be used to signal the CLIST to stop reading. This could be based upon some naturally occurring value in the last data record that was unique. The CLIST could test for that value, and when found, stop file input. Where the data does not accommodate such a test, a unique record could be added as the last record of the data set. The unique value, like all nines, could still be tested to determine when to stop reading.

The final method for handling end-of-file conditions is to add statements to the CLIST that detect when such an error occurs but keep the CLIST from terminating. This can be accomplished using an error routine, and will be discussed in the next section.

Error handling

When a GETFILE statement is executed causing a read past end of file, an error situation is created. This is true despite a message indicating that normal end of file has been reached. Under normal circumstances, the return code is set to 400, and processing is halted immediately. An error exit can be included, however, that would allow the CLIST to continue processing. The error exit is an instruction or a special DO GROUP that is placed before code where an error could be anticipated. In this case, the *ERROR* routine is placed somewhere before the GETFILE statement. An error is sensed when a command or statement issues a high return code. When an error is encountered, control branches to the last previously executed error routine. The error routine only takes effect in the event of an error. That is to say, even though error code is encountered in the normal execution-flow sequence, it is not actually activated until there is an error.

An ERROR routine can execute any number of TSO commands and CLIST statements. With no other direction, the next sequential instruction will be executed after the error routine is executed. In this case, the next sequential instruction would be the one immediately following the error routine itself, and not the statement following the statement causing the error. Control can, however, also be directed to the instruction following the one that caused the error. This is done with the RETURN statement.

```
        .
        .
        .
ERROR +
    DO
        SET &ERROR_CNT = &ERROR_CNT + 1
        RETURN
    END
        .
        .
        .
```

The ERROR routine above includes a DO group. That allows more than a single statement to be executed when the routine is activated. After a variable used as an error counter is incremented, control is directed to the statement following the one that caused the error. The branch back is mandated by the RETURN statement.

Below is the previous complete example of reading from one file and writing to another. An ERROR routine has been added to better handle an end-of-file condition while reading data from the input data set. The code that has been added is highlighted.

```
CONTROL MAIN NOFLUSH
ALLOCATE FILE(TRANSACT) DATASET('TS01234.INPUT.DATA') SHR REUSE
ALLOCATE FILE(HISTORY) DATASET('TS01234.OUTPUT.DATA') MOD REUSE
OPENFILE TRANSACT
OPENFILE HISTORY OUTPUT
SET &RC = 0
ERROR +
   DO
      SET &RC = &LASTCC
      IF &RC   = 400 THEN   +
      WRITE     NORMAL END OF CLIST
      ELSE   +
         DO
            WRITE     UNEXPECTED END OF CLIST
            WRITE     RETURN CODE IS &RC
            EXIT
         END
   END
DO WHILE &RC = 0
   GETFILE TRANSACT
   SET &HISTORY = &STR(&SYSDATE &TRANSACT)
   PUTFILE HISTORY
END
CLOSFILE TRANSACT
CLOSFILE HISTORY
FREE FILE(TRANSACT HISTORY)
```

An ERROR statement has been added to the code and the DO WHILE statement has been changed. Statements to close and free the files have also been added. Remember that in the previous GETFILE example, the CLIST would have been flushed before such statements could have been executed. When an error is encountered, control immediately branches to the error routine. Because the branch is immediate, the first statement placed in the ERROR routine above saves the return code for further testing.

In the case of a GETFILE error, the return code will have the value of 400. The ERROR routine has a section of code that deals specifically with that particular error code. Notice that the error routine also

has some logic that would apply to errors that result from other causes. Errors can occur, for example, trying to open a file that was not
previously allocated or reading from or writing to files that were not
opened. The code included in the example to deal with all other errors
is very much simplified, and would halt the CLIST execution since
such errors would not have been anticipated and would likely be more
severe than reading past end-of-file.

When the error routine finishes executing, control falls through to
the next sequential instruction. For a GETFILE error in the previous
example, that would be the DO WHILE test. That test would fail due
to the value in variable &RC (which at that point would be 400). That,
in turn, would cause control to fall through the loop to code that closes
and frees the files.

It is also possible to include an ERROR statement that contains no
other instructions. In this case execution continues with the next
sequential instruction (following the statement that produced the
error). Used in this fashion, the ERROR statement will display the
command or statement that caused the error. The display may also
include explanatory text.

Branching to an ERROR statement in the event of an error only
becomes possible after the error statement code is encountered.
Multiple error routines can be included in a CLIST, and the last one
executed will replace any ERROR routine previously in effect. The
subsequent branching after an error can be also be turned off. This
enables the CLIST developer to decide when to try to correct errors,
and when to let them terminate the CLIST. The following statement

```
ERROR OFF
```

would turn error processing off, and might be used when a high
return code is anticipated. In the following code, for example, it would
not be unusual to receive a high return code from the DELETE command.

```
.
.
ERROR OFF
DELETE TEMP.DATA
ERROR +
  DO
    SET &RC = &LASTCC
    WRITE   UNEXPECTED END OF CLIST
    WRITE   RETURN CODE IS &RC
    EXIT
```

```
END
  .
  .
```

Such a high return code would be generated when the data set did not already exist, and therefore, could not be deleted. This certainly would not be a critical error, and so the ERROR function is turned off before the command is executed. The ERROR function is then reactivated in anticipation of subsequent errors.

The CONTROL statement parameters NOFLUSH and MAIN should be used to prevent CLIST code from being flushed. This will help to insure that a branch is made to the error routine after an error is encountered, rather than the immediate termination of the CLIST.

The next chapter deals with some specialized CLIST functions. The reader will find that the first of those functions, the attention routine, is very similar to the error routine that we just discussed.

Special Functions

There are some special functions within the CLIST language that do not fit readily into the major categories we have covered so far. Some of these functions were made available as the language evolved, and greatly simplified the task of coding a CLIST program. Often, they served to expedite tasks that CLISTs had performed for some time. Among these are functions to check for the presence of data sets, and trap TSO command output for further use with the CLIST. The first topic of discussion, however, is a function that is not otherwise available. The first topic of discussion is the *attention routine.*

THE ATTENTION ROUTINE

A CLIST user is usually able to terminate a CLIST using the PA1 (Program Access 1) or ATTN (Attention) keys. In most instances, the CLIST is terminated immediately. The attention routine, however, provides an exit to branch to after such an interrupt. This is very similar to the function that the ERROR routine provides after a processing error. Like the ERROR routine, a CLIST may have multiple ATTN routines. The ability to branch to an attention routine exists only after ATTN code has been executed. Also, the attention routine code does not become active until after an attention interrupt has been sensed. At that point, a branch is made to the last previously executed attention routine code. The ability to branch to such code can be turned off at any point in the CLIST by including the following statement.

```
ATTN OFF
```

Unlike the ERROR routine, only a single TSO command or subcommand may be executed in the ATTN routine. An ATTN routine can include multiple statements, but the execution of a TSO command or subcommand within the routine will cause control to branch back to the statement that was interrupted. A null statement can be used in place of either of the above. To execute more than a single TSO command or subcommand, a subordinate CLIST can be invoked. That secondary CLIST is not restricted to the number of TSO commands and subcommands that it can execute. Upon return from the subordinate CLIST, control will branch back to the statement that was interrupted.

Below is a sample ATTN routine. It uses a null statement, represented by the variable &NULL, that has not been given an initial value. If the PA1 or ATTN keys are used during the CLIST execution, control will branch to this code. This specific ATTN routine asks the CLIST user if he or she wants to terminate the CLIST. If the answer is *Y,* for yes, the CLIST takes care of its termination processing, and ends. If any other response is made, control is returned to the statement that was interrupted. This is effected by including a null statement in the false path of the IF statement test.

```
CONTROL MAIN
   .
   .
ATTN DO
   WRITE   DO YOU WANT TO TERMINATE THE CLIST?
   WRITENR   ENTER Y OR NO ===>
   READ &ANS
   IF &ANS = Y THEN +
     DO
        CLOSEFILE INDATA
        FREE FILE(INDATA)
        EXIT
     END
   ELSE &NULL
END
   .
   .
```

CONTROL MAIN is included to identify the CLIST as the main procedure in use and to keep it from flushing the remainder of the CLIST when the attention exit is used. The RETURN statement can also be used to cause control to branch back. With the RETURN statement, however, execution resumes with the statement following the one that was interrupted. Below is the same ATTN routine with the RETURN statement included in place of the null statement.

```
CONTROL MAIN

·

·

ATTN DO
   WRITE    DO YOU WANT TO TERMINATE THE CLIST?
   WRITENR   ENTER Y OR N ===>
   READ &ANS
   IF &ANS = Y THEN +
      DO
         CLOSEFILE INDATA
         FREE FILE(INDATA)
         EXIT
      END
   ELSE RETURN
END

·

·
```

Note that neither of the last two examples contains a TSO command or subcommand. Such a command would end the ATTN routine.

DETECTING DATA SET PRESENCE

The next function to be discussed is *&SYSDSN*. It can be used to determine the presence or absence of a cataloged data set. The function assumes different values that reflect the status of the data set. If the data set exists, the value that is reflected is "OK." If the data set does not exist, the value is "DATASET NOT FOUND." This is true even if there is a catalog entry but no data set. When testing for the latter value, the spacing between words should be exact. The following is an example of how the function is used.

```
SET &DSNTEST = &SYSDSN(SEQ.DATA)
```

In the example, the variable &DSNTEST is set by the &SYSDSN function. The variable &DSNTEST could then be tested for the value

"OK." The function value need not be placed in a separate variable, however, to be used.

```
IF &SYSDSN(&DSNAME) = OK THEN +
  ALLOC FILE(SYSUT2) DATASET(&DSNAME) OLD REUSE
ELSE ALLOC FILE(SYSUT2) DATASET(&DSNAME) NEW CATALOG +
  UNIT(3380) VOLUME(SYSTM4) RECFM(F B) LRECL(80) BLKSIZE(6240) +
  TRACKS SPACE(3 1) REUSE
```

This example also shows another way to determine whether a file can be allocated to an existing data set, or if a new data set must be created. Notice too, that throughout this last example, the data set name is handled within a variable. The format of a data set name in the &SYSDSN function is the same as it is for any TSO data set name. It therefore may or may not need to be fully qualified.

The &SYSDSN function can also be used to test for the presence of a member within a data set. When the combination of data set and member name both exist, the value of the function is still "OK." If the data set exists, but the member does not, the function value is "MEMBER NOT FOUND." In cases where a member name should not be included, the &SYSDSN function would return the value "MEMBER SPECIFIED, BUT DATASET IS NOT PARTITIONED." Again, the user should be careful to test for the exact literal content. Other values issued by the &SYSDSN function include:

INVALID DATASET NAME   This message indicates that the syntax of the data set name specified is incorrect. This could be due to the use of invalid special characters, unbalanced parentheses or single quotes, or too many characters in the name itself or in one of the simple qualifiers. The actual message issued includes the data set name as it was included in the &SYSDSN function. Testing for this condition is, therefore, not a straightforward matter. There are two fairly common ways to conduct such a test. The first is to test the first twenty bytes of the message which will always be a constant value

```
SET &MESS = &SYSDSN(&DSN)
IF &SUBSTR(1:20,&MESS) = +
  &STR(INVALID DATASET NAME)
```

An alternative is to include the same from of the data set name in the condition test. Here, the data set name is contained in the variable &DSN.

```
SET &MESS = &SYSDSN(&DSN)
IF &MESS = +
   &STR(INVALID DATASET NAME, &DSN)
```

The same variable could be used to specify the data set name to the &SYSDSN function and test the message it issues.

MISSING DATASET NAME

This message indicates that the &SYSDSN function was executed without a data set name value.

UNAVAILABLE DATASET

This message indicates that a lock has been placed on the data set due to its use elsewhere, and the data set cannot currently be used.

VOLUME NOT ON SYSTEM

This message indicates that the volume containing the data set in question (as indicated by information in the system catalog) is not mounted or is not available. The disk VTOC, therefore, cannot be searched for data set information.

PROTECTED DATASET

This message indicates that the terminal user's access is insufficient to allow the directory to be opened to obtain member information.

CAPTURING COMMAND OUTPUT

Another special function allows a CLIST to *capture* the output of many TSO commands. Traditionally, TSO command output is directed to the screen. There are a few commands, like LISTCAT, that allow command output to be directed elsewhere. The LISTCAT command OUTFILE parameter would, for example, allow catalog information to be written to a data set or hardcopy file rather than to the terminal. Except for the few exceptions like this, CLISTs had to be content to control whether such output was displayed or suppressed. The SYSOUT trap function allows much of the TSO command output to be captured and used within the CLIST.

Before attempting to capture command output, it is important to

ensure that message output will be produced. The following CON-
TROL statement can be used to enable message production.

```
CONTROL MSG
```

After having ensured that messages will be produced, it is necessary to set the trap. In doing so, the maximum number of lines to trap
is specified. It is often a good idea to make this number larger than
what is normally anticipated to allow for expansion or unusual circumstances.

```
SET &SYSOUTTRAP = 10
```

The statement above turns the trap on and sets the line limit to ten
lines. Any message output in excess of the set limit, in this case ten
lines, will not be captured, nor will it display at the terminal as it
would if the trap had never been set. Any subsequent command that
the CLIST executes will have its output trapped until the trap is
turned off. The trap is turned off by setting variable &SYSOUTTRAP
back to zero. The CLIST can then go back to suppressing or displaying
message output. Below is an example of what we have discussed:

```
PROC 1 DSNAME
CONTROL MSG
SET &SYSOUTTRAP = 10
LISTDS &DSNAME
SET &SYSOUTTRAP = 0
CONTROL NOMSG
.
.
```

In the example, a data set name is brought in as a positional
parameter. The messages and the SYSOUT trap are turned on. The
data set name becomes part of a LISTDS command whose message
output is trapped, and finally, the trap and messages are turned off.
At this point we have not yet accessed the trapped information. The
trapped information is contained in variables which all have the name
&SYSOUTLINEx. In the variable name, x represents the relative line
number. Having set the maximum line number to ten, if all lines were
used, the information for the last line of message output would be
stored in variable &SYSOUTLINE10.

The LISTDS command is used to list data set attributes. A sample
of output from the command follows.

```
TS01234.PDS.DATA
--RECFM-LRECL-BLKSIZE-DSORG
  FB    80    6160    PO
--VOLUMES--
  DISK04
```

The CLIST should anticipate not only the particular line that the desired information will appear on, but also the columns from which to extract the information. If we wanted to determine the data set organization, we would want to extract the two bytes starting in column 23 of line 3 of the message output.

```
SET &DSORG = &SUBSTR(23:24,&SYSOUTLINE3)
```

The variable &SYSOUTLINE3 contains the entire third line of LISTDS output. The above statement sets the variable &DSORG to the two bytes, 23 and 24, of that line. That variable can then be tested to direct logic concerning the data set's organization. Similar logic can be applied to a previous example:

```
PROC 1 DSNAME
CONTROL MSG
SET &SYSOUTTRAP = 10
LISTDS &DSNAME
SET &SYSOUTTRAP = 0
CONTROL NOMSG
IF &SUBSTR(23:24,&SYSOUTLINE3) = PO  THEN  +
   DO
      WRITE ENTER NAME OF MEMBER
      READ &MEMBER
   END
   .
   .
```

The example above represents part of a CLIST that would accept a data set name as its only positional parameter. The CLIST traps the LISTDS output and tests the part of the output that represents the data set organization. The value "PO" stands for partitioned organization and indicates that the data set is a PDS. Sensing this, the logic prompts the terminal user to enter a member name. The CLIST would then typically go on to do other processing. Other information about the data set's characteristics can be obtained in a similar manner.

The SYSOUT trap can also be used to trap error messages. This type of information can often provide more information to guide CLIST processing than the return codes that are routinely available. The error messages can then be tested to determine what is wrong and make "intelligent" decisions about recovery from the errors.

Another SYSOUT trap variable allows the CLIST to determine the last line trapped. When the trap is started, the maximum number of lines to trap is specified. Not necessarily all such lines, however, would contain trapped output. The variable &SYSOUTLINE contains the line number of the last line to contain trapped data after the trap is turned off. The variable can, therefore, be used to control iterative or loop processing. Such is the case in the example below. The following code is designed to capture a list of all PDS members and display them at the terminal. The output is formatted to list seven members on a single line as opposed to the normal member-per-line output of the LISTDS command.

```
PROC 1 DSN COUNT(6)
SET &SPACES = &STR(          )
SET &SYSOUTTRAP = 999
LISTDS &DSN    M
SET &SYSOUTTRAP = 0
WRITE
WRITE THE MEMBERS IN DATA SET    &DSN    ARE:
WRITE
LOOP: SET &COUNT = &COUNT + 1
IF &COUNT > &SYSOUTLINE THEN END
SET &LINE = &SYSOUTLINE&COUNT
SET &LEN = &LENGTH(&LINE)
SET &MEMBER = &LINE&SUBSTR(&LEN+1:9,&SPACES)
IF (&COUNT-6) // 7 = 0  THEN WRITE &MEMBER
ELSE   WRITENR &MEMBER
GOTO LOOP
```

Actual loop processing starts with the seventh line of output. This is effected by starting with a counter value of six and incrementing it immediately at the top of the loop. This allows the CLIST to bypass the data set characteristics and start with the first member name. The same counter is used to test against the last line used value contained in variable &SYSOUTLINE, and it serves as the numeric portion of the variables used to address the actual trapped output.

The member names are all padded to be a uniform length so that they will line up when displayed at the terminal. Multiple members are written on a single line of the terminal by simply using the no-return option of the WRITE statement, WRITENR. Every seventh WRITE statement is a normal write which finishes off one line and positions itself below for the next line. The remainder function is used to detect every seventh WRITE statement (after subtracting the number six because of the unusual starting position). That seventh occurrence is determined when the &COUNT (minus 6) is evenly divisible by seven.

Notice that the variable that contains the last line used, &SYSOUT-LINE, is very similar to the variables that actually contain the trapped output. These latter variables are distinguished by the numeric value that is the variable-name suffix. This example shows the line variables handled as if they were in a single dimension table. The double "&" in the variable name &&SYSOUTLINE&COUNT is the key to handling the variable in this way and making it ideally suited to loop processing.

TABLE PROCESSING WITH VARIABLES

As we have just seen, CLIST variables can be treated as if they were in a *table* or array. This is especially helpful when variable information is handled during loop processing. This structure can be implemented by starting the variable name with a double ampersand. Where loop processing is concerned, it is helpful to include a numeric variable within that name which would serve as an index value. For example, the variable name &&VARIABLE&NUM would resolve to &VARIABLE1 when &NUM has a value of 1. By incrementing the variable &NUM during loop processing, it would be possible to create variable &VARIABLE2, &VARIABLE3, and so on. Below is a complete CLIST example of how table like variables can be used in loop processing.

```
SET &NUMBER = 1
SET &SYSDVAL = 31 28 31 30 31 30 31 31 30 31 30 31
READDVAL &MONTH1 &MONTH2 &MONTH3 &MONTH4 &MONTH5 &MONTH6 +
         &MONTH7 &MONTH8 &MONTH9 &MONTH10 &MONTH11 &MONTH12
DO WHILE &DATATYPE(&NUMBER) = NUM
   WRITE    ENTER THE MONTH AS A VALUE FROM 1 TO 12
   WRITENR   OR ENTER A BLANK TO TERMINATE ===>
   READ &NUMBER
   IF &NUMBER > 0 AND &NUMBER < = 12 THEN +
      DO
         SET &DAYS = &&MONTH&NUMBER
         WRITE    THAT MONTH CONTAINS &DAYS DAYS
      END
END
```

The CLIST above reads values into twelve different month variables. Each variable then contains the number of days that month normally contains. Within the loop, the CLIST user is prompted to enter the numeric month value. That value becomes part of the variable name to reference one of the twelve variables. The variable value is then placed in another variable that can be written out, displaying the number of days in that month. The process is repeated until the CLIST user enters a null value.

A double ampersand is not used when the variable appears in the left half of a SET statement.

```
SET &NUMBER = 12
SET &MONTH&NUMBER = 31
```

The second statement in the example above would set the variable &MONTH12 to a value of 31.

BATCH EXECUTION OF A CLIST

The program IKJEFT01 supports the execution of TSO commands and subcommands in a background mode. The TSO command EXEC, in turn, allows a CLIST to be executed explicitly or implicitly. That means that, depending on its design, a CLIST can also be run in the background. It can be combined with TSO commands and other CLISTs. This would leave the terminal free to do other work while the CLIST is executing in the background, and is particularly useful when working with larger amounts of data. Running in the background also allows CLIST functions to be run overnight when there is less likely to be contention over resources. This is especially true where exclusive control of a data set is required. Yet another reason for executing a CLIST in the background is to capture command output that is normally only written to the screen. Output from a batch-submitted CLIST can be written to SYSOUT or to a data set.

The user-ID of the CLIST user can be propagated through the TSO SUBMIT command to the CLIST as it executes in the background. The PROFILE command can also be used to change the prefix that is used with data sets that are not fully qualified. A CLIST running in background mode cannot make use of the READ and TERMIN statements. An interactive function based upon those statements, therefore, cannot be maintained.

Invoked using JCL, the CLIST becomes an initiated task, executed by the program IKJEFT01. Only two DD statements are required for execution. These statements describe the input and output, and can be specified in any order. The DD statement that describes the pro-

cessing output has a file name of SYSTSPRT. It can be directed to
SYSOUT or to a data set.

The DD statement that describes the input to program IKJEFT01
has a file name of SYSTSIN. It can describe instream data or can
refer to a data set. Either form of input can be used to execute CLISTs
as well as TSO commands. In the example below, the commands to be
executed are specified as instream data. This is possible, because only
TSO commands and subcommands are included.

```
//TS01234A JOB account,parameters,
//  CLASS=A,MSGCLASS=A,NOTIFY=TS01234
//BATCHTSO EXEC PGM=IKJEFT01
//SYSTSPRT DD  SYSOUT=*
//SYSTSIN  DD  *
EDIT 'TS01234.AUDIT.REPORT' OLD DATA NONUM
C * 999 '01/01/92' '02/10/92' ALL
LIST
END SAVE
```

When CLIST statements are to be executed, the statements must
be included in a CLIST data set and invoked with some form of the
EXEC command.

```
//TS01234A JOB account,parameters,
//  CLASS=A,MSGCLASS=A,NOTIFY=TS01234
//BATCHTSO EXEC PGM=IKJEFT01
//SYSPROC  DD  DSN=TS01234.CLIST,DISP=SHR
//SYSTSPRT DD  SYSOUT=*
//SYSTSIN  DD  *
%HARDCOPY 'TS01234.PRINT.TEXT' COPIES(3) CLASS(T)
```

In the example above, an implicit form of the EXEC command is
used. The percent sign dictates that only the SYSPROC file will be
used to search for the CLIST called HARDCOPY. A SYSPROC DD
statement has been included that references the data set that contains the HARDCOPY CLIST. This allows the implicit form of the
command to be used, and works the same way in background execution as it does in foreground execution. In addition to the SYSPROC
file, other DD statements can be added when it is necessary to simulate other environments.

If system CLISTs are also to be accessed, then the data sets that
contain those CLISTs should also be concatenated to the SYSPROC
file. The following example shows how to effect such a concatenation
using JCL.

```
//SYSPROC  DD  DSN=TS01234.CLIST,DISP=SHR
//         DD  DSN=PUBLIC.CLIST,DISP=SHR
//         DD  DSN=SYS1.CLIST,DISP=SHR
```

Data set concatenation is effected in JCL when multiple DDs are used with a single file or DD name. Just as with the ALLOCATE command, the data set attributes must be compatible, and the data set with the largest blocksize must be specified first. If the data set blocksizes are not a factor, most CLIST users prefer to include their own CLIST libraries ahead of the system libraries. This is the way that the DD statement above is coded and gives the CLIST user the opportunity to create and utilize modified versions of system-provided software.

CONTROL STATEMENT OPTIONS

Various *CONTROL statement parameters* have been shown in the previous three chapters to support the examples. These parameters are important in setting up the proper execution environment, whether that entails allowing the CLIST to continue executing after an error or supporting lowercase data. The CONTROL statement parameters are summarized below.

MSG NOMS	This CONTROL statement option determines whether or not messages are issued. The default is to display messages. CONTROL NOMSG can be specified to suppress message output. CONTROL MSG can then be used to enable the display of messages.
LIST NOLIST	This CONTROL statement option determines whether or not TSO commands and subcommands within the CLIST are listed at the terminal as they are executed. NOLIST is the default. This option can also be specified as an EXEC command option when the CLIST is invoked.
SYMLIST NOSYMLIST	This CONTROL statement option determines whether or not CLIST statements are to be listed. With this particular option, statements are listed before symbolic substitution of variables has occurred and before the statement is executed. By default, this listing function is turned off.
COLIST NOCONLISTLIST	This CONTROL statement option determines whether or not CLIST statements are to be listed. With this particular option, statements are listed after symbolic substitution of variables has occurred

and before the statement is executed. By default, this listing function is turned off.

PROMPT   This CONTROL statement option determines
NOPROMPT   whether or not commands and statements are able to
             prompt the terminal user. This option can also be
             specified as an EXEC command option when the
             CLIST is invoked. The following example shows the
             sequence of events that might occur when the
             PROMPT option is in effect.

```
CONTROL PROMPT
ALLOC DA(NEW.DATA) SPACE
.

.
```

Because the information specified in the CLIST is insufficient for allocating a new data set, a prompt is issued to the terminal.

```
ENTER SPACE VALUE AND IF ANY, INCREMENT VALUE -
```

The CLIST user is prompted to enter the space value(s) that would normally accompany the space parameter keyword.

```
1
```

To the prompt, the CLIST user has specified the value *1*. This value will be interpreted as the primary space amount, and the secondary amount will be considered a null value. Another prompt is written to the terminal.

```
ENTER UNIT OF SPACE KEYWORD WITH VALUE, IF ANY -
```

This prompt asks for the space unit type. This is asking if the space is to be allocated in blocks, tracks, or cylinders. When blocks are specified, the size of the blocks in bytes should also be specified.

```
TRACK
```

The CLIST user has responded to this prompt with the value TRACK. After this last value is entered, there is enough information to allocate the new data set and execution would proceed to the next sequential instruction.

FLUSH   This CONTROL statement option determines
NOFLUSH   whether or not the command stack will be flushed
when an error is encountered. FLUSH is the default.
This causes a CLIST to terminate immediately. CONTROL NOFLUSH is typically added when the CLIST
contains code that allows it to recover from error situations.

MAIN   This CONTROL statement option identifies the current CLIST as the primary procedure. As such it also
sets up the environment achieved by using CONTROL NOFLUSH to protect the command stack in
the event of an error.

CAPS   This CONTROL statement option controls whether or
NOCAPS   not data is converted to uppercase characters.
ASIS   Conversion to uppercase is the default. When CONTROL NOCAPS or CONTROL ASIS is specified, data
is not converted. Either CONTROL statement option
maintains the data as it is first encountered in both
upper- and lowercase. Specifying CONTROL CAPS
would only be necessary to switch back to an uppercase conversion mode.

END   This CONTROL statement option provides a one-to-
four character string to be used in place of the string
END, to end a DO statement. In the following example the CONTROL statement is used to substitute the
string STOP for the string END. All subsequent DO
groups within the CLIST are terminated with the
string STOP unless the string is again changed using
the CONTROL statement.

```
CONTROL END(STOP)
DO
     .
     .
     .
STOP
```

Virtually all of the examples in this book use the
string ENDO in place of END in the belief that whatever value is chosen, it should be used consistently.

SWITCHING TO TERMINAL INPUT

The *TERMIN statement* can be used to suspend CLIST execution and switch the source of input back to the terminal. The terminal user can then enter TSO commands and subcommands and return to the suspended CLIST at their discretion. The following statement would be used to switch control from the CLIST to the terminal.

```
TERMIN
```

CLIST users may or may not get a READY mode prompt to indicate that they are in the TSO environment. In either case they are then able to enter whatever TSO commands and subcommands they want. Control will return to the CLIST when a null line is entered. Other delimiters can be used to determine when to return to the CLIST. These delimiters or character strings are specified on the TERMIN statement. Below is an example where the return delimiter has been changed from a null line to the character string, RETURN.

```
.
.
WRITE   ENTER TSO COMMAND(S) BELOW
WRITE   WHEN FINISHED, ENTER THE WORD  RETURN
WRITE   TO RETURN TO CLIST EXECUTION
TERMIN RETURN
.
.
```

Write statements have been added to the CLIST above in addition to the changed delimiter. These WRITE statements are used to inform the CLIST user that the execution mode is changing and what the user can do to return to the CLIST. This sort of information should be supplied to the CLIST user no matter what delimiters are used. The user would then type RETURN rather than entering a null line to return to the CLIST.

It is also possible to include multiple-return delimiters. One reason for doing this is to give the terminal user more control of what happens when the CLIST resumes execution. The variable &SYSDLM can be used to determine which character string was used to cause a return to the CLIST. The variable contains a numeric value that indicates which delimiter was entered to effect the return to the CLIST. This value indicates the order of the delimiter on the TERMIN statement. The previous example has been altered to include multiple return delimiters:

```
.
.
WRITE    ENTER TSO COMMAND(S) BELOW
WRITE    WHEN FINISHED, ENTER  CONT  TO CONTINUE
WRITE                     OR    STOP  TO TERMINATE CLIST EXECUTION
TERMIN CONT STOP
IF &SYSDLM = 2 THEN EXIT
.
.
```

In this example, the delimiters have been paired with the choice of continuing CLIST execution or having the CLIST terminate. If the terminal user enters the string CONT, the CLIST will continue executing. If the string STOP is entered, the true path of an IF statement test will terminate the CLIST.

The system variable &SYSDVAL would contain the text, if any, that the terminal user entered following the delimiter that was used to return to the CLIST. Often, the TERMIN statement is used to allow the CLIST user to access TSO commands to obtain information that is needed for the CLIST. The variable &SYSDVAL provides a vehicle for the communication of this information and can be utilized once control has returned to the CLIST.

9

CLIST Design Strategy

PLANNING CLIST REQUIREMENTS

Before any effort is spent on CLIST design, it is important to consider if foreground execution is the only feasible mode of execution. If the answer is no, then is it at least the best execution mode? If the answer is still no, then an alternate solution should be investigated. There are considerations that support the use of the CLIST language. These include the requirement of interacting with the application user, providing a timely result, and interfacing with other real-time products or programs.

The first design consideration will generally be to determine the flow of information. This is particularly important with the CLIST language because of the many ways it has of incorporating information. Each method of communicating information has a different set of characteristics that make it better suited for a particular circumstance. Consideration should also be given to what information is required for execution and what information is optional. Where information is optional, defaults can be designed that will suit the needs of most individuals who will be using the CLIST. This will serve to make the CLIST easier to use by reducing the amount of information that has to be supplied.

KNOWING THE CLIST AUDIENCE

Because the CLIST language allows for such diverse applications to be built, there are additional factors to take under consideration. Some of these involve the expected makeup of CLIST users. One such consideration is how many individuals will use the CLIST being developed. Another consideration is how sophisticated those individuals are. As a general rule, the larger the user population, and the less sophisticated they are, the greater the effort that should be expended in the development of a CLIST, since this combination increases the possibility of misuse or encountering an error.

Larger user populations generally also require greater CLIST flexibility because, as a whole, they will try to do more with a given CLIST. A successful CLIST design will anticipate this need and provide the means to handle a wide variety of user requests. Greater CLIST flexibility, in turn, generally promotes wider use. Take for example the hardcopy CLIST that was first mentioned in Chap. 3. The only function of the CLIST was to print a disk data set. Not much flexibility would be required when creating such a CLIST for a few people who always wanted to print the same data set. When trying to satisfy the print needs of many individuals, however, the CLIST would need to be made flexible enough to print one of many different data sets. In addition, many different print characteristics and print destinations may apply.

Use by less sophisticated individuals generally requires more thorough handling of error conditions. This sometimes requires guarding against potential misuse of the CLIST. A CLIST is not really effective, for example, if it allows users to inadvertently delete all of their data sets much faster than they could have otherwise. One of the worst scenarios imaginable is when an application program of any sort, even through misuse, does more harm than good.

One of the considerations in developing CLIST code is to anticipate the consequence of errors. Intuitively, the greater the consequence, the greater the effort that should be expended to address potential errors. This is an important consideration in CLIST design and coding because accounting for and dealing with such errors consumes a disproportionate amount of time and effort.

Also relevant, CLISTS are often installed in a less formal environment or created for personal use only. In this context, error handling takes on less importance. Indeed, when creating a CLIST for personal use, familiarity alone will keep the user from making most usage errors. Below is a CLIST created for personal use. It is designed to simplify the task of creating *Generation Data Group* (GDG) indexes. The CLIST uses the DEFINE TSO command to create the GDG index structure within the system catalog. This in turn allows reference to data sets within the catalog structure by the base data set name and either a relative or absolute generation number.

```
PROC 2 DSN ENTRIES SCRATCH EMPTY
DEFINE GENERATIONDATAGROUP  +
  (NAME(&DSN)  LIMIT(&ENTRIES)  &SCRATCH  &EMPTY)
WRITE RETURN CODE IS &LASTCC
```

The CLIST makes it easier to enter the information required to build the index, but the user would be expected to know what input information is required to run it. If the CLIST were invoked without any parameters, it would issue prompts for the two positional parameters. The CLIST user should also know how to interpret the numeric return code that is displayed at the terminal at the end of the CLIST.

The CLIST can be made easier to use by a larger population by better indicating what information is required. To this end, the CLIST is modified below to prompt for information that it uses in the DEFINE command.

```
CONTROL NOFLUSH
WRITE ENTER THE FULLY QUALIFIED
WRITENR GDG INDEX NAME ===>
READ &DSN
WRITENR ENTER THE NUMBER OF GDG ENTRIES ===>
READ &ENT
WRITENR ENTER OPTIONAL PARAMETERS (SCRATCH OR EMPTY) ===>
READ &OPT
DEFINE GENERATIONDATAGROUP +
  (NAME('&DSN')  LIMIT(&ENT) &OPT)
IF &LASTCC = 0 THEN +
  WRITE THE GDG INDEX '&DSN' HAS BEEN CREATED
ELSE WRITE UNABLE TO CREATE THE GDG INDEX '&DSN'
```

The CLIST now contains a minimum of prompt information and no error checking. Its use is appropriate for someone who has a fairly good understanding of the process.

The CLIST below has minimal error checking added. When an error is detected, additional information is written out and a branch is made back to the original WRITE and READ statements so the needed information can be reentered. Even when the code is reused in this fashion, the CLIST is now three to four times longer than the previous version, and much longer than the original. The following code that has been added to the previous CLIST is highlighted.

```
CONTROL NOFLUSH
DSN: +
WRITE ENTER THE FULLY QUALIFIED
WRITENR GDG INDEX NAME ===>
READ &DSN
IF &DSN =  THEN +
  DO
    WRITE THE NAME OF THE GENERATION DATA GROUP INDEX WAS OMITTED.
    GOTO DSN
  END
ENT: +
WRITENR ENTER THE NUMBER OF GDG ENTRIES ===>
READ &ENT
IF &STR(&ENT) = THEN +
  DO
    WRITE THE NUMBER OF GDG ENTRIES WAS OMITTED.
    GOTO ENT
  END
ELSE +
  DO
    IF &DATATYPE(&ENT) NE NUM THEN +
      DO
        WRITE THE ENTRIES VALUE WAS NOT NUMERIC.
        GOTO ENT
      END
    ELSE +
      DO
        IF &ENT < 1 OR &ENT > 255 THEN +
          DO
            WRITE THE ENTRIES VALUE MUST BE IN RANGE 1 TO 255.
            GOTO ENT
          END
      END
  END
OPT: +
WRITENR ENTER OPTIONAL PARAMETERS (SCRATCH OR EMPTY) ===>
READ &OPT
IF &OPT NE THEN +
  IF &OPT = SCRATCH OR &OPT = EMPTY THEN
  ELSE +
    DO
      WRITE THE OPTION ENTERED IS INVALID.
      WRITE VALID OPTIONS ARE SCRATCH OR EMPTY.
      GOTO OPT
```

```
    END
DEFINE GENERATIONDATAGROUP +
  (NAME('&DSN') LIMIT(&ENT) &OPT)
IF &LASTCC = 0 THEN +
  WRITE THE GDG INDEX '&DSN' HAS BEEN CREATED
ELSE WRITE UNABLE TO CREATE THE GDG INDEX '&DSN'
```

Error checks have been added that check for missing information, the wrong class of information, and that numeric values are within the proper range. By validating the information that is entered, the CLIST should be easier to user by a wider range of individuals. It might also be advisable to add a narrative explaining the CLIST function and required data. This could be displayed before the first prompt.

INCREASING CLIST USABILITY

We have just seen how the design of a CLIST can make it easier to use. Much of this type of information can surface while the CLIST is being tested. The amount of effort that goes into testing is often indicative of how easy the finished CLIST will be to use.

There are several other factors that affect the usability of a given CLIST. The proper use and communication of variable information is perhaps the single most important of these. When used effectively, variables can allow the CLIST user the ability to tailor each execution to the needs of the moment. How the variable information is communicated between the terminal user and the CLIST is also an important consideration.

There are several ways to facilitate the communication of variable information. For the more basic CLIST, this might involve using understandable variable names. If the variable name is descriptive of the information it contains, the CLIST user will be more likely to supply the correct information. This is especially important when a CLIST user is prompted for positional parameter information since the variable name becomes part of the prompt displayed at the terminal.

```
ENTER POSITIONAL PARAMETER PRINTDATASETNAME
```

To increase the ability to communicate variable information, the user could decide to issue his or her own prompts using READ and WRITE statements. That would allow the user to display whatever explanation is deemed necessary to fully describe the information being requested.

```
PLEASE ENTER THE NAME OF THE DATA SET TO BE PRINTED.
THE DATA SET NAME MUST BE FULLY QUALIFIED
AND MUST NOT CONTAIN QUOTES.
```

Keeping user-supplied input to a minimum will also increase the usability of a CLIST. This does not mean cutting into the flexibility provided to the CLIST user, but supplying information that can be obtained in other ways. If a CLIST can create an output data set based upon the characteristics of another data set, that is preferable to forcing users to create the data set themselves before executing the CLIST or even prompting them for the data set characteristics.

BUILDING UPON WHAT WORKS

Many individuals develop new programs from old ones. This practice is independent of what language is being used, and can be an efficient way to create code. This is also useful in creating new CLISTs. This practice takes on a new meaning for CLIST programs, however, that stems from the ease of executing a CLIST. Because a CLIST can be run without compiling and is not broken into arbitrary segments, it is often very simple to create code and test it immediately. Running in the foreground, immediate feedback is obtained. The CLIST developer can then switch back to the editor and make corrections to the code, or, if satisfied with the results, proceed to add additional code. This latter instance is building upon what works. If it does not work, stop and fix it now, before the code gets any more convoluted and difficult to change. This takes advantage of a unique CLIST characteristic. It is typically relatively easy to execute parts of a CLIST, a concept which in other languages might be called unit or modular testing.

This same feature also allows users to build the CLIST in the order they want to. That very well may entail creating the most difficult code first, and adding the surrounding code later. That has the distinct advantage of allowing users to work with the code without the distractions that the surrounding code may present. Creating the most difficult code first can also serve as a sort of feasibility study. It would allow coders to find out early in the development process if the CLIST language provides the functions they need to arrive at a solution.

Part of the strategy for building upon what works includes saving the versions that work. This can be done very simply with most editors, saving the different versions under different member or data set names. Using a numbering sequence within the member or data set name can be very effective, and will help to mark the natural progression of the code. When added code causes a failure, the previous version can be used for comparison or as a starting point to reapply any changes.

TESTING

Testing is an important part of the development process when creating a program that will be used by other individuals. The best time to create a test plan is while the CLIST code is being created. As the developer finishes with a particular piece of code, it should be easy to devise the data that will test the function performed by that particular section. In fact, if at all possible, the code should be tested right away. That way errors can be eliminated before the code becomes too complex and complicates the testing process. In some languages, this is called *modular testing*. After testing the pieces of a program, *integrated testing* is called for. The pieces of code are brought together and so are the pieces of data that were used to test them.

Once developers are sure that they have accounted for the known situations, they should concentrate their efforts on handling unexpected conditions. While working closely with the code itself it should not be difficult to come up with ideas like executing the CLIST with an empty input file to see what it does, or entering the data out of proper sequence. This is also referred to as trying to "break the code." As mentioned earlier in this chapter, the determination about the consequences of an error in the execution of the CLIST will determine how much effort, if any, is spent on this sort of activity.

CLIST DOCUMENTATION

A CLIST can be documented internally using comment statements. Comments are designated using the slash character immediately followed by an asterisk. They are ignored during the execution of the CLIST code.

```
/*THIS IS A SAMPLE COMMENT STATEMENT
```

Like other CLIST statements, comments may be continued on subsequent lines.

```
/*THIS IS A SAMPLE COMMENT STATEMENT. IT IS USED TO SHOW +
  HOW A COMMENT CAN BE CONTINUED OVER MULTIPLE LINES BY +
  USING STANDARD CONTINUATION CHARACTERS.
```

Starting each comment line with /*, however, makes it much easier to identify comment lines from executable statements.

```
/* THIS IS A SAMPLE COMMENT STATEMENT. IT IS USED TO SHOW
/* HOW A COMMENT CAN BE CONTINUED OVER MULTIPLE LINES WITHOUT
/* USING CONTINUATION CHARACTERS.
```

Comment lines can also be terminated with an asterisk immediately followed by a slash character. This is optional except when a command or statement follows the comment.

```
/* INCREMENT THE LOOP COUNTER */   SET &COUNT = &COUNT + 1
```

There are several reasons for using comments to document a CLIST. The first is that these comments might assist a user who is looking for a particular CLIST or is looking for any CLIST that performs a particular function. Comments can also assist the CLIST user by explaining how the CLIST is used, and help the CLIST coder to remember what processing takes place. Maintenance of the code by other individuals can also be made easier by adding comments.

The comments that are added to a CLIST can be directed toward specific aspects of the CLIST. These might include:

1. describing the CLIST function

2. describing positional and keyword parameters

3. describing logic flow or processing

4. describing non conventional code

Below is an example taken from Chap. 8. To the example we have added comments (highlighted statements) from the four categories above.

```
      PROC 1 DSN COUNT(6)
1 ⌈  /* FUNCTION: THIS CLIST PRINTS PDS MEMBER NAMES IN SEVEN
  ⌊  /*           COLUMNS ACROSS THE SCREEN.
      /*
2 ⌈  /* INPUT VARIABLES
  |  /*   DSN   (POSITIONAL) - SPECIFIED IN TSO FORMAT, CONTAINING
  |  /*         A PDS NAME
  |  /*   COUNT (KEYWORD) - INCLUDED FOR INITIALIZATION ONLY,
  ⌊  /*         NOT TO BE ENTERED BY USER.
      /*
3 [  /* SET VARIABLE THAT IS USED TO PAD THE MEMBER NAME WITH BLANKS
      SET &SPACES = &STR(       )
3 [  /* TRAP MEMBER LIST FROM LISTD COMMAND OUTPUT
```

```
      SET &SYSOUTTRAP = 999
      LISTDS &DSN M
      SET &SYSOUTTRAP = 0
      WRITE
      WRITE THE MEMBERS IN DATA SET  &DSN  ARE:
      WRITE
      LOOP: SET &COUNT = &COUNT + 1
      IF &COUNT > &SYSOUTLINE THEN END
      SET &LINE = &&SYSOUTLINE&COUNT
      SET &LEN = &LENGTH(&LINE)
  3 ⎡  /* PAD MEMBER NAME WITH SPACES SO THE COLUMNS OF MEMBER
    ⎣  /* NAMES WILL LINE UP
      SET &MEMBER = &LINE&SUBSTR(&LEN+1:9,&SPACES)
  3 [  /* SUBTRACT 6 FROM COUNT TO ADJUST FOR STARTING SYSOUT LINE
      /*
  4 ⎡  /* WHEN EVENLY DIVISIBLE BY 7 USE THE NORMAL WRITE
    ⎮  /* STATEMENT TO ESTABLISH POSITION ON THE NEXT
    ⎣  /* LINE OF TERMINAL OUTPUT.
      IF (&COUNT - 6) // 7 = 0  THEN WRITE &MEMBER
      ELSE  WRITENR &MEMBER
      GOTO LOOP
```

Other useful information could be included. This might include change history information to detail when and why the CLIST was changed. Different computer installations may well have standard formats for what documentation is included in a CLIST. Whatever documentation is included should be added carefully so that it does not interfere with functional CLIST code. When adding comments to a CLIST, it is important not to interrupt the continuation of existing statements or to allow the comment's continuation to affect subsequent statements. After comments are added, the CLIST should be retested before it is put into service.

There are generally other forms that documentation may take other than placing comments in the CLIST itself. Instructions for how to execute a particular CLIST might be found in an installation's training materials or standard's manual. It is also possible to make the information available on-line. This includes the possibility of placing the documentation with the information for standard TSO commands, making it accessible to all TSO users through the HELP command.

INCREASING CLIST MAINTAINABILITY

The documentation methods just presented can greatly enhance the maintainability of CLIST code. Maintainability can also be enhanced by making the code easier to read and understand. There are several things that can be done in this direction. Perhaps the most important of these is to use meaningful variable names. This often takes more time to code, but is well worth the effort.

Using a structured format can also improve the readability of a CLIST program. A structured format implies the alignment of related statements with dependent statements indented. Since the CLIST language supports a free formatting of commands and statements, statement alignment affects only the readability of the code. This does, however, make the code much easier to read. This in turn should result in fewer coding errors and less time required to make coding changes.

The following code is taken from an example used earlier in this chapter. Vertical lines have been drawn to the left of certain statements to help show their alignment.

```
   .
   .
   .
 IF &STR(&ENT) = THEN +
   DO
      WRITE THE NUMBER OF GDG ENTRIES WAS OMITTED.
      GOTO ENT
   END
 ELSE +
   DO
      IF &DATATYPE(&ENT) NE NUM THEN +
         DO
         WRITE THE ENTRIES VALUE WAS NOT NUMERIC.
            GOTO ENT
         END
      ELSE +
         DO
            IF &ENT < 1 OR &ENT > 255 THEN +
               DO
                  WRITE THE ENTRIES VALUE MUST BE IN RANGE 1 TO 255.
                  GOTO ENT
               END
         END
   END
   .
   .
   .
```

Notice that all related IF and ELSE clauses are lined up. This is also true with DO and END statements. On the other hand, all code that is dependent upon other code is indented from that other code.

GUIDELINES FOR CLIST USAGE

We have mentioned many advantages to using the CLIST language. There are also conditions under which its use is not recommended. When a complex flowchart is needed to represent the intended logic, the use of a compiled language would generally be preferred. CLISTs are also generally not used with tape applications. This is because of the delays inherent in trying to locate and have tapes mounted so they can be used. CLISTs are better left for applications where such delays will not be encountered.

Perceived delays can also occur where very large amounts of data are to be processed or contention over a resource, such as a data set, may exist. Alternate solutions should be considered here, too, or at least running the CLIST in background mode. Running the CLIST in background mode would not only allow the terminal to remain free for other uses, but it would allow the background execution to be scheduled for a time when resource contention would not be a problem.

PROGRAM CONSIDERATIONS

When a CLIST is created to execute a program, its requirements are driven by that program. One of the most important of these is the file requirements. The program is typically written to obtain data and output it through files. Unless the program is written to obtain these dynamically, the resources for these files must be obtained by the CLIST before calling the program.

There are several sources of information for determining the file and resource requirements of a program. If the program source code is available, it can be examined for input and output statements. Depending on the language, these may be functions like read and write, get and put, and list and display. Another source of information is documentation that may be distributed with the program. This is especially true of vendor-supplied utility programs. If the program already runs using JCL, as mentioned earlier, the JCL can be translated into the CLIST language. As a last resort, it is often possible to execute a program with only some or even none of its files allocated, and determine from the error messages issued what files need to be allocated.

The examples in Chap. 5 and 10 use utility programs because they are so familiar to many and because their file requirements are contained in documentation supplied by the program vendor. We also see in those same two chapters how JCL statements can be converted into the CLIST language. Without sources such as these, however, the user would need to inspect the program source statements to see what the file requirements were. Source statements taken from a COBOL program are listed below. The statements that are responsible for establishing a connection between the program and the input data that it utilizes are highlighted.

```
IDENTIFICATION DIVISION.
PROGRAM-ID. SAMPLE1.
ENVIRONMENT DIVISION.
 .
 .
INPUT-OUTPUT SECTION.
FILE-CONTROL.
     SELECT   INPUT-FILE  ASSIGN TO UT-S-DATAIN.
     SELECT   OUTPUT-FILE ASSIGN TO UT-S-DATAOUT.
     SELECT   PRINT-FILE  ASSIGN TO UT-S-REPORT.
DATA DIVISION.
FILE SECTION.
FD  INPUT-FILE
    RECORD CONTAINS 100 CHARACTERS
    BLOCK CONTAINS 0 RECORDS
    LABEL RECORDS ARE STANDARD.
01  INRECORD                PIC X(100).
 .
 .
```

The source statements above show that this COBOL program uses three files. The SELECT statements are used to connect the program's view of the data (*FD* or *File Description*) to a file name. In the case of the single input file that we have highlighted, the file description INPUT-FILE is paired with a file name of DATAIN. The CLIST would then need to provide whatever resources were required for that file. If we isolate the statements that effect this connection and add the related CLIST statement, it would look like this.

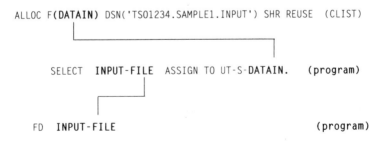

```
ALLOC F(DATAIN) DSN('TSO1234.SAMPLE1.INPUT') SHR REUSE  (CLIST)


     SELECT  INPUT-FILE  ASSIGN TO UT-S-DATAIN.   (program)


     FD  INPUT-FILE                               (program)
```

The complete CLIST that would be used to execute that COBOL program is shown below:

```
ALLOC F(DATAIN)  DSN('TSO1234.SAMPLE1.INPUT') SHR REUSE
ALLOC F(DATAOUT) DSN('TSO1234.SAMPLE1.OUTPUT') CAT REUSE +
  UNIT(3380) VOL(TEST01) SP(10 2) TRACK +
  RECFM(F B) BLKSIZE(23400)
ALLOC F(REPORT)  SYSOUT(T) FCB(STD4) DEST(R17) REUSE
CALL TEST(SAMPLE1)
FREE F(DATAIN DATAOUT REPORT)
```

Notice that there is an **ALLOCATE** command for each file resource that must be obtained. The record length was omitted from the output file DATAOUT because it will be obtained from the characteristics defined in the program.

The source statements of other programming languages can be examined to determine the program's file requirements. Below is a simple FORTRAN program, called EXPONENT, that is used to raise one real number to the power of a second real number.

```
      CHARACTER *72 MESSAGE
      MESSAGE = 'NUMBERS ENTERED MAY CONTAIN UP TO 2 DECIMAL
        PLACES'
      WRITE (8)MESSAGE
      MESSAGE = 'THE VALUE 0 CAN BE ENTERED AFTER ANY PROMPT TO STOP'
      WRITE (8)MESSAGE
100   MESSAGE = 'ENTER A REAL NUMBER'
      WRITE (8)MESSAGE
      READ (3,310)REALNUM1
      IF (REALNUM1 .EQ. 0) GO TO 200
      MESSAGE = 'ENTER THE EXPONENT'
      WRITE (8)MESSAGE
      READ (3,310)REALNUM2
      IF (REALNUM2 .EQ. 0) GO TO 200
      ANSWER=REALNUM1**REALNUM2
      WRITE (9,320)ANSWER
      GO TO 100
200   CONTINUE
310   FORMAT(F8.2)
320   FORMAT(F16.4)
      STOP
      END
```

The program was designed specifically to be accessed from a terminal. As such, logic to interact with the terminal user was moved from the CLIST to the program. Rather than have the CLIST obtain the two numbers and CALL the program each time a pair of numbers is entered, the program is invoked only once. The program was designed to use its own read and write facilities to communicate with the terminal user. This is important because it makes the function more efficient to execute. The ALLOCATE commands are used to direct the data read and written by the program to and from the terminal.

Below is a READ statement from the FORTRAN program. It uses the standard file designation, where the first number represents the file number. (The second number in this example refers to the statement number of a format statement that will define what the data looks like.)

```
READ (3,310)REALNUM1
```

The file number is a one- or two-digit number. In this case, the file number is 3. That number then becomes part of the file name as shown below:

```
FT03F001
```

In the file name, the file number is always two digits and a leading zero is added when necessary. That file name is then used in the ALLOCATE command FILE parameter. If the FORTRAN OPEN statement is used to change the file name, that file name can be used directly. The complete CLIST that would be used to execute the FORTRAN program EXPONENT is shown below:

```
ALLOC F(FT03F001) DA(*) REUSE
ALLOC F(FT08F001) DA(*) REUSE
ALLOC F(FT09F001) DA(*) REUSE
ALLOC F(FT06F001) DUMMY REUSE
CALL 'TS01234.FORT.LOAD(EXPONENT)'
FREE F(FT03F001 FT08F001 FT09F001 FT06F001)
```

The three files used in the program, 3, 8, and 9, are allocated to the terminal. A fourth file, FT06F001, has been added. This file is routinely used to list FORTRAN error messages. The output to file FT06F001 is negated using the DUMMY parameter to suppress any such error messages.

Another consideration for program execution is the amount of memory that a program requires. If the program needs more memory than is provided by a typical TSO session, terminal users should ensure that additional memory is made available when they LOGON to TSO.

The amount of memory (also called *REGION*) necessary to support the program execution can be specified using the LOGON TSO command SIZE parameter. With newer versions of TSO/E, this value can also be specified on a screen that contains fields that are used to specify LOGON parameters. Regardless of the manner in which it is entered, a numeric value representing the number of kilobytes (1024 bytes) of memory is entered. If the following command is used to access TSO

```
LOGON TSO1234 SIZE(1088)
```

1088K or 1,114,112 bytes of memory is requested. It is important that a value smaller than the normal default not be used since this may well impair the functioning of TSO and other common program products. The amount of region requested must also be tempered by what is available. If the requested region is not available, TSO users would not be able to enter TSO. They would then have to restart the LOGON process requesting a smaller region.

The next chapter provides detailed descriptions of CLIST examples. Among them are CLISTs that support program execution.

Chapter

10

CLIST Examples

This chapter contains examples of CLIST code. All examples are complete. A general description of the CLIST function is given, and then each line of the CLIST is discussed. Line sequence numbers have been added to the examples. These line sequence numbers are not required, but have been added to facilitate reference to the code itself. Where appropriate, invoking parameters, as well as samples of input and output data is supplied.

As mentioned before, there are many approaches to take in creating an application with the CLIST language. The examples in this chapter illustrate coding structures that have been covered so far. They do not necessarily represent the most expedient coding solutions, but rather try to represent the topics that have been discussed so far in the framework of a logical, if not familiar, application.

The following CLIST examples include:

Example 1 (pp 154-155). Submits a JCL jobstream after variable substitution. This CLIST illustrates the use of the TSO EDIT command to modify a data set with variables supplied through a PROC statement. The modified jobstream is then submitted for background execution.

Example 2 (pp. 156-159). Submits a JCL jobstream after variable substitution. This CLIST illustrates the use of PUTFILE statements to create a data set containing job-control statements. Again, variables are supplied through a PROC statement, and the jobstream created is submitted for background execution using the TSO SUBMIT command.

Example 3 (pp. 160-161). Link edits object code. This CLIST invokes the linkage-editor program using the TSO LINK COMMAND. Variable substitution is used to provide a consistent member name for three of the data sets used in the process.

Example 4 (pp.162-165). Link edits object code. This CLIST also invokes the linkage-editor program. It does this using the CALL COMMAND to access the program directly and illustrates how parm information is conveyed. The functionality of the previous CLIST example is replicated.

Example 5 (pp. 166-169). Divides one number by another, displaying the result to four decimal places. This CLIST illustrates code to perform an arithmetic function as well as perform condition testing. &STR and &SUBSTR functions are used to prepare the result for display to the terminal.

Example 6 (pp. 170-173). Isolates the first qualifier of a data set name. This CLIST illustrates iterative processing using labels and the GOTO statement. It also uses the &SUBSTR and &LENGTH functions.

Example 7 (pp. 174-178). Sends multiple-line messages to multiple TSO users. This CLIST illustrates two types of loops as well as the &LENGTH function. Data is read from the terminal using &SYSDVAL and incorporated as the message text within the TSO SEND command.

Example 8 (pp. 180-185). Performs a PDS compress in place. This CLIST illustrates how resources can be obtained and released to provide for program execution. The equivalent JCL code is presented to demonstrate how to translate from one language to another.

Example 9 (pp. 186-193). Creates a report, with headings, from data that is extracted from a disk data set. This CLIST illustrates the use of PUTFILE statements to create SYSOUT or report output with carriage-control characters. DO WHILE and ERROR structures are included to effect iterative processing and handle end-of-file conditions. In addition, the &SUBSTR function is used to extract "fields" of data from fixed format records.

Example 10 (pp. 194-203). Cuts fixed-length records into smaller or larger record lengths. This CLIST illustrates the remainder function, nested DO WHILE structures, and the ERROR routine used to handle end-of-file conditions. The CLIST also extracts information from the system date and time variables to use in building a unique, new data set name, and calculates the blocksize for the new data set.

Example 11 (pp. 204-207). Writes data entered at the terminal to a data set. This CLIST illustrates the use of terminal interactive statements as well as the system variable &SYSDVAL to handle data with spaces and special characters. Data is also maintained in upper- and lowercase. An ATTN routine is included so the CLIST processing can be interrupted. The attention routine includes the TERMIN statement to switch back to TSO mode to enable the CLIST user to access other information before returning to the CLIST.

Example 12 (pp. 208-215). Writes TSO command output to a data set. This CLIST illustrates the use of the sysout trap function, variables used in table fashion and iterative processing.

Example 1: The submit CLIST

This CLIST is used to incorporate variable information into a JCL job-stream and then submit it for batch execution. When executed, the jobstream will use the utility IEBGENER to copy data from one place to another. A print function is created by copying the data from a disk data set to a sysout or print file. The CLIST uses a simple PROC statement to provide a data set name and output print class in variables &DSN and &CLASS, respectively. The TSO EDIT command is used to modify an existing data set. That data set is numbered and contains a two-line job statement. Lines are added to the job statement to create a print jobstream. The jobstream is then submitted for background execution and EDIT is ended without saving the changed version (thus retaining the original data).

It would not be a good idea to use SUBMIT as the name of this CLIST. The reason for that is that SUBMIT is also a TSO command. The CLIST could still be invoked under that name using %SUBMIT since that would limit the search to the SYSPROC file. Another alternative would be to use the explicit form of the EXEC command. The name BATCHPRT will be used instead because it avoids the potential conflict just mentioned and is more descriptive of the ultimate CLIST purpose.

The CLIST could be invoked in the following fashion.

```
BATCHPRT TSO1234.COBOL(PAYROLL) CLASS(P)
```

This would print the disk data set TSO1234.COBOL(PAYROLL), to sysout class *P*. It is necessary here to specify a fully qualified data set name without quotes. This is contrary to the way that TSO handles data set names. The difference here is that the data set name will ultimately be used in JCL rather than CLIST code.

```
PROC 1 DSN CLASS(A)                              0001
EDIT 'TSO1234.CNTL(JOBCARD)' OLD CNTL             0002
003 //STEP1 EXEC PGM=IEBGENER                     0003
004 //SYSPRINT DD SYSOUT=&CLASS                   0004
005 //SYSUT1   DD DISP=SHR,DSN=&DSN               0005
006 //SYSUT2   DD SYSOUT=&CLASS                   0006
007 //SYSIN    DD DUMMY,DCB=BLKSIZE=80            0007
SUBMIT                                            0008
END NOSAVE                                        0009
```

Line 1   The first line of this CLIST is a PROC statement. It specifies that one positional parameter is required for the CLIST to execute. That positional parameter is the name of the disk data set that is to be printed. As mentioned before, for the JCL to be successful, the data set name supplied should be a fully qualified data set name without quotes.The PROC statement also specifies a keyword parameter, CLASS. This variable is supplied with a default value of A. That value will be in effect if no value is supplied to the CLASS keyword when the CLIST is invoked. The value of the variable will subsequently be used as the output class in two different places in the JCL jobstream.

Line 2   This line uses the TSO command EDIT to activate the editor. Parameters on the statement identify the data set to be edited, its disposition, and the data set type. The data set type need not be specified in this case because it is identical to the data set name descriptive qualifier (last qualifier) and is a standard descriptive qualifier for use by the editor. As such, it carries with it certain data set characteristics that will be used by the editor. The data set TSO1234.CNTL(JOBCARD), contains a two-line JCL job statement.

```
//TSO1234P JOB '0','SUBMIT EXAMPLE',
// CLASS=A,MSGCLASS=A,NOTIFY=TSO1234
```

Lines 3   These lines contain data that will be inserted by the editor.
through 7 The statements being inserted are numbered on the left so they do not interfere with the statements already in the data set. The actual result will be to add these five JCL statements after the two that are already in the data set. That will create a complete jobstream after variable substitution occurs. The variable &CLASS will provide the output class value for two different SYSOUT parameters. The variable &DSN will provide the name of the data set to be printed on the SYSUT1 DD statement. To be appropriate for JCL purposes, it should be a fully qualified data set name without quotes.

Line 8   This line contains the EDIT subcommand SUBMIT. This subcommand reads the edited result into the system for background execution.

Line 9   This line contains the EDIT subcommand END. This subcommand ends the edit session. The NOSAVE parameter indicates that the edited result should not be written back to the permanent disk data set. This will allow data set TSO1234.CNTL(JOBCARD) to retain its original value. It can then be used subsequently to run the same or a similar process that can utilize a two-line JCL job statement.

Example 2: The submit II CLIST

This CLIST is an alternate method used to incorporate variable information into a JCL jobstream and then submit it for batch execution. The JCL included performs the same function as that in the previous example. The jobstream is the same, too, except that this CLIST also includes the two-line job statement. Just as in the previous example, variables are supplied through a PROC statement. This CLIST uses PUTFILE statements to create a data set containing job control statements. If the data set already exists, it is reused. Otherwise, a new data set is created and written to. The jobstream created is submitted for background execution using the TSO SUBMIT command. Yet another process for submitting jobstreams to execute in the background will be discussed in Chap. 12. It provides for instream submittal of JCL and is available with TSO/E release 1.3.

```
PROC 1 DSN CLASS(U)                                             0001
CONTROL NOFLUSH NOMSG                                           0002
ALLOC F(CNTLDATA) DA(SUBMIT.CNTL) OLD REUSE                     0003
IF &LASTCC > 0 THEN +                                           0004
   ALLOC F(CNTLDATA) DA(SUBMIT.CNTL) SP(1 1) TR UNIT(SYSTDA) +  0005
      LRECL(80) RECFM(F B) BLK(3120) CATALOG REUSE              0006
CONTROL  MSG                                                    0007
OPENFILE CNTLDATA OUTPUT                                        0008
SET &CNTLDATA = &STR(//&SYSUID.M JOB '0','SUBMIT EXAMPLE',)     0009
PUTFILE CNTLDATA                                                0010
SET &CNTLDATA = &STR(// CLASS=A,MSGCLASS=&CLASS,NOTIFY=&SYSUID) 0011
PUTFILE CNTLDATA                                                0012
SET &CNTLDATA = &STR(//STEP1 EXEC PGM=IEBGENER)                 0013
PUTFILE CNTLDATA                                                0014
SET &CNTLDATA = &STR(//SYSPRINT DD SYSOUT=&CLASS)               0015
PUTFILE CNTLDATA                                                0016
SET &CNTLDATA = &STR(//SYSUT1   DD DISP=SHR,DSN=&DSN)           0017
PUTFILE CNTLDATA                                                0018
SET &CNTLDATA = &STR(//SYSUT2   DD SYSOUT=&CLASS)               0019
PUTFILE CNTLDATA                                                0020
SET &CNTLDATA = &STR(//SYSIN    DD DUMMY,DCB=BLKSIZE=80)        0021
PUTFILE  CNTLDATA                                               0022
CLOSFILE CNTLDATA                                               0023
FREE F(CNTLDATA)                                                0024
SUBMIT  SUBMIT.CNTL                                             0025
```

Line 1	The first line of this CLIST is a PROC statement. It specifies that one positional parameter is required for the CLIST to execute. That positional parameter is the name of the disk data set that is to be printed. The data set name supplied should be a fully qualified data set name without quotes.
Line 2	This line is a CONTROL statement. The options that it specifies, NOFLUSH and NOMSG, are included for the ALLOCATE commands that follow. They will ensure that no messages are issued to the terminal and that the CLIST will continue to execute.
Line 3	This line allocates the data set that the JCL will be written to. The disposition is OLD, which means that the data set must already exist, and that its contents will be completely overwritten. There is, of course, the chance that the data set does not yet exist, which is why the CONTROL statement options NOFLUSH and NOMSG have been used. This condition will be handled by the next two statements. If the data set does exist, it will be allocated to file CNTLDATA for subsequent use with the PUTFILE statement.
Line 4	This line tests the return code from the previous ALLOC command. If the return code is greater than zero, it is assumed that the data set does not already exist. The true path of this statement will be to allocate the data set as a new data set.
Lines 5 and 6	These lines are the true path of the previous IF statement test. It is a single ALLOCATE command continued on to a second line. The command creates a data set that will be connected to file CNTLDATA to make it available for PUTFILE processing. The REUSE parameter is included in case the file CNTLDATA is already in use.
Line 7	This line uses the CONTROL statement to allow messages to be displayed at the terminal. Messages were turned off while the output data set was being created because the CLIST would handle any problems. With that processing complete, any error messages would be unexpected and should be displayed at the terminal.
Line 8	This line opens the file CNTLDATA for output processing. This file is connected to the data set just allocated.
Line 9	This line sets the variable &CNTLDATA to the value that corresponds to the first line of the JCL. The variable &CNTLDATA corresponds to the file name CNTLDATA, to allow data to be written to the file. The data contains the system variable &SYSUID. The value for that variable, the terminal user's user-ID, will be substituted before the data is written out.
Line 10	This line writes the data contained in variable &CNTLDATA to the data set that is connected to file CNTLDATA.

Example 2: The submit II CLIST *(Continued)*

```
PROC 1 DSN CLASS(U)                                              0001
CONTROL NOFLUSH NOMSG                                            0002
ALLOC F(CNTLDATA) DA(SUBMIT.CNTL) OLD REUSE                      0003
IF &LASTCC > 0 THEN +                                            0004
   ALLOC F(CNTLDATA) DA(SUBMIT.CNTL) SP(1 1) TR UNIT(SYSTDA) +   0005
   LRECL(80) RECFM(F B) BLK(3120) CATALOG REUSE                  0006
CONTROL  MSG                                                     0007
OPENFILE CNTLDATA OUTPUT                                         0008
SET &CNTLDATA = &STR(//&SYSUID.M JOB '0','SUBMIT EXAMPLE',)      0009
PUTFILE CNTLDATA                                                 0010
SET &CNTLDATA = &STR(// CLASS=A,MSGCLASS=&CLASS,NOTIFY=&SYSUID)  0011
PUTFILE CNTLDATA                                                 0012
SET &CNTLDATA = &STR(//STEP1 EXEC PGM=IEBGENER)                  0013
PUTFILE CNTLDATA                                                 0014
SET &CNTLDATA = &STR(//SYSPRINT DD SYSOUT=&CLASS)                0015
PUTFILE CNTLDATA                                                 0016
SET &CNTLDATA = &STR(//SYSUT1   DD DISP=SHR,DSN=&DSN)            0017
PUTFILE CNTLDATA                                                 0018
SET &CNTLDATA = &STR(//SYSUT2   DD SYSOUT=&CLASS)                0019
PUTFILE CNTLDATA                                                 0020
SET &CNTLDATA = &STR(//SYSIN    DD DUMMY,DCB=BLKSIZE=80)         0021
PUTFILE  CNTLDATA                                                0022
CLOSFILE CNTLDATA                                                0023
FREE F(CNTLDATA)                                                 0024
SUBMIT  SUBMIT.CNTL                                              0025
```

Lines 11 through 22	These lines change the value of variable &CNTLDATA and write that value to the output data set. Each pair of SET and PUTFILE statements represent a line of JCL code. Substitution of variable values occurs before the data is output.
Line 23	This line uses the CLOSFILE statement to close the output file.
Line 24	This line uses the FREE command to free the output file.
Line 25	This line uses the SUBMIT command to read the JCL in the data set into the system for background execution.

Example 3: The link CLIST

This CLIST combines the standard TSO LINK command with the variable handling capabilities of a CLIST. A single variable, &MEM-NAME, is entered as positional parameter input. It identifies the object code to be link-edited as it is applied to three separate data sets in a process that turns compiler output into an executable load module. The variable adds to the flexibility of the CLIST allowing it to be used for many different load modules by merely changing the member name each time it is invoked.

```
PROC 1 MEMNAME                                         0001
LINK 'TSO1234.OBJ(&MEMNAME)' +                         0002
   LOAD('TSO1234.TEST.LOAD(&MEMNAME)') +              0003
   LIB('TSO1234.DEV.LOAD' +                            0004
     'COMMON.LOADLIB' +                                0005
     'SYS1.FORTLIB') +                                 0006
   PRINT('TSO1234.TEST.LINKLIST(&MEMNAME)') +         0007
   XREF                                                0008
WRITE RETURN CODE IS &LASTCC                           0009
```

Line 1   The first statement of this CLIST is a PROC statement. Its only function is to communicate the variable value for the member name that is to be used in the object, load, and print data sets. That variable &MEMNAME was included as a positional parameter because the information it will convey is required for the CLIST to execute.

Line 2   This statement invokes the linkage-editor program using the TSO LINK command. On the same line, it specifies the data set that contains object code or instruction input to the linkage editor program. This data set name is a positional subparameter of the LINK command and must be specified before any other parameters. The member name specified when the CLIST was invoked will be substituted to complete the data set name.

Line 3   This statement is a continuation of the one used to invoke the linkage-editor program. It uses the LOAD-keyword parameter to specify the data set that the load module is to be written to. Here, too, the member name specified when the CLIST was invoked will be substituted to complete the data set name.

Lines 4 through 6   These are also continuation lines. They use the LIB-keyword parameter to specify automatic-call libraries. The automatic-call libraries are used by the linkage-editor program to resolve external references. Here, three data sets are concatenated so that any of the three can supply subroutines that are necessary to supplement the load module being created.

Line 7   This is also a continuation line. It uses the PRINT keyword parameter to specify the data set that the message output is to be written to. Just as with the object input and load output, the member name specified when the CLIST was invoked will be substituted to complete the data set name. This keyword parameter can also be used to direct message output to the terminal.

Line 8   This is the last continuation line of the TSO LINK command. It is used to request that a module cross reference be included in the program's message output. Other linkage-editor options can be specified in a similar fashion.

Line 9   This statement writes the system variable &LASTCC to the terminal. The variable contains the numeric return code passed back from the TSO LINK command. This provides feedback on the success of the command since all other informational output was directed to the data set specified in the PRINT keyword.

Example 4: The link II CLIST

This CLIST is also designed to turn compiler output, known as *object code*, into an executable load module. The process is almost identical to that performed by the previous CLIST except that the link-editor program is invoked directly rather than using a TSO command. Another difference is the use of parm information to communicate link-edit options to the program. Additional parameters to specify residence mode, addressing mode, and the use of automatic call for subroutine references have been added to show how multiple options can be specified. As in the previous CLIST, a single variable, &MEMNAME, is applied as the member name to three separate data sets. These data sets are allocated to the terminal session before the linkage-editor program is invoked. All ALLOCATE commands make use of the REUSE parameter to ensure that a particular file can be allocated even if it is already in use.

```
PROC 1 MEMNAME                                                   0001
ALLOC F(SYSLIN)  DA('TSO1234.OBJ(&MEMNAME)') SHR REUSE           0002
ALLOC F(SYSLMOD) DA('TSO1234.TEST.LOAD(&MEMNAME)') OLD REUSE     0003
ALLOC F(SYSLIB)  DA('TSO1234.DEV.LOAD' +                         0004
                 'COMMON.LOADLIB' +                              0005
                 'SYS1.FORTLIB') SHR REUSE                       0006
ALLOC F(SYSPRINT) DA('TSO1234.TEST.LINKLIST(&MEMNAME)') OLD REU  0007
ALLOC F(SYSUT1)  UNIT(SYSDA)  SPACE(15 15) TRACK REUSE           0008
CALL 'SYS1.LINKLIB(IEWL)' +                                      0009
  'AMODE=31,RMODE=ANY,XREF,CALL'                                 0010
WRITE RETURN CODE IS &LASTCC                                     0011
FREE F(SYSLIN SYSLMOD SYSLIB SYSPRINT SYSUT1)                    0012
```

Line 1   The first line of this CLIST is a PROC statement. Its only function is to communicate the variable value for the member name that is to be used in the object, load, and print data sets. That variable, &MEMNAME, was included as a positional parameter because the information it will convey is required for the CLIST to execute.

Line 2   This line allocates the SYSLIN file to the data set TSO1234.OBJ. Whatever member name is supplied when the CLIST is invoked will be substituted for the variable &MEMNAME. Object code or instructions will be read from the SYSLIN file as input to the linkage-editor program.

Line 3   This line allocates the SYSLMOD file to the data set TSO1234.TEST.LOAD. Whatever member name is supplied when the CLIST is invoked will be substituted for the variable &MEMNAME. The load module, whether fully resolved or not, will be written to this file and placed in the member specified. A disposition of OLD is used to place the proper enqueue on the PDS member to allow it to be written to.

Lines 4   These lines allocate three data sets to the SYSLIB file. The
through 6   SYSLIB file supports the automatic call feature of the linkage-editor program's attempt to resolve external references. The three data sets are concatenated so that any of the three can supply subroutines that are necessary to supplement the load module being created. The libraries are searched, in the order specified, for a given load-module member. This is an important consideration when a given member name exists in more than one of the libraries. Obviously, the first such member encountered in the search is the one that will be used. The disposition is SHR since copies will be made of the existing subroutines for inclusion in the load module being constructed.

Example 4: The link II CLIST (Continued)

```
PROC 1 MEMNAME                                                  0001
ALLOC F(SYSLIN)  DA('TSO1234.OBJ(&MEMNAME)') SHR REUSE          0002
ALLOC F(SYSLMOD) DA('TSO1234.TEST.LOAD(&MEMNAME)') OLD REUSE    0003
ALLOC F(SYSLIB)  DA('TSO1234.DEV.LOAD' +                        0004
                 'COMMON.LOADLIB' +                             0005
                 'SYS1.FORTLIB') SHR REUSE                      0006
ALLOC F(SYSPRINT) DA('TSO1234.TEST.LINKLIST(&MEMNAME)') OLD REU 0007
ALLOC F(SYSUT1)  UNIT(SYSDA)  SPACE(15 15) TRACK REUSE          0008
CALL 'SYS1.LINKLIB(IEWL)' +                                     0009
 'AMODE=31,RMODE=ANY,XREF,CALL'                                 0010
WRITE RETURN CODE IS &LASTCC                                    0011
FREE F(SYSLIN SYSLMOD SYSLIB SYSPRINT SYSUT1)                   0012
```

Line 7	This line allocates the SYSPRINT file to the data set TSO1234.TEST.LINKLIST. Whatever member name is supplied when the CLIST is invoked will be substituted for the variable &MEMNAME. The message output from the linkage-editor program is written to this file. This includes messages about the task outcome as well as other information like cross reference and map output that can be requested. A disposition of OLD is used to place the proper enqueue on this PDS member to allow it to be written to.
Line 8	This line allocates the SYSUT1 file. The file is used only to provide work space for the link-editor program, and so it includes only space and unit information.
Lines 9 and 10	These lines cause the linkage-editor program to be loaded and executed. As it is invoked, execution options are passed to the program as parm information. In this particular case, 31-bit addressing is established (AMODE=31) with a residence mode of mode of any (RMODE=ANY). The parm information also requests that a cross-reference listing be produced (XREF) and specifies that external references are to be resolved using the automatic call feature (CALL).
Line 11	This line writes the system variable &LASTCC to the terminal. At this point, the variable contains the numeric return code passed back from the linkage-editor program. This provides feedback on the success of the link operation since all other informational output was directed to the SYSPRINT data set. It is also common to omit this statement and direct SYSPRINT output to the screen.
Line 12	This line frees the five files that were allocated in the CLIST prior to invoking the linkage-editor program. The files would otherwise remain attached to the terminal session until they were reused or the terminal user logged off of TSO.

The JCL that would be used to perform the same link-edit function is listed below:

```
//TSO1234L JOB '0','LINK EDIT',
// CLASS=A,MSGCLASS=A,NOTIFY=TSO1234
//LKED EXEC PGM=IEWL,
//         PARM='AMODE=31,RMODE=ANY,XREF, CALL'
//SYSPRINT DD DSN=TSO1234.TEST.LINKLIST(UPDTPROG),DISP=OLD
//SYSUT1   DD UNIT=SYSDA,SPACE=(TRK,(15,15))
//SYSLIB   DD DSN=TSO1234.DEV.LOAD,DISP=SHR
//         DD DSN=COMMON.LOADLIB,DISP=SHR
//         DD DSN=SYS1.FORTLIB,DISP=SHR
//SYSLIN   DD DSN=TSO1234.OBJ(UPDTPROG),DISP=SHR
//SYSLMOD  DD DSN=TSO1234.TEST.LOAD(UPDTPROG),DISP=OLD
```

A specific member name, UPDTPROG, has been used to identify the member to be used in the object, load, and print data sets.

Example 5: The divide CLIST

Part of this CLIST was shown in Chap. 6 as a way to simulate decimal arithmetic when dividing one number by another. This is accomplished by multiplying the dividend by a factor of 10 for each decimal place that we would like to retain. This CLIST has logic that places a period four places in from the end of the result to represent the decimal point. Provision is also made for a result that is less than one. Additional code has been added to handle results as small as .001. A PROC statement has also been added to complete the CLIST, and to make it easier to invoke. The CLIST could be invoked, for example, in the following fashion.

```
DIVIDE 547 BY 13
```

Only integer numbers are acceptable as input. Numbers entered with periods or even commas would be treated as character data and cause the SET statement to fail.

```
PROC 3 NUM1 OPER NUM2                                      0001
CONTROL END(ENDO)                                          0002
SET &NUM1 = &NUM1 * 10000                                  0003
SET &ANS = &NUM1 / &NUM2                                   0004
SET &LEN = &LENGTH(&ANS)                                   0005
IF &LEN > 4 THEN +                                         0006
  SET &ANS = &SUBSTR(1:&LEN - 4,&ANS).+                    0007
    &SUBSTR(&LEN - 3:&LEN,&ANS)                            0008
ELSE  IF &LEN = 4  THEN  SET &ANS = .&ANS                  0009
ELSE  IF &LEN = 3  THEN  SET &ANS = .0&ANS                 0010
ELSE  IF &LEN = 2  THEN  SET &ANS = .00&ANS                0011
ELSE  +                                                    0012
  DO                                                       0013
    WRITE  RESULT IS TOO SMALL FOR THIS FUNCTION TO DISPLAY 0014
    END                                                    0015
  ENDO                                                     0016
WRITE &ANS                                                 0017
```

Line 1	The first line of the CLIST is a PROC statement. It specifies that three positional parameters are required for the CLIST to execute. Those parameters include the dividend, the operation code, and the divisor. Whether the CLIST user types "BY", "/", or virtually anything else for the second parameter is of little consequence since the positional parameter OPER is never subsequently used by the CLIST. This parameter merely allows the information to be entered in a more readable fashion. The other two positional parameters, NUM1 and NUM2, will contain the numeric values used in the SET statement expression.
Line 2	This line changes the delimiter END to the string ENDO for all subsequent DO groups.
Line 3	This line multiples the variable &NUM1 by 10,000. This is like adding four zeroes to the number initially entered. This will allow four more significant digits to be retained when the number is divided.
Line 4	This line uses the expanded number (still in variable &NUM1) as the dividend and the original value entered for &NUM2 as the divisor. The result of the expression is placed in variable &ANS.
Line 5	This line uses the &LENGTH built-in function to determine the length of the number in variable &ANS. The length value is placed in variable &LEN.
Line 6	This line uses an IF statement test to see that the result is greater than four bytes in length.
Lines 7 and 8	These lines are the true path of the IF statement test continued over two lines. Noting that the answer is more than four digits, it places a period four places in from the right. The stored length value is used to place all but the last four digits on the left side of the period, and the last four digits on the right side.
Line 9	This line is the false path of the IF statement. It also tests the length of the result stored in variable &LEN. If the result is four digits, a period is placed in front of the result.

Example 5: The divide CLIST *(Continued)*

```
PROC 3 NUM1 OPER NUM2                                           0001
CONTROL END(ENDO)                                              0002
SET &NUM1 = &NUM1 * 10000                                      0003
SET &ANS = &NUM1 / &NUM2                                       0004
SET &LEN = &LENGTH(&ANS)                                       0005
IF &LEN > 4 THEN +                                            0006
  SET &ANS = &SUBSTR(1:&LEN - 4,&ANS).+                       0007
    &SUBSTR(&LEN - 3:&LEN,&ANS)                                0008
ELSE  IF &LEN = 4  THEN  SET &ANS = .&ANS                     0009
ELSE  IF &LEN = 3  THEN  SET &ANS = .0&ANS                    0010
ELSE  IF &LEN = 2  THEN  SET &ANS = .00&ANS                   0011
ELSE  +                                                       0012
  DO                                                          0013
    WRITE  RESULT IS TOO SMALL FOR THIS FUNCTION TO DISPLAY   0014
    END                                                       0015
  ENDO                                                        0016
WRITE &ANS                                                    0017
```

Lines 10 and 11	These lines also test the variable length, and in the true path, string a period and leading zeroes in front of the value. Both statements are the false path of the IF statement before it. That means that if any of the previous IF statement tests are true, these statements will not be executed. In either statement, enough zeroes are added to the result to provide four digits.
Lines 12 through 16	At this point all variable lengths greater than one have been accounted for. This means the result is .0009 or less. Additional code could be added to account for results from .0009 to .0001, but for most applications, it would not be worth the effort. This section of code writes a message to the screen to tell the CLIST user that the answer is too small for the CLIST to handle. The CLIST is then terminated so that the statement that displays the division result is not executed. The END command to terminate the CLIST is not confused with the END statement to end the DO group because the latter was changed to the string ENDO on line 2 of the CLIST.
Line 17	This line displays the result of the division (which is now character data) at the terminal.

Example 6: The data set name qualifier
CLIST

This CLIST searches for the first period in a fully qualified data set name and then uses the &SUBSTR function to extract the data set name high-level qualifier. The first qualifier of the data set name is written to the terminal. A more practical application for the extracted information might be to compare the data set qualifier against the CLIST user's user-ID contained in system variable &SYSUID. That process could be used to determine ownership of the data set and direct other processing accordingly.

The CLIST expects a fully qualified data set name without quotes as positional parameter input. Additional checks to help ensure that these conditions are true could also be added to the example shown. A loop is established to step through the data set name one position at a time while searching for a period that would separate one data set name qualifier from another. If the end of the data set name is reached before a period is found, an error message is written to the terminal and the CLIST is terminated.

```
PROC 1 DSN                                              0001
CONTROL END(ENDO)                                       0002
SET &MAX = &LENGTH(&DSN)                                0003
SET &INDEX = 0                                          0004
LOOP:  SET &INDEX = &INDEX + 1                          0005
IF &INDEX > &MAX   THEN +                               0006
  DO                                                    0007
    WRITE                                               0008
    WRITE THE DATA SET NAME PROVIDED DOES NOT CONTAIN   0009
    WRITE VALID MULTIPLE QUALIFIERS.                    0010
    WRITE                                               0011
    END                                                 0012
  ENDO                                                  0013
IF &SUBSTR(&INDEX:&INDEX,&DSN)  NE  . THEN +            0014
  GOTO LOOP                                             0015
SET &TO = &INDEX - 1                                    0016
SET &QUAL = &SUBSTR(1:&TO,&DSN)                         0017
WRITE THE DATA SET FIRST QUALIFIER IS &QUAL            0018
```

Line 1	The first line of the CLIST is a PROC statement. Its positional specification number indicates that a single positional parameter will follow. That parameter is a data set name and is information that is required for the CLIST to execute. The CLIST is constructed to make use of a fully qualified data set name (of at least two qualifiers) that does not contain quotes.
Line 2	This line is a CONTROL statement. It is used to change the DO group delimiter from END to the string ENDO.
Line 3	This line uses the built-in function, &LENGTH, to set the value of variable &MAX to the number of characters in the passed data set name. This value will be used to stop the loop if the end of the data set name is reached before the first period is located.
Line 4	This line initializes the variable &INDEX. This variable will serve to control loop processing as well as index or reference individual bytes within the data set name.
Line 5	This line represents the top of the loop, and increments the loop counter &INDEX by one each time the loop is executed. The label LOOP provides a point that the execution sequence can branch back to.
Line 6	This line is a condition test to see if the loop counter &INDEX exceeds the number of characters in the data set name that was entered when the CLIST was invoked. The IF statement has a true condition, but has no false path logic.
Lines 7 through 13	These lines represent the true path of the IF statement test. To provide a single imperative to the true condition, several statements are included in a DO group. The function of the group is to write a message to the screen and terminate the CLIST.

Example 6: The data set name qualifier
CLIST *(Continued)*

```
PROC 1 DSN                                              0001
CONTROL END(ENDO)                                       0002
SET &MAX = &LENGTH(&DSN)                                0003
SET &INDEX = 0                                          0004
LOOP:  SET &INDEX = &INDEX + 1                          0005
IF &INDEX > &MAX  THEN +                                0006
  DO                                                    0007
    WRITE                                               0008
    WRITE THE DATA SET NAME PROVIDED DOES NOT CONTAIN   0009
    WRITE VALID MULTIPLE QUALIFIERS.                    0010
    WRITE                                               0011
    END                                                 0012
  ENDO                                                  0013
IF &SUBSTR(&INDEX:&INDEX,&DSN)  NE  .  THEN +           0014
  GOTO LOOP                                             0015
SET &TO = &INDEX - 1                                    0016
SET &QUAL = &SUBSTR(1:&TO,&DSN)                         0017
WRITE THE DATA SET FIRST QUALIFIER IS &QUAL            0018
```

Line 14   This line uses the &SUBSTR function to test a position within the data set name against the symbol for a period. The position that is tested varies based on the variable that also serves as the loop counter. While the IF statement has only a true path, the branch that it mandates makes all following statements identical to a false path.

Line 15   This line is the true path imperative for the preceding IF statement test. When the position tested does not contain a period, a branch is made to the top of the loop by way of the label LOOP. This allows the next position in the data set name to be tested.

Line 16   At this point in the logic, a period has been located in the data set name. The value in &INDEX points to the position of the period relative to the start of the data set name string. This statement subtracts one from that value to mark the last usable position of information that will become the data set high-level qualifier. That ending byte value is placed in the variable &TO.

Line 17   This line extracts the high-level qualifier of the data set name starting in the first position of the string. The value that was just derived for variable &TO is used to specify the last byte to be extracted. The extracted information is placed in variable &QUAL.

Line 18   This line displays the extracted qualifier at the terminal by combining literal and variable information in a WRITE statement.

Example 7: The message CLIST

This CLIST is used to send messages to one or more TSO users. The CLIST user is prompted to enter the message, and the CLIST will continue to accept message input until a blank line is entered. One or more user-IDs is passed as a positional parameter to designate who the message is to be sent to. The CLIST could be invoked in the following fashion.

```
MESSAGE TS00273TS00394TS00595
```

Because a positional parameter was chosen to convey the user-ID information, the information must be entered. If the information was not specified at the time the CLIST was invoked, the user would be prompted to enter the positional parameter USERID. Since it is a positional parameter, embedded spaces or commas are not allowed in the parameter value. That is why the three user-IDs specified in the example above are run together. The CLIST code will have to break the information up into separate, usable user-IDs.

```
PROC 1 USERID   LOGON(LOGON)                              0001
CONTROL ASIS                                             0002
SET &LEN   = &LENGTH(&USERID)                            0003
SET &FIRST = 1                                           0004
SET &LAST  = 7                                           0005
DO WHILE &LAST LE &LEN                                   0006
   SET &C = &C &SUBSTR(&FIRST:&LAST,&USERID)             0007
   SET &FIRST = &FIRST + 7                               0008
   SET &LAST  = &LAST + 7                                0009
END                                                     0010
WRITE ENTER MESSAGE OR BLANK TO STOP                     0011
LOOP: +                                                  0012
READ                                                    0013
```

Line 1   The first line of the CLIST is a PROC statement. It specifies that a single positional parameter is required for the CLIST to execute. That parameter, USERID, is intended to include the TSO user-ID of the individual that the message is being sent to. As we shall see later, the CLIST is designed to handle multiple user-IDs.

The PROC statement also defines a keyword parameter, LOGON. The main intent here is to initialize the variable &LOGON to the value LOGON. This will be used as a parameter on the SEND command. The CLIST user also has the option of negating this parameter value. That can be done if the CLIST is invoked in the following fashion.

```
MESSAGE TS00273TS00394TS00595 LOGON('')
```

The variable &LOGON was handled in this way because the default value of LOGON would be used most of the time. If the opposite were true, the PROC statement could have been coded like the following statement.

```
PROC 1 USERID  LOGON
```

This would provide a null default value for the variable &LOGON while providing a way to establish its value as the character string LOGON. This value would result when the modified keyword LOGON is used on the invoking statement.

```
MESSAGE TS00273TS00394TS00595 LOGON
```

Line 2   This line stops data from automatically being translated to uppercase. This would allow data entered in lowercase characters to remain that way as it is sent as messages to different individuals.

Line 3   This line determines the length of the variable &USERID and places the length value in variable &LEN.

Line 4   This line initializes the variable &FIRST to a value of 1. This variable will be used to point to the start of user-ID values as they are parsed from the positional parameter &USERID.

Line 5   This line initializes the variable &LAST to a value of 7. This variable will be used to point to the end of user-ID values which will all be seven bytes long.

Line 6   This line forms the start of a loop to parse user-IDs from the list of user-IDs in variable &USERID. Assuming that at least one valid user-ID of seven characters was entered, the loop will be executed at least once. The loop will stop when the user-ID end pointer &LAST has a value greater than the length of the string being parsed. At that point, the WRITE statement on line 11 will be executed.

Example 7: The message CLIST *(Continued)*

```
PROC 1 USERID  LOGON(LOGON)                                 0001
CONTROL ASIS                                                0002
SET &LEN   = &LENGTH(&USERID)                               0003
SET &FIRST = 1                                              0004
SET &LAST  = 7                                              0005
DO WHILE &LAST LE &LEN                                      0006
   SET &C = &C &SUBSTR(&FIRST:&LAST,&USERID)                0007
   SET &FIRST = &FIRST + 7                                  0008
   SET &LAST  = &LAST + 7                                   0009
END                                                         0010
WRITE ENTER MESSAGE OR BLANK TO STOP                        0011
LOOP: +                                                     0012
READ                                                        0013
IF &STR(&SYSDVAL) =   THEN END                              0014
SEND '&SYSDVAL' U(&C)  &LOGON                               0015
GOTO LOOP                                                   0016
```

Line 7   This line constructs a new variable, &C. Each time the loop is executed, another seven-character user-ID is added to the variable. The space between the variable and the &SUBSTR expression causes each added user-ID to be separated from the previous user-IDs by a space. This is the objective of the loop: to separate the user-IDs so they will conform to proper command syntax. The &SUBSTR function is used to extract user-IDs from variable &USERID. The pointers &FIRST and &LAST are used to specify the start and end positions of the data to be extracted.

Line 8   This line increments the variable &FIRST by seven. This will allow it to point to the start of the next user-ID if another iteration of the loop code is executed.

Line 9   This line increments the variable &LAST by seven. This will allow it to point to the end of the next user-ID if another iteration of the loop code is executed.

Line 10   This line ends the DO WHILE loop. At this point, control branches back to the top to again test the conditions that perpetuate the loop.

Line 11   Control falls through to this statement when the loop test is no longer true. This statement writes information to the terminal. The written text is intended to prompt the CLIST user to enter the message text, and describe to them how to terminate processing.

Line 12   This line provides a label that is referenced by a GOTO statement later in the CLIST. The two statements form another type of loop to iteratively process input text. The label is not followed by a command or CLIST statement, and so contains a continuation character. That allows the subsequent code to be included on the next line.

Line 13   This line reads the message text from the terminal. Because a variable name is not used, the information read in must be subsequently accessed from the system variable &SYSDVAL. This allows the entire text read to be handled as a single-variable value. The use of any other variable would have truncated the text at the first space or comma delimiter.

Example 7: The message CLIST *(Continued)*

```
PROC 1 USERID  LOGON(LOGON)                                    0001
CONTROL ASIS                                                   0002
SET &LEN   = &LENGTH(&USERID)                                  0003
SET &FIRST = 1                                                 0004
SET &LAST  = 7                                                 0005
DO WHILE &LAST LE &LEN                                         0006
  SET &C = &C &SUBSTR(&FIRST:&LAST,&USERID)                    0007
  SET &FIRST = &FIRST + 7                                      0008
  SET &LAST  = &LAST + 7                                       0009
END                                                           0010
WRITE ENTER MESSAGE OR BLANK TO STOP                          0011
LOOP: +                                                       0012
READ                                                          0013
IF &STR(&SYSDVAL) =   THEN END                                0014
SEND '&SYSDVAL' U(&C)  &LOGON                                 0015
GOTO LOOP                                                     0016
```

Line 14   This line tests the value just read in. If that was a blank line, the CLIST is terminated by executing the END command. Otherwise, execution is allowed to continue with the next sequential instruction. The &STR function is used with the variable &SYSDVAL in case that variable happens to contain special characters that might be misinterpreted as an attempt to do arithmetic. This avoids errors that might otherwise result from a combination of characters that would be invalid as an arithmetic operation.

Line 15   This line is the TSO SEND command. The message content is contained in the system variable &SYSDVAL. Its value was read in from the terminal. The keyword U( ) is the abbreviated form of the parameter used to specify message recipients. The variable &C contains the list of user-IDs after spaces were "inserted" to delimit one user-ID from another. The last variable, &LOGON, is used to represent another parameter when the default value is left to apply. This parameter value specifies that if the recipient is not currently logged on or accepting messages, the messages will be held until the next time that individual enters the TSO function.

Line 16   This line branches backup to the label LOOP to allow additional messages to be entered.

Example 8: The compress CLIST

This CLIST is used to perform an in-place compress of a partitioned data set. Such a process is periodically required to reorganize a PDS and free previously used space. That space is then available for subsequent use. The primary function of the CLIST is to obtain resources prior to program execution. Once the proper environment is established, the program IEBCOPY is invoked. Upon return from program execution, the resources allocated by the CLIST are freed. The JCL code to perform the same function is also presented. It is discussed first, and then used to demonstrate how to translate from JCL to CLIST code.

```
//TSO1234C JOB '0', 'PDS COMPRESS',                      0010
//  CLASS=A,MSGCLASS=A,NOTIFY=TSO1234                    0020
//COMPRESS EXEC PGM=IEBCOPY                              0030
//SYSPRINT DD SYSOUT=*                                   0040
//PDS      DD DISP=OLD,DSN=TSO1234.FULL.PDS              0050
//SYSUT3   DD UNIT=SYSDA,SPACE=(TRK,(15,15))             0060
//SYSUT4   DD UNIT=SYSDA,SPACE=(TRK,(15,15))             0070
//SYSIN    DD DISP=SHR,DSN=TSO1234.CNTL(COMPRESS)        0080


ALLOC F(PDS) DA('TSO1234.FULL.PDS') OLD REUSE            0001
ALLOC F(SYSUT3) SP(15 15) TRACK UNIT(SYSDA) REUSE        0002
ALLOC F(SYSUT4) SP(15 15) TRACK UNIT(SYSDA) REUSE        0003
ALLOC F(SYSPRINT) DA(*) REUSE                            0004
ALLOC F(SYSIN) DA('TSO1234.CNTL(COMPRESS)' SHR REUSE     0005
CALL 'SYS1.LINKLIB(IEBCOPY)'                             0006
FREE F(PDS SYSUT3 SYSUT4 SYSPRINT SYSIN)                 0007
```

Line 10   This line is the first line of a two-line JOB statement. It identi-
             fies the jobname and specifies the first two positional parame-
             ters that, at most installations, contain accounting informa-
             tion.

Line 20   This line is the second line of the two-line JOB statement. It
             identifies the input class that the job is to run in as well as the
             print class that is to be used for part of the job output. The
             NOTIFY parameter causes a message to be sent to the user-ID
             specified at the end of the job execution.

Line 30   This line invokes the program IEBCOPY that will compress
             the PDS. The program is used to copy PDS data from one place
             to another. A compress takes place when the data is copied
             back to the original data set. If the program had not been spe-
             cially defined to the operating system, a STEPLIB DD state-
             ment would have also been required to point to the location of
             the data set that contains the program. The statement also
             specifies a stepname, which in this case is COMPRESS.

Line 40   This line contains a DD statement for the file SYSPRINT.
             SYSPRINT is the file name that the IEBCOPY messages are
             written to. In this case, the file output is directed to SYSOUT
             processing to the same output class as job message output (as
             determined by the JOB statement MSGCLASS= parameter).

Line 50   This line contains a DD statement that will be referenced from
             the control-statement parameters. Here, control statement
             refers to parameter data that is used to control the IEBCOPY
             utility program. This statement is used to identify both the
             input and output data set (since the data is copied over itself
             during a compress).

Line 60   This line contains a DD statement for the file SYSUT3.
             SYSUT3 is a file that is used to allocate temporary work space
             for the program. In this case, space is allocated in tracks with a
             primary quantity of 15 as well as a secondary quantity of 15.
             The space will be obtained from an eligible volume that has
             been defined to the esoteric name SYSDA.

Line 70   This line contains a DD statement for the file SYSUT4.
             SYSUT4, just like SYSUT3, is a file that is used to allocate
             temporary work space for the program. The allocation parame-
             ters are identical to those of the SYSUT3 file.

Example 8: The compress CLIST *(Continued)*

```
//TSO1234C JOB 'O', 'PDS COMPRESS',                        0010
//   CLASS=A,MSGCLASS=A,NOTIFY=TSO1234                     0020
//COMPRESS EXEC PGM=IEBCOPY                                0030
//SYSPRINT DD SYSOUT=*                                     0040
//PDS      DD DISP=OLD,DSN=TSO1234.FULL.PDS                0050
//SYSUT3   DD UNIT=SYSDA,SPACE=(TRK,(15,15))               0060
//SYSUT4   DD UNIT=SYSDA,SPACE=(TRK,(15,15))               0070
//SYSIN    DD DISP=SHR,DSN=TSO1234.CNTL(COMPRESS)          0080


ALLOC F(PDS) DA('TSO1234.FULL.PDS') OLD REUSE             0001
ALLOC F(SYSUT3) SP(15 15) TRACK UNIT(SYSDA) REUSE         0002
ALLOC F(SYSUT4) SP(15 15) TRACK UNIT(SYSDA) REUSE         0003
ALLOC F(SYSPRINT) DA(*) REUSE                             0004
ALLOC F(SYSIN) DA('TSO1234.CNTL(COMPRESS)') SHR REUSE     0005
CALL 'SYS1.LINKLIB(IEBCOPY)'                              0006
FREE F(PDS SYSUT3 SYSUT4 SYSPRINT SYSIN)                  0007
```

Line 80   This line contains a DD statement for the file SYSIN. The
           SYSIN file, for the IEBCOPY program, contains control state-
           ment data. In this case, the control statement data is stored in
           a data set called TSO1234.CNTL(COMPRESS). That data set
           contains the following copy statement.

```
COPY INDD=PDS,OUTDD=PDS
```

The control statement parameters both make reference to the
previous DD statement PDS. The CLIST statements are
detailed below. They are shown with the equivalent JCL statement to highlight how similar the two types of statements can
be. Every ALLOCATE command in this CLIST makes use of
the REUSE parameter to ensure that the file it allocates will
be available. There is no JCL facility for this since resources
are obtained and freed automatically at the step level.

Line 1   This line is used to allocate the data set that will be both input
           and output for the IEBCOPY program. The data set is allocat-
           ed with a disposition of OLD to gain exclusive control while it
           is being rewritten. Control statement parameters read into the
           SYSIN file, reference the file name of PDS, to define the file as
           both input and output to the utility. The process of writing the
           PDS back onto itself is what causes it to be compressed.

```
(CLIST)
    ALLOC F(PDS) DA('TSO1234.FULL.PDS') OLD REUSE
(JCL)
    //PDS      DD DISP=OLD,DSN=TSO1234.FULL.PDS
```

Line 2   This line allocates file SYSUT3. SYSUT3 is a file that is used
           to allocate temporary work space for the program. With the
           absence of a permanent data set name, a system temporary
           data set name for this file will be generated. The data set cre-
           ated here will be deleted when the file is freed. Primary and
           secondary space of fifteen tracks each will be obtained from an
           eligible volume that has been defined to the esoteric name
           SYSDA.

```
(CLIST)
    ALLOC F(SYSUT3) SP(15 15) TRACK UNIT(SYSDA) REUSE
(JCL)
    //SYSUT3   DD UNIT=SYSDA,SPACE=(TRK,(15,15))
```

Example 8: The compress CLIST *(Continued)*

```
//TS01234C JOB '0', 'PDS COMPRESS',                          0010
//   CLASS=A,MSGCLASS=A,NOTIFY=TS01234                       0020
//COMPRESS EXEC PGM=IEBCOPY                                  0030
//SYSPRINT DD SYSOUT=*                                       0040
//PDS       DD DISP=OLD,DSN=TS01234.FULL.PDS                 0050
//SYSUT3    DD UNIT=SYSDA,SPACE=(TRK,(15,15))                0060
//SYSUT4    DD UNIT=SYSDA,SPACE=(TRK,(15,15))                0070
//SYSIN     DD DISP=SHR,DSN=TS01234.CNTL(COMPRESS)           0080


ALLOC F(PDS) DA('TS01234.FULL.PDS') OLD REUSE               0001
ALLOC F(SYSUT3) SP(15 15) TRACK UNIT(SYSDA) REUSE           0002
ALLOC F(SYSUT4) SP(15 15) TRACK UNIT(SYSDA) REUSE           0003
ALLOC F(SYSPRINT) DA(*) REUSE                               0004
ALLOC F(SYSIN) DA('TS01234.CNTL(COMPRESS)' SHR REUSE        0005
CALL 'SYS1.LINKLIB(IEBCOPY)'                                0006
FREE F(PDS SYSUT3 SYSUT4 SYSPRINT SYSIN)                    0007
```

Line 3   This line is the same as the previous statement except that the
                work space that it obtains is used under the file name of
                SYSUT4.

                (CLIST)
                    ALLOC F(SYSUT4) SP(15 15) TRACK UNIT(SYSDA) REUSE
                (JCL)
                    //SYSUT4   DD UNIT=SYSDA,SPACE=(TRK,(15,15))

Line 4   This line allocates the utility SYSPRINT file. That is the file
                that the IEBCOPY messages are written to. This statement
                directs those statements to display at the terminal.

                (CLIST)
                    ALLOC F(SYSPRINT) DA(*) REUSE
                (JCL)
                    //SYSPRINT DD SYSOUT=*

Line 5   This line allocates the SYSIN file. This file is used to convey
                control statement instructions to the IEBCOPY program. The
                statement   makes   reference   to   the   data   set
                TSO1234.CNTL(COMPRESS), where the control statements
                are stored. That data set contains the copy statement

                    COPY INDD=PDS,OUTDD=PDS

                which identifies the "from" and "to" file names to be used in the
                copy operation. In this case, both parameters refer to the same
                file name, PDS, that was allocated earlier in the CLIST.

                (CLIST)
                    ALLOC F(SYSIN) DA('TSO1234.CNTL(COMPRESS)') SHR REUSE
                (JCL)
                    //SYSIN   DD DISP=SHR,DSN=TSO1234.CNTL(COMPRESS)

Line 6   This line causes the IEBCOPY program to be loaded and exe-
                cuted. It was necessary to find which system library contained
                the utility program and include that data set name on the
                CALL statement.

                (CLIST)
                    CALL 'SYS1.LINKLIB(IEBCOPY)'
                (JCL)
                    //COMPRESS EXEC PGM=IEBCOPY

Line 7   This line frees five files that were allocated in the CLIST. This
                will also free the data sets that were allocated to these files.
                There is no equivalent JCL statement because resources are
                freed at the termination of every background job step.

                (CLIST)
                    FREE F(PDS SYSUT3 SYSUT4 SYSPRINT SYSIN)

Example 9: The report CLIST

This CLIST creates a phone list report from extracted data. The data is obtained from various positions on multiple lines of input data. Below is a layout of what the input data looks like.

```
EMPNO: xxxx DEPT: xx NAME: xxxxxxxxxxxxxxxxxxxxxxxxxxxxxx
SSN  : xxx xx xxxx PHONEW: xxx xxx-xxxx PHONEH: xxx xxx-xxxx
ADDR1: xxxxxxxxxxxxxxxxxxxxxxxxxxxxxxxxxxxxxxxxx
ADDR2: xxxxxxxxxxxxxxxxxxxxxxxxxxxxxxxxxxxxxxxxx
ADDR3: xxxxxxxxxxxxxxxxxxxxxxxxxxxxxxxxxxxxxxxxx
```

These five lines represent the information for one individual. Information for the phone list will be extracted from lines one and two. Capital letters and special characters are actually part of the input data. Positions occupied by the variable portion of the data are represented using a lowercase letter *x*. When all data is obtained for any individual, the information is written out in sixty-line pages with headings. A print counter is maintained to determine when heading lines should be written.

Information is output using the PUTFILE statement. The ALLO-CATE command for the file being written, RPTFILE, directs the output to a printer rather than a disk data set. The ALLOCATE command also specifies the use of carriage-control for the print file. A skip to new page and double spacing is included in the heading by placing the appropriate characters in column one of the data that is written out. Below is a detailed description of each line of the CLIST:

```
PROC 0  HEADING1('1              PHONE LIST') +          0001
HEADING2('          SORTED BY EMPLOYEE NAME')  +          0002
HEADING3('0 NAME            EMP NUMBER DEPART+          0003
MENT  PHONE')                                            0004
CONTROL NOFLUSH                                          0005
SET &PAGE_CNT = 60                                       0006
SET &RC = 0                                              0007
ALLOC F(EMPFILE) DA('EMPLOYEE.DATA') SHR REUSE          0008
```

(Code continued on page 188.)

Lines 1 through 4	The first four lines of this CLIST form a PROC statement. The PROC statement specifies that there are no positional parameters. The statement does, however, specify three keyword parameters: HEADING1, HEADING2, and HEADING3. These variables will be used to create the report heading. The intent is not to supply three variables that could be used to change the report heading. Although those variables could be used for that purpose, it would not be an effective use of the CLIST user's time. The variables appear on the PROC statement because it is more efficient to establish their values there than to use SET statements. The variable values are enclosed in quotes to allow the use of embedded spaces.
Line 1	This portion of the PROC statement contains the first heading variable HEADING1. The value it contains will be used as the first heading line every time there is a page break. The page break is determined in part by the number 1 in position one of the variable. This will also be position one of the written data and will serve as the carriage-control character, causing a skip to the head of the form.
Line 2	This portion of the PROC statement contains the second heading variable, HEADING2. The value it contains will be used as the second heading line every time there is a page break. The leading spaces in this variable value as well as the other two are to center the significant portion of the heading text within the report.
Lines 3 and 4	This portion of the PROC statement contains the third heading variable, HEADING3. The value it contains will be used as the third heading line or column heading every time there is a page break. The 0 in the first position will serve as a carriage-control character to cause double spacing before the line is printed.
Line 5	This line is a CONTROL statement. It specifies that the command stack not be flushed when an error is encountered. This is added in anticipation of the error that will undoubtedly occur when end of file is reached while reading the input file.
Line 6	This line sets the variable &PAGE_CNT to a value of 60. This variable will be used to keep track of how many lines have been written and, therefore, when to break to a new page. The initial value is set high to force the headings to be written on a new page immediately. Although sixty is the number of lines that will be written on each page, it is not the number that will be tested for.
Line 7	This line sets the variable &RC which will control the read loop. The initial value of 0 will ensure that the loop is executed at least once.
Line 8	This line allocates the data set containing employee information EMPLOYEE.DATA, to the input file EMPFILE. This file will later be read for the employee information to generate the report.

Example 9: The report CLIST *(Continued)*

```
ALLOC F(EMPFILE) DA('EMPLOYEE.DATA') SHR REUSE              0008
ALLOC F(RPTFILE) SYSOUT(A) RECFM(F B A) LRECL(80)          0009
OPENFILE EMPFILE                                            0010
OPENFILE RPTFILE OUTPUT                                     0011
GETFILE EMPFILE                                             0012
ERROR +                                                     0013
  DO                                                        0014
    SET &RC = &LASTCC                                       0015
    IF &RC  NE 400 THEN  +                                  0016
      DO                                                    0017
        WRITE    UNEXPECTED END OF CLIST                    0018
        WRITE    RETURN CODE IS &RC                         0019
        EXIT                                                0020
      END                                                   0021
  END                                                       0022
DO WHILE &RC  = 0                                           0023
  IF &SUBSTR(1:5,&EMPFILE) = EMPNO  THEN +                  0024
    DO                                                      0025
      SET &EMP_NO = &SUBSTR(8:12,&EMPFILE)                  0026
      SET &DEPT   = &SUBSTR(19:20,&EMPFILE)                 0027
      SET &NAME   = &SUBSTR(28:57,&EMPFILE)                 0028
    END                                                     0029
  ELSE IF &SUBSTR(1:3,&EMPFILE) = SSN  THEN +               0030
    DO                                                      0031
      SET &PHONE  = &SUBSTR(28:39,&EMPFILE)                 0032
      IF &PAGE_CNT > 55 THEN +                              0033
        DO                                                  0034
          SET &PAGE_CNT = 0                                 0035
          SET &RPTFILE = &STR(&HEADING1)                    0036
          PUTFILE RPTFILE                                   0037
          SET &RPTFILE = &STR(&HEADING2)                    0038
          PUTFILE RPTFILE                                   0039
          SET &RPTFILE = &STR(&HEADING3)                    0040
          PUTFILE RPTFILE                                   0041
        END                                                 0042
      SET &RPTFILE = &STR(  &NAME  &EMP_NO    DEPT    &PHONE) 0043
      PUTFILE RPTFILE                                       0044
      SET &PAGE_CNT = &PAGE_CNT + 1                         0045
    END                                                     0046
  GETFILE EMPFILE                                           0047
END                                                         0048
```

Line 9	This line allocates a SYSOUT data set to the file RPTFILE. The information written to this file will be printed as eighty-byte fixed-length records. It will be printed to class A, utilizing carriage-control characters in column one of the data.
Line 10	This line opens the file EMPFILE for input processing. The information read from this file will be available in variable &EMPFILE.
Line 11	This line opens the file RPTFILE for output processing. Information will be accumulated in variable &RPTFILE before it is written to this file.
Line 12	This line reads the first record from the data set containing employee information.
Lines 13 through 22	These lines form an ERROR routine. That ERROR routine immediately precedes a DO WHILE condition test that supports iterative processing until an end-of-file error is encountered.
Line 13	This line identifies the beginning of ERROR routine code. Control will branch to this statement if an error occurs. The ERROR routine was not placed before the initial GETFILE statement since an end-of-file error there would indicate a completely empty data set. Under that circumstance, it would be appropriate to let the CLIST terminate.
Line 14	This line starts a DO group that will allow more than a single statement to be executed when a error is encountered.
Line 15	This line captures the error return code contained in system variable &LASTCC. That return code is saved in variable &RC. This must be the first statement of the ERROR routine to capture the &LASTCC value before it changes.
Line 16	This line tests the saved return code for a value of 400. This value indicates that an attempt was made to read past the end of the input file. This is an expected condition, after which the CLIST will be terminated normally. For any other error, the CLIST will be terminated immediately.
Line 17	This line starts a DO group that will be executed when the return code is not equal to 400.
Lines 18 and 19	These lines write a message to the screen that an unexpected error has been encountered. The return code saved in variable &RC is written with that message.
Line 20	This line terminates the CLIST after the unexpected error.
Line 21	This line ends the inner DO group for processing all errors except that encountered by reading past end of file.
Line 22	This line ends the DO group that defines the ERROR routine.

Example 9: The report CLIST *(Continued)*

```
ERROR +                                                    0013
   DO                                                      0014
      SET &RC = &LASTCC                                    0015
      IF &RC  NE 400 THEN  +                               0016
         DO                                                0017
            WRITE    UNEXPECTED END OF CLIST               0018
            WRITE    RETURN CODE IS &RC                    0019
            EXIT                                           0020
            END                                            0021
      END                                                  0022
DO WHILE &RC  = 0                                          0023
   IF &SUBSTR(1:5,&EMPFILE) = EMPNO  THEN +                0024
   DO                                                      0025
      SET &EMP_NO = &SUBSTR(8:12,&EMPFILE)                 0026
      SET &DEPT   = &SUBSTR(19:20,&EMPFILE)                0027
      SET &NAME   = &SUBSTR(28:57,&EMPFILE)                0028
   END                                                     0029
   ELSE IF &SUBSTR(1:3,&EMPFILE) = SSN  THEN +             0030
   DO                                                      0031
      SET &PHONE  = &SUBSTR(28:39,&EMPFILE)                0032
      IF &PAGE_CNT > 55 THEN +                             0033
         DO                                                0034
            SET &PAGE_CNT = 0                              0035
            SET &RPTFILE = &STR(&HEADING1)                 0036
            PUTFILE RPTFILE                                0037
            SET &RPTFILE = &STR(&HEADING2)                 0038
            PUTFILE RPTFILE                                0039
            SET &RPTFILE = &STR(&HEADING3)                 0040
            PUTFILE RPTFILE                                0041
            END                                            0042
      SET &RPTFILE = &STR(  &NAME  &EMP_NO    DEPT    &PHONE)  0043
      PUTFILE RPTFILE                                      0044
      SET &PAGE_CNT = &PAGE_CNT + 1                        0045
   END                                                     0046
   GETFILE EMPFILE                                         0047
END                                                        0048
CLOSFILE EMPFILE                                           0049
CLOSFILE RPTFILE                                           0050
FREE F(EMPFILE RPTFILE)                                    0051
```

Line 23	This line defines a DO loop that will execute while the return code saved in variable &RC is zero. The value of that variable was set to zero before the first record was read to cause the loop to execute. After all input records have been read, a GET-FILE error will change the variable value to 400. That value will cause the loop test to fail, and iterative processing to stop.
Line 24	This line tests the first five bytes of the input record to see if it is equal to the character string EMPNO.
Line 25	This line starts a DO group that will be executed when the the preceding IF statement test is true. This indicates that the first of five records that make up the information for any given employee is now stored in variable &EMPFILE.
Lines 26 through 28	These lines extract information from the input record contained in variable &EMPFILE. The &SUBSTR function is used to take information from particular columns of the input record and place it in variables &EMP_NO, &DEPT, and &NAME.
Line 29	This line ends the DO group that defines the true path of the previous IF statement test. That condition test was used to determine when the first record of employee information is obtained.
Line 30	This line tests for the second record of employee information. It will only execute in the false path of the previous IF statement (which tests for the first record of employee information).
Line 31	This line starts a DO group that will be executed when the the preceding IF statement test is true. This indicates that the second of five records that make up the information for any given employee is now stored in variable &EMPFILE. Subsequent logic will format the extracted information and write it to the output file.
Line 32	This line extracts the employee phone number from data read into variable &EMPFILE. That data is placed in variable &PHONE.
Line 33	This line tests the variable used to keep track of the number of lines written to a given page. The intent is to print sixty lines on each page. The line count variable is tested against the value 55 because, including the double-spaced line, the heading accounts for four print lines. In the true path of this condition test, headings will be written, and the counter reset to keep track of the lines written to the new page.
Line 34	This line starts a DO group that will be executed in the true path of the preceding IF statement test.
Line 35	This line sets the line count variable to zero to start tracking the number of lines written to a new page.

Example 9: The report CLIST *(Continued)*

```
ERROR +                                                         0013
  DO                                                            0014
    SET &RC = &LASTCC                                           0015
    IF &RC   NE 400 THEN  +                                     0016
      DO                                                        0017
        WRITE    UNEXPECTED END OF CLIST                        0018
        WRITE    RETURN CODE IS &RC                             0019
        EXIT                                                    0020
      END                                                       0021
  END                                                           0022
DO WHILE &RC  = 0                                               0023
  IF &SUBSTR(1:5,&EMPFILE) = EMPNO  THEN +                      0024
    DO                                                          0025
      SET &EMP_NO = &SUBSTR(8:12,&EMPFILE)                      0026
      SET &DEPT   = &SUBSTR(19:20,&EMPFILE)                     0027
      SET &NAME   = &SUBSTR(28:57,&EMPFILE)                     0028
    END                                                         0029
  ELSE IF &SUBSTR(1:3,&EMPFILE) = SSN  THEN +                   0030
    DO                                                          0031
      SET &PHONE  = &SUBSTR(28:39,&EMPFILE)                     0032
      IF &PAGE_CNT > 55 THEN +                                  0033
        DO                                                      0034
          SET &PAGE_CNT = 0                                     0035
          SET &RPTFILE = &STR(&HEADING1)                        0036
          PUTFILE RPTFILE                                       0037
          SET &RPTFILE = &STR(&HEADING2)                        0038
          PUTFILE RPTFILE                                       0039
          SET &RPTFILE = &STR(&HEADING3)                        0040
          PUTFILE RPTFILE                                       0041
        END                                                     0042
      SET &RPTFILE = &STR(  &NAME  &EMP_NO    DEPT    &PHONE)    0043
      PUTFILE RPTFILE                                           0044
      SET &PAGE_CNT = &PAGE_CNT + 1                             0045
    END                                                         0046
  GETFILE EMPFILE                                               0047
END                                                             0048
CLOSFILE EMPFILE                                                0049
CLOSFILE RPTFILE                                                0050
FREE F(EMPFILE RPTFILE)                                         0051
```

Line 36   This line places the first heading line in the output file variable in preparation of writing that information to file RPTFILE. The data in the first heading line includes the character "1" in column one to cause a skip to a new page when the information is printed.

Line 37   This line uses the PUTFILE statement to write the first heading line to file RPTFILE.

Line 38   This line places the second heading line in the output file variable in preparation of writing that information to file RPTFILE.

Line 39   This line uses the PUTFILE statement to write the second heading line to file RPTFILE.

Line 40   This line places the third heading line in the output-file variable in preparation of writing that information to file RPTFILE. The data in the third heading line includes the character "0" in column one to cause double spacing before the information is printed.

Line 41   This line uses the PUTFILE statement to write the third heading line to file RPTFILE.

Line 42   This line ends a DO group that was used to write headings to a new page of the report.

Line 43   This line formats a detail line of the report, placing the data in the output file variable &RPTFILE.

Line 44   This line uses the PUTFILE statement to write a detail line to the report.

Line 45   This line increments the line count variable by 1 to reflect that another detail line has been written.

Line 46   This line ends a DO group that was used to complete detail-line formatting and printing, and it includes the logic to determine whether or not headings should be written.

Line 47   This line uses the GETFILE statement to obtain another record from the employee information file. If such a GETFILE is attempted after the last record, control will branch up to the ERROR routine.

Line 48   This line ends the DO group that controls iterative processing.

Line 49   This line closes the input, employee-information file.

Line 50   This line closes the output, report file.

Line 51   This line frees the input and output files that were used in processing employee information.

Example 10: The cut CLIST

This CLIST is used to cut most fixed-length record data sets into data sets with smaller record lengths. When a new data set record length is chosen that is smaller than the record length of the current data set, the data is divided up and written to the smaller length records. To do this, a write counter is set by dividing the current record length by the new record length. The result is the number of times records will have to be written out to account for one input record. In addition, the remainder function is used to determine if any of the input record remains to be written out. This not only accounts for uneven division, but also accounts for a new record length that is larger than the record length of the current data set. The CLIST, therefore, also has the ability to create larger record lengths in the data set being created.

The *CUT CLIST* extracts the numeric portion of the the system date and time variables (**&SYSDATE** and **&SYSTIME**) to use in building a unique, new data set name to give to the new data set being created. It also calculates the blocksize for the new data set based upon the new record length. That record length can be specified as a keyword variable, or left to default to a value of 80. The following is an example of how the CLIST might be invoked.

```
CUT 'TSO1234.LONG.DATA' LRECL(50)'
```

The above example would read the data from data set 'TSO1234.LONG.DATA' and reformat the records into fifty-byte record lengths. If the data set currently contained eighty-byte records, for example, each record read would cause two fifty-byte records to be written. The first such record would contain the first fifty bytes of the input data set, while the second record would contain the next thirty bytes of data followed by twenty bytes of spaces.

The CLIST contains nested DO WHILE structures. The outer structure controls reading of the input file. An ERROR routine is included to handle normal end of file processing. The inner DO WHILE structure controls iterative output processing.

```
PROC 1 DSN LRECL(80)                                          0001
CONTROL NOFLUSH                                               0002
SET &RC = 0                                                   0003
ALLOC F(CUT) DA(&DSN) SHR REUSE                               0004
SET &DATE = D&SUBSTR(1:2,&SYSDATE)+                           0005
   &SUBSTR(4:5,&SYSDATE)&SUBSTR(7:8,&SYSDATE)                 0006
SET &TIME = T&SUBSTR(1:2,&SYSTIME)+                           0007
   &SUBSTR(4:5,&SYSTIME)&SUBSTR(7:8,&SYSTIME)                 0008
```

(Code continued on page 196.)

Line 1   The first line of this CLIST is a PROC statement. It specifies that one positional parameter is required for the CLIST to execute. That positional parameter is the name of the disk data set that is to be cut up. A value for the new record length can optionally be specified using the keyword parameter LRECL. If no value is specified for the LRECL keyword, the default of 80, which is coded on the PROC statement, will apply.

Line 2   This line uses the CONTROL statement to keep the CLIST statements from being flushed in the event of an error. In particular, such an error is anticipated when end of file is reached reading the input data set.

Line 3   This line sets variable &RC to a value of zero. This variable will be used to control iterative processing via the DO WHILE statement.

Line 4   This line allocates the data set whose name is conveyed as a positional parameter to the file CUT. This file will be used to read input data into the CLIST.

Lines 5 and 6   These lines extract the numeric portion of the system date variable &SYSDATE. The string 102892 would, for example, be extracted from the date 10/28/92. The SET statement places this string behind the letter D and places the result in variable &DATE. The intent is to create a valid data set qualifier that will form a unique data set name when combined with other qualifiers.

Lines 7 and 8   These lines extract the numeric portion of the system time variable &SYSTIME. The string 115734 would, for example, be extracted from the time 11:57:34. The SET statement places this string behind the letter T and places the result in variable &TIME. Again, the intent is to create a valid data set qualifier that will form a unique data set name when combined with other qualifiers.

Example 10: The cut CLIST (Continued)

```
SET &DATE = D&SUBSTR(1:2,&SYSDATE)+                              0005
  &SUBSTR(4:5,&SYSDATE)&SUBSTR(7:8,&SYSDATE)                     0006
SET &TIME = T&SUBSTR(1:2,&SYSTIME)+                              0007
  &SUBSTR(4:5,&SYSTIME)&SUBSTR(7:8,&SYSTIME)                     0008
SET &DSN2 = &SYSUID..&DATE..&TIME                                0009
SET &BLKSIZE = 23476 / &LRECL * &LRECL                           0010
ALLOC F(NEWDATA) DA('&DSN2') SPACE(5 5) TRACK RELEASE CATALOG +  0011
  RECFM(F B) LRECL(&LRECL) BLKSIZE(&BLKSIZE) REUSE               0012
OPENFILE CUT                                                     0013
OPENFILE NEWDATA OUTPUT                                          0014
GETFILE CUT                                                      0015
SET &LEN = &LENGTH(&STR(&CUT))                                   0016
SET &LOOP_COUNT = &LEN /  &LRECL                                 0017
SET &REMAIN   = &LEN // &LRECL                                   0018
ERROR +                                                          0019
  DO                                                             0020
    SET &RC = &LASTCC                                            0021
    IF &RC  NE 400 THEN  +                                       0022
      DO                                                         0023
        WRITE    UNEXPECTED END OF CLIST                         0024
        WRITE    RETURN CODE IS &RC                              0025
        EXIT                                                     0026
      END                                                        0027
  END                                                            0028
DO WHILE &RC  = 0                                                0029
  SET &COUNT  = 0                                                0030
  SET &START  = 1                                                0031
  SET &END    = &LRECL                                           0032
  DO WHILE &COUNT < &LOOP_COUNT                                  0033
    SET &NEWDATA = &SUBSTR(&START:&END,&CUT)                     0034
    SET &COUNT = &COUNT + 1                                      0035
    SET &START = &START + &LRECL                                 0036
    SET &END   = &END   + &LRECL                                 0037
    PUTFILE NEWDATA                                              0038
  END                                                            0039
  IF &REMAIN > 0 THEN +                                          0040
    DO                                                           0041
      SET &NEWDATA = &SUBSTR(&START:&LEN,&CUT)                   0042
      PUTFILE NEWDATA                                            0043
    END                                                          0044
```

Line 9   This line combines the data set qualifiers, developed in the previous two SET statements, with the user-ID contained in system variable &SYSUID to form a new, unique data set name. That data set name is placed in variable &DSN2. Elements of the current date and time were used to ensure that the data set name is unique. This is similar to formats used in temporary data set names created by the operating system. The CLIST user's user-ID is used as the high-level qualifier of the data set name to avoid potential access problems. Such problems can arise when the TSO session is prefixed to a different high-level qualifier where there is insufficient authority to create a data set.

Line 10   This line calculates an optimum blocksize for the data set that will be created in the next statement. The calculation uses the record length that was entered (or left to default) as keyword variable &LRECL. An assumption is made here that the optimum blocksize is that which is closest to half of a 3380 disk track. That number is 23,476 bytes. The calculation takes advantage of the inability to carry decimal places, that is, to multiply the integer result of division back by the record length. The result is the largest number that is an even multiple of the record length but does not exceed the number 23,476.

Lines 11   These lines use the ALLOCATE command to create a new data
and 12   set and connect it to the file name NEWDATA. The data set name used is one that was created in previous statements to be unique. The blocksize used was calculated in the previous statement, and the primary and secondary space values are both arbitrarily set at five tracks.

Line 13   This line uses the OPENFILE statement to open the input file CUT. Records will be read from this file to supply the data written to the output file.

Line 14   This line uses the OPENFILE statement to open the output file NEWDATA. Data read from the input file will be written to this file. If the file is allocated to a data set with a different record length, the data will be written out in multiple lines or padded as it is written out.

Line 15   This line uses the GETFILE statement to obtain the first input record.

Line 16   This line uses the built-in function &LENGTH to determine the length of the data read. The &STR function is used to retain trailing spaces. This ensures that a valid length value is obtained.

Line 17   This line sets a variable that is used to control a DO WHILE loop for iterative processing. The loop is an inner loop that determines how many output lines must be formatted for each input line read.

Example 10: The cut CLIST *(Continued)*

```
OPENFILE CUT                                              0013
OPENFILE NEWDATA OUTPUT                                   0014
GETFILE CUT                                               0015
SET &LEN = &LENGTH(&STR(&CUT))                            0016
SET &LOOP_COUNT = &LEN /  &LRECL                          0017
SET &REMAIN    = &LEN // &LRECL                           0018
ERROR +                                                   0019
  DO                                                      0020
    SET &RC = &LASTCC                                     0021
    IF &RC  NE 400 THEN  +                                0022
      DO                                                  0023
        WRITE    UNEXPECTED END OF CLIST                  0024
        WRITE    RETURN CODE IS &RC                       0025
        EXIT                                              0026
      END                                                 0027
  END                                                     0028
DO WHILE &RC  = 0                                         0029
  SET &COUNT  = 0                                         0030
  SET &START  = 1                                         0031
  SET &END    = &LRECL                                    0032
  DO WHILE &COUNT < &LOOP_COUNT                           0033
    SET &NEWDATA = &SUBSTR(&START:&END,&CUT)              0034
    SET &COUNT = &COUNT + 1                               0035
    SET &START = &START + &LRECL                          0036
    SET &END   = &END   + &LRECL                          0037
    PUTFILE NEWDATA                                       0038
  END                                                     0039
  IF &REMAIN > 0 THEN +                                   0040
    DO                                                    0041
      SET &NEWDATA = &SUBSTR(&START:&LEN,&CUT)            0042
      PUTFILE NEWDATA                                     0043
    END                                                   0044
  GETFILE                                                 0045
END                                                       0046
CLOSFILE CUT                                              0047
CLOSFILE NEWDATA                                          0048
FREE F(CUT NEWDATA)                                       0049
WRITE DATA HAS BEEN PLACED IN DATA SET '&DSN2'            0050
```

Line 18 This line uses the remainder function, essentially, to see if there are any bytes left after the input-record length is divided by the new record length (the record length to be attributed to the output data set). The remainder value is placed in variable &REMAIN. This value will used to process any data that remains after all complete output lines are written out.

Line 19 This line defines an ERROR routine which is included to account for end-of-file errors. Processing will continue after such an error, but will terminate after any other type of error since it has not been anticipated.

Line 20 This line starts a DO group that will allow more than a single statement to be executed when a error is encountered.

Line 21 This line captures the error return code contained in system variable &LASTCC. That return code is saved in variable &RC. This must be the first statement of the ERROR routine to capture the &LASTCC value before it changes.

Line 22 This line tests the saved return code for a value of 400. This value indicates that an attempt was made to read past the end of the input file. This is an expected condition, after which the CLIST will be terminated normally. For any other error, the CLIST will be terminated immediately.

Line 23 This line starts a DO group that will be executed when the return code is not equal to 400.

Lines 24 and 25 These lines write a message to the screen that an unexpected error has been encountered. The return code saved in variable &RC is written with that message.

Line 26 This line terminates the CLIST after the unexpected error.

Line 27 This line ends the inner DO group for processing all errors except that encountered by reading past end of file.

Line 28 This line ends the DO group that defines the ERROR routine.

Line 29 This line defines a DO loop that will execute while the return code saved in variable &RC is zero. The value of that variable was set to zero before the first record was read to cause the loop to execute. After all input records have been read, a GET-FILE error will change the variable value to 400. That value will cause the loop test to fail, and the loop to be bypassed.

Line 30 This line initializes the variable &COUNT. The variable will be incremented during loop processing and tested against variable &LOOP_COUNT to control the loop.

Line 31 This line initializes the variable &START. The variable will be used in the &SUBSTR function to point to the first byte of data to be extracted from the input record. The variable is incremented during loop processing to subsequently reference other portions of the input record.

Example 10: The cut CLIST *(Continued)*

```
OPENFILE CUT                                          0013
OPENFILE NEWDATA OUTPUT                               0014
GETFILE CUT                                           0015
SET &LEN = &LENGTH(&STR(&CUT))                        0016
SET &LOOP_COUNT = &LEN / &LRECL                       0017
SET &REMAIN    = &LEN // &LRECL                       0018
ERROR +                                               0019
  DO                                                  0020
    SET &RC = &LASTCC                                 0021
    IF &RC  NE 400 THEN  +                            0022
      DO                                              0023
        WRITE    UNEXPECTED END OF CLIST              0024
        WRITE    RETURN CODE IS &RC                   0025
        EXIT                                          0026
      END                                             0027
  END                                                 0028
DO WHILE &RC  = 0                                     0029
  SET &COUNT  = 0                                     0030
  SET &START  = 1                                     0031
  SET &END    = &LRECL                                0032
  DO WHILE &COUNT < &LOOP_COUNT                       0033
    SET &NEWDATA = &SUBSTR(&START:&END,&CUT)          0034
    SET &COUNT = &COUNT + 1                           0035
    SET &START = &START + &LRECL                      0036
    SET &END   = &END   + &LRECL                      0037
    PUTFILE NEWDATA                                   0038
  END                                                 0039
  IF &REMAIN > 0 THEN +                               0040
    DO                                                0041
      SET &NEWDATA = &SUBSTR(&START:&LEN,&CUT)        0042
      PUTFILE NEWDATA                                 0043
    END                                               0044
  GETFILE                                             0045
END                                                   0046
CLOSFILE CUT                                          0047
CLOSFILE NEWDATA           .                          0048
FREE F(CUT NEWDATA)                                   0049
WRITE DATA HAS BEEN PLACED IN DATA SET '&DSN2'        0050
```

Line 32	This line initializes the variable &END to the record length of the new data set. That value is contained in variable &LRECL. The variable &END will be used in the &SUBSTR function to point to the last byte of data to be extracted from the input record. The variable is also incremented during loop processing to reference other portions of the input record.
Line 33	This line uses a DO WHILE structure to form an inner loop that determines how many output lines must be formatted for each input line read. It is possible that the inner loop will not be executed at all. This would be true when the output-record length is greater than the input-record length.
Line 34	This line extracts data from the input record. That data will be written out to the output file at the end of the inner loop. The &SUBSTR function is used with variables that are initialized before the inner loop is executed. At that point, the initial portion of the input record (contained in variable &CUT) is referenced. The variables are incremented inside the loop so that subsequent execution will reference other portions of the input record.
Line 35	This line uses the SET statement to increment the variable &COUNT which is used to control loop processing.
Line 36	This line uses the SET statement to increment the variable &START which is used to reference the first byte of data to be extracted using the &SUBSTR function. The variable value is incremented by the value contained in the record length variable &LRECL. This allows the data for multiple output lines to be extracted during subsequent executions of the inner loop.
Line 37	This line uses the SET statement to increment the variable &END which is used to reference the last byte of data to be extracted using the &SUBSTR function. The variable value is incremented by the value contained in the record length variable &LRECL. This allows the data for multiple output lines to be extracted during subsequent executions of the inner loop.
Line 38	This line uses the PUTFILE statement to write the data in variable &NEWDATA to the output file. This data was previously extracted from the data read into the input file.
Line 39	This line uses the END statement to end the inner DO WHILE loop.
Line 40	This line tests to see if the value of variable &REMAIN is greater than zero. If it is, then the input record length was not evenly divisible by the new record length and there is additional input data to be written out after inner loop processing is completed.
Line 41	This line defines the start of a DO group that will execute in the true path of the preceding IF statement test.

Example 10: The cut CLIST *(Continued)*

```
OPENFILE CUT                                        0013
OPENFILE NEWDATA OUTPUT                             0014
GETFILE CUT                                         0015
SET &LEN = &LENGTH(&STR(&CUT))                       0016
SET &LOOP_COUNT = &LEN /  &LRECL                     0017
SET &REMAIN    = &LEN // &LRECL                      0018
ERROR +                                             0019
  DO                                                0020
    SET &RC = &LASTCC                               0021
    IF &RC  NE 400 THEN  +                          0022
      DO                                            0023
        WRITE     UNEXPECTED END OF CLIST           0024
        WRITE     RETURN CODE IS &RC                0025
        EXIT                                        0026
      END                                           0027
  END                                               0028
DO WHILE &RC  = 0                                    0029
  SET &COUNT  = 0                                    0030
  SET &START  = 1                                    0031
  SET &END    = &LRECL                               0032
  DO WHILE &COUNT < &LOOP_COUNT                       0033
    SET &NEWDATA = &SUBSTR(&START:&END,&CUT)         0034
    SET &COUNT = &COUNT + 1                           0035
    SET &START = &START + &LRECL                      0036
    SET &END   = &END   + &LRECL                      0037
    PUTFILE NEWDATA                                 0038
  END                                               0039
  IF &REMAIN > 0 THEN +                              0040
    DO                                              0041
      SET &NEWDATA = &SUBSTR(&START:&LEN,&CUT)       0042
      PUTFILE NEWDATA                               0043
    END                                             0044
  GETFILE                                           0045
END                                                 0046
CLOSFILE CUT                                         0047
CLOSFILE NEWDATA                                     0048
FREE F(CUT NEWDATA)                                 0049
WRITE DATA HAS BEEN PLACED IN DATA SET '&DSN2'       0050
```

Line 42   This line extracts the remaining data from the input record. That data will also be written out to the output file. This &SUBSTR function, like the previous one, uses the variable &START to identify the start of data to be extracted. The last byte of data, however, is identified by the variable &LEN that identifies the total length of the input record. This ensures that all data is accounted for and that no reference is made beyond the addressable bytes of input data.

Line 43   This line uses the PUTFILE statement to write the data in variable &NEWDATA, to the output file. This is data that was not extracted from the input-file data during loop processing.

Line 44   This line ends the DO group for processing the remaining input data.

Line 45   This line uses the GETFILE statement to read the next input record. If such a GETFILE is attempted after the last record, control will branch up to the ERROR routine.

Line 46   This line ends the DO WHILE group that serves to control outer loop processing.

Line 47   This line is the first line of normal termination processing. It is executed when outer loop processing terminates and when it uses the CLOSFILE statement to close the input file.

Line 48   This line uses the CLOSFILE statement to close the output file.

Line 49   This line uses the FREE command to free both the input and output files.

Line 50   This line writes a message to the terminal. The message includes the name of the output data set, since it was created internally and would not be obvious to the CLIST user.

Example 11: The data-entry CLIST

This CLIST takes data that is entered at the terminal and writes it to a disk data set. The data entered either appends to the bottom of existing data, replaces an existing data set, or is used to create a new data set. The keyword DISP with a value of MOD is used for the first mode while a value of OLD is used for the other two. If the data set does not currently exist, it is created by the CLIST. The data set to be written to is specified by way of a positional parameter. The following is an example of how the CLIST might be invoked.

```
%WRITDATA AUDIT.DATA DISP(MOD)
```

Data would be added to the end of the existing data in data set AUDIT.DATA. Notice that it is not necessary to fully qualify the data set name. It should be noted, too, that the disposition of MOD would not be valid when working with PDS members. This is a restriction of the operating system as opposed to a limitation of the CLIST language.

When the CLIST is invoked, the following prompt is written to the screen.

```
ENTER DATA OR STOP (IN COLUMN 1) TO TERMINATE
```

Following the prompt, input is accepted from the screen. Upper- and lowercase data read from the screen is written to the specified data set until the word *STOP* or *stop* is typed starting in column one. The test for the word STOP uses both upper- and lowercase since the data brought into the CLIST is not translated to uppercase. The CLIST includes ATTN and TERMIN functions that allow the CLIST user to interrupt the CLIST. They then enter normal TSO mode where they can use TSO commands to gather information to bring back to the CLIST.

```
PROC 1 DSN DISP(OLD)                                      0001
CONTROL NOFLUSH NOMSG ASIS                                0002
ALLOC F(NEWDATA) DA(&DSN) &DISP REUSE                     0003
IF &LASTCC > 0 THEN +                                     0004
  ALLOC F(NEWDATA) DA(&DSN) CAT SP(1 1) TRACK REUSE +     0005
    RECFM(F B) LRECL(80) BLKSIZE(6160)                    0006
OPENFILE NEWDATA OUTPUT                                   0007
ATTN DO                                                   0008
  WRITE   ENTER THE WORD EXIT TO RETURN                   0009
  TERMIN  EXIT                                            0010
  RETURN                                                  0011
END                                                       0012
```

(Code continued on page 206.)

Line 1	This first line of the CLIST includes a PROC statement. The PROC statement defines a positional parameter that is used to name the output data set. This information is required for execution. The statement also includes a keyword that can be used to specify the disposition of the output data set. Expected values are OLD and MOD (although the use of MOD could not be supported when writing to a PDS member). These will cause an existing data set to be written over or for the data entered to be appended to the end of the existing data, respectively. If no value is entered for the DISP keyword when the CLIST is invoked, the default of OLD, which is coded on the PROC statement, will apply.
Line 2	This line uses the CONTROL statement to set the CLIST processing options. The NOFLUSH parameter is used to ensure that the CLIST code is not flushed if the CLIST is interrupted (to make use of the ATTN routine). NOMSG is specified to suppress the display of messages, and ASIS prevents data from being translated to uppercase.
Line 3	This line allocates the specified data set using the disposition value in variable &DISP. If the data set does not already exist, the data set will not be allocated and the ALLOCATE command will issue a return code of twelve.
Line 4	This line tests the return code issued by the ALLOCATE command. The only concern is for a nonzero code. Under this condition, the data set will be allocated as if it were a new, sequential data set.
Line 5 and 6	These lines form the true path of the previous IF statement test. They allocate a new, sequential data set. The data set is allocated with minimal space and eighty-byte fixed-length records.
Line 7	This line uses the OPENFILE statement to open the file just allocated for output processing.
Line 8	This line defines the start of the attention routine and the DO group that will allow that routine to include more than a single statement.
Line 9	This line writes a message to the terminal describing what the CLIST user would enter to return to the CLIST from TSO mode.
Line 10	This line contains the TERMIN statement as well as a return delimiter, the character string EXIT. When this statement is executed, the CLIST user will be placed in TSO mode. They will be returned to the CLIST when they enter the character string EXIT.
Line 11	This line includes the RETURN statement to return control back to the statement that was interrupted.

Line 12   This line ends the ATTN routine.

Example 11: The data-entry CLIST
(Continued)

```
PROC 1 DSN DISP(OLD)                                            0001
CONTROL NOFLUSH NOMSG ASIS                                      0002
ALLOC F(NEWDATA) DA(&DSN) &DISP REUSE                           0003
IF &LASTCC > 0 THEN +                                           0004
  ALLOC F(NEWDATA) DA(&DSN) CAT SP(1 1) TRACK REUSE +           0005
    RECFM(F B) LRECL(80) BLKSIZE(6160)                          0006
OPENFILE NEWDATA OUTPUT                                         0007
ATTN DO                                                         0008
  WRITE   ENTER THE WORD EXIT TO RETURN                         0009
  TERMIN  EXIT                                                  0010
  RETURN                                                        0011
END                                                            0012
WRITE ENTER DATA  OR  STOP (IN COLUMN 1) TO TERMINATE          0013
REPEAT: +                                                       0014
READ                                                           0015
IF &STR(&SYSDVAL) = STOP OR &STR(&SYSDVAL) = stop THEN +       0016
  DO                                                           0017
    CLOSFILE NEWDATA                                           0018
    EXIT                                                       0019
  END                                                          0020
SET &NEWDATA = &STR(&SYSDVAL)                                   0021
PUTFILE NEWDATA                                                 0022
GOTO REPEAT                                                     0023
```

Line 13   This line writes a message to the terminal to tell the CLIST user how to end the CLIST.

Line 14   This line contains only a label to provide a place to branch to at the completion of normal processing. That process forms the loop that supports iterative processing. A continuation character follows the label because there is not an executable statement on the line.

Line 15   This line reads data from the terminal. The system variable &SYSDVAL is used rather than a named variable because the data entered by the CLIST user is likely to contain embedded spaces or commas. The &SYSDVAL variable provides the greatest flexibility for reading data of this type.

Line 16   This line tests the data read for a value of "STOP." This character string would be entered when the CLIST user is finished entering data and wants to terminate the CLIST. Both upper- and lowercase characters are tested since the value could have been entered in either form. Remember that the CONTROL statement option ASIS was used to keep lowercase data from being translated to uppercase.

Line 17   This line starts a DO group that will allow more than a single statement to be executed in the true path of the IF statement test. This will include statements to terminate the CLIST.

Line 18   This line closes the output file.

Line 19   This line terminates the CLIST.

Line 20   This line ends the DO group that executes in the true path of the previous IF statement test.

Line 21   This line places the value read from the terminal (contained in system variable &SYSDVAL) into the variable used for output file processing &NEWDATA.

Line 22   This line uses the PUTFILE statement to write the data to the data set connected to file NEWDATA.

Line 23   This line uses the GOTO statement to cause control to branch back to the label REPEAT. This establishes the loop that supports iterative processing. The process will continue until the CLIST user enters the string, STOP.

Example 12: The TSO command trap CLIST

This CLIST will trap the output of most TSO commands. The CLIST is invoked without any initial parameters. A prompt is then issued for the CLIST user to enter a TSO command. The command is entered as it would be if it were executed outside of the CLIST. The CLIST uses the number of trapped output lines to calculate how much disk space will be used before writing the output lines to a disk file. Before terminating, The TSOTRAP CLIST will write a message to the screen to indicate how many lines of output were written to the disk data set as well as the name of the data set that they were written to.

Some TSO commands use a different mode of output that cannot be captured. When such a command is entered, an appropriate message is issued and the command output is displayed at the terminal in normal fashion.

```
CONTROL END(ENDO) NOFLUSH                                    0001
SET &SYSOUTTRAP = 9999                                       0002
WRITENR  ENTER TSO COMMAND = = =>                            0003
READ                                                         0004
&SYSDVAL                                                     0005
SET &SYSOUTTRAP = 0                                          0006
SET &ENDLINE = &SYSOUTLINE                                   0007
IF  &ENDLINE = 0 THEN  +                                     0008
  DO                                                         0009
    WRITE                                                    0010
    WRITE                                                    0011
    WRITE  UNABLE TO TRAP TSO COMMAND OUTPUT FOR THE COMMAND 0012
    WRITE          &SYSDVAL                                  0013
    WRITE                                                    0014
    END                                                      0015
  ENDO                                                       0016
ELSE +                                                       0017
  DO                                                         0018
    SET &PRIM = &ENDLINE / 504                               0019
    IF &PRIM = 0 THEN  SET &PRIM = 1                         0020
    IF (&PRIM * 504) < &ENDLINE THEN SET &PRIM = &PRIM + 1   0021
  ENDO                                                       0022
CONTROL NOMSG                                                0023
FREE FILE(OUTDATA) DATASET('&SYSUID..COMMAND.OUTPUT')        0024
DEL '&SYSUID..COMMAND.OUTPUT'                                0025
CONTROL MSG                                                  0026
ALLOC FILE(OUTDATA) DATASET('&SYSUID..COMMAND.OUTPUT')  +    0027
  SPACE(&PRIM 1) TRACK                                       0028
OPENFILE  OUTDATA  OUTPUT                                    0029
```

Line 1	The first line of the CLIST is a CONTROL statement. It specifies a different string, ENDO, to replace END as the end delimiter for DO groups. At the same time, the statement specifies that the command stack not be flushed when an error is encountered.
Line 2	This line sets the SYSOUT trap limit at 9,999 lines. The number is set high to accommodate a wide variety of commands and the amount of output they might generate.
Line 3	This line writes to the terminal and remains positioned after the text. The text is a request for the CLIST user to enter the TSO command whose output is to be trapped.
Line 4	This line reads the TSO command being entered. Conspicuously, it does not supply a variable to store the response in. This was done to accommodate multiple word commands as well as those that might contain special characters that might be confused as delimiters. The entire response will be stored in variable &SYSDVAL.
Line 5	This line contains that &SYSDVAL variable. Since there is nothing preceding it, it will become its own executable statement. Whatever TSO command was entered following the prompt will, then, be executed at this point.
Line 6	This line turns the SYSOUT trap off. Whatever output would have been produced by the TSO command has already been trapped.
Line 7	This line moves the value of variable &SYSOUTLINE to the variable &ENDLINE. Both variables now contain a numeric value that represents the last line of command output trapped. That value will be used to control iterative processing later in the CLIST. The variable &SYSOUTLINE could have been used for this purpose since the trap function will not be used again in this CLIST. The variable &ENDLINE is created and used, however, since its name is more descriptive of the function that it serves.
Line 8	This line tests the last line value to see if it is equal to zero. If it is, then no lines of output were trapped, and an appropriate message will be issued.
Lines 9 through 16	These lines form a DO group that is executed in the true path of the previous IF statement test. A formatted message is written to the screen to let the user know that the CLIST was not able to capture any command output. The original command is then written out and the CLIST is terminated with the END statement. The DO group is terminated with the changed string ENDO. This string allows the END command to be placed within the DO group without being misinterpreted as the end of the DO group itself.

Example 12: The TSO command trap CLIST
(Continued)

```
SET &SYSOUTTRAP = 9999                                          0002
WRITENR  ENTER TSO COMMAND = = =>                               0003
READ                                                           0004
&SYSDVAL                                                       0005
SET &SYSOUTTRAP = 0                                            0006
SET &ENDLINE = &SYSOUTLINE                                     0007
IF &ENDLINE = 0 THEN  +                                        0008
  DO                                                          0009
    WRITE                                                     0010
    WRITE                                                     0011
    WRITE  UNABLE TO TRAP TSO COMMAND OUTPUT FOR THE COMMAND   0012
    WRITE            &SYSDVAL                                  0013
    WRITE                                                     0014
    END                                                       0015
  ENDO                                                        0016
ELSE +                                                        0017
  DO                                                          0018
    SET &PRIM = &ENDLINE / 504                                0019
    IF &PRIM = 0 THEN  SET &PRIM = 1                          0020
    IF (&PRIM * 504) < &ENDLINE THEN SET &PRIM = &PRIM + 1     0021
  ENDO                                                        0022
CONTROL NOMSG                                                 0023
FREE FILE(OUTDATA) DATASET('&SYSUID..COMMAND.OUTPUT')         0024
DEL '&SYSUID..COMMAND.OUTPUT'                                 0025
CONTROL MSG                                                   0026
ALLOC FILE(OUTDATA) DATASET('&SYSUID..COMMAND.OUTPUT')  +      0027
  SPACE(&PRIM 1) TRACK                                        0028
OPENFILE  OUTDATA  OUTPUT                                     0029
SET &COUNT = 0                                                0030
LOOP: SET &COUNT = &COUNT + 1                                 0031
SET &LINE = &&SYSOUTLINE&COUNT                                0032
SET &OUTDATA = &STR(&LINE)                                    0033
PUTFILE  OUTDATA                                             0034
IF &COUNT < &ENDLINE  THEN  GOTO LOOP                         0035
CLOSFILE  OUTDATA                                           0036
FREE FILE(OUTDATA)                                           0037
WRITE                                                       0038
WRITE                                                       0039
WRITE   &ENDLINE LINES OF COMMAND OUTPUT HAVE BEEN            0040
WRITE   PLACED IN '&SYSUID..COMMAND.OUTPUT'                   0041
WRITE                                                       0042
```

Line 17	This line represents the false path of the IF statement test on line 8. This statement is not really required since there is an END command in the true path. That means that subsequent code could have been made unconditional since an &ENDLINE value equal to zero would have stopped the CLIST before this point, anyway.
Lines 18 through 22	These lines form a DO group that is executed in the false path of the IF statement test. Within the DO group, the number of tracks required to write all command output is calculated.
Line 19	This line calculates the number of tracks of primary space that should be allocated to hold the command output. Testing has shown that 504 records will be written to each track when the default blocksize is left to apply. The number of output lines already trapped (contained in variable &ENDLINE) is divided by the number of records per track (504) to arrive at the number of tracks required. That number is stored in variable &PRIM. Since decimal arithmetic is not supported, the value of &PRIM is an integer number. That is appropriate for use in the ALLOCATE SPACE parameter.
Line 20	This line tests for a calculated track value of zero. This will be true when the number of trapped lines of output is less than 504. At this point in the CLIST, however, we know that the number of lines produced is greater than zero. Because of this, the primary track amount is set to 1, which is the minimum space allocation for a data set.
Line 21	This line tests to see if the number of primary tracks (&PRIM) multiplied by the number of records per track (504) is less than the number of lines of output. When this is true, the number of primary tracks is incremented by one. This is accomplished by setting variable &PRIM to itself plus one. This is like rounding up after the division in line 19. In essence, the number of lines of output was not evenly divisible by 504. Another track of space should be provided for those output lines that would be represented as the division remainder. The remainder function could, in fact, be used to determine when it was necessary to add another track (when the remainder and the first value of &PRIM were greater than zero).
Line 23	This line uses the CONTROL function to suppress messages using the parameter NOMSG. Specifically, the messages are being turned off before the FREE and DELETE statements that immediately follow. The messages from either of the next two statements are of little consequence, and will not be displayed.
Line 24	This line uses the FREE command to release the use of the file named OUTDATA and the data set COMMAND.OUTPUT. Both file and data set are freed since either resource could have been previously allocated separate from the other.

Example 12: The TSO command trap CLIST
(Continued)

```
SET &SYSOUTTRAP = 9999                                            0002
WRITENR  ENTER TSO COMMAND = = =>                                 0003
READ                                                              0004
&SYSDVAL                                                          0005
SET &SYSOUTTRAP = 0                                               0006
SET &ENDLINE = &SYSOUTLINE                                        0007
IF  &ENDLINE = 0 THEN  +                                          0008
  DO                                                              0009
    WRITE                                                         0010
    WRITE                                                         0011
    WRITE  UNABLE TO TRAP TSO COMMAND OUTPUT FOR THE COMMAND      0012
    WRITE             &SYSDVAL                                    0013
    WRITE                                                         0014
    END                                                           0015
  ENDO                                                            0016
ELSE +                                                            0017
  DO                                                              0018
    SET &PRIM = &ENDLINE / 504                                    0019
    IF &PRIM = 0 THEN  SET &PRIM = 1                              0020
    IF (&PRIM * 504) < &ENDLINE THEN SET &PRIM = &PRIM + 1        0021
  ENDO                                                            0022
CONTROL NOMSG                                                     0023
FREE FILE(OUTDATA) DATASET('&SYSUID..COMMAND.OUTPUT')             0024
DEL '&SYSUID..COMMAND.OUTPUT'                                     0025
CONTROL MSG                                                       0026
ALLOC FILE(OUTDATA) DATASET('&SYSUID..COMMAND.OUTPUT')  +         0027
  SPACE(&PRIM 1) TRACK                                            0028
OPENFILE  OUTDATA  OUTPUT                                         0029
SET &COUNT = 0                                                    0030
LOOP: SET &COUNT = &COUNT + 1                                     0031
SET &LINE = &&SYSOUTLINE&COUNT                                    0032
SET &OUTDATA = &STR(&LINE)                                        0033
PUTFILE  OUTDATA                                                  0034
IF &COUNT < &ENDLINE  THEN  GOTO LOOP                             0035
CLOSFILE  OUTDATA                                                 0036
FREE FILE(OUTDATA)                                                0037
WRITE                                                             0038
WRITE                                                             0039
WRITE   &ENDLINE LINES OF COMMAND OUTPUT HAVE BEEN               0040
WRITE   PLACED IN '&SYSUID..COMMAND.OUTPUT'                       0041
WRITE                                                             0042
```

Line 25	This line uses the DELETE command to delete the data set that TSO command output will be written to. It is normally more efficient to reuse an existing data set. In this case, however, the space needed for each command issued can be calculated and incorporated in the ALLOCATE command. This allows commands with widely varying amounts of output to be processed. In some cases, the data set will not be present to delete. That is certainly acceptable to the processing in this CLIST. Under this circumstance, the DELETE command will issue a high return code and processing will continue.
Line 26	This line uses the CONTROL function with the MSG parameter to turn messages back on.
Lines 27 and 28	This ALLOCATE command recreates the data set previously deleted. The data set name is forced to contain the current user's user-ID (from system variable &SYSUID) to avoid any access problems. The space request is tailored with the number of tracks needed. This was previously calculated using the known number of output lines as well as the number of lines per track, and is contained in variable &PRIM. System defaults for unit and volume residence are left to apply. DCB information will be supplied when the data set is opened and written to.
Line 29	This line opens the file just allocated, OUTDATA. The file is opened for output processing since information from the TSO command will be written to it.
Line 30	This line sets the variable &COUNT to an initial value of zero. The variable will be used as a loop counter. This statement is for documentation as much as anything else since it is not necessary to initialize the variable for the way that it will be used subsequently.
Line 31	This line represents the top of a loop. It contains a label LOOP that will be used for branching back. The rest of the statement increments the counter variable &COUNT by 1 each time through the loop.
Lines 32 and 33	These lines set the variable &OUTDATA to what is contained in each of the &SYSOUTLINEx variables. This is done through the intermediate variable &LINE. The loop-counter variable &COUNT becomes part of the variable name and allows a different SYSOUT line to be referenced each time through the loop.
Line 34	This line writes a line to the file OUTDATA. The data written to the file is that contained in variable &OUTDATA which at this point is set to the value of one of the SYSOUT lines.

Example 12: The TSO command trap CLIST
(Continued)

```
SET &SYSOUTTRAP = 9999                                               0002
WRITENR  ENTER TSO COMMAND = = =>                                    0003
READ                                                                 0004
&SYSDVAL                                                             0005
SET &SYSOUTTRAP = 0                                                  0006
SET &ENDLINE = &SYSOUTLINE                                           0007
IF  &ENDLINE = 0 THEN  +                                             0008
  DO                                                                 0009
    WRITE                                                            0010
    WRITE                                                            0011
    WRITE  UNABLE TO TRAP TSO COMMAND OUTPUT FOR THE COMMAND         0012
    WRITE            &SYSDVAL                                        0013
    WRITE                                                            0014
    END                                                              0015
  ENDO                                                               0016
ELSE +                                                               0017
  DO                                                                 0018
    SET &PRIM = &ENDLINE / 504                                       0019
    IF &PRIM = 0 THEN  SET &PRIM = 1                                 0020
    IF (&PRIM * 504) < &ENDLINE THEN SET &PRIM = &PRIM + 1           0021
  ENDO                                                               0022
CONTROL NOMSG                                                        0023
FREE FILE(OUTDATA) DATASET('&SYSUID..COMMAND.OUTPUT')               0024
DEL '&SYSUID..COMMAND.OUTPUT'                                        0025
CONTROL MSG                                                          0026
ALLOC FILE(OUTDATA) DATASET('&SYSUID..COMMAND.OUTPUT')  +           0027
  SPACE(&PRIM 1) TRACK                                               0028
OPENFILE  OUTDATA  OUTPUT                                            0029
SET &COUNT = 0                                                       0030
LOOP: SET &COUNT = &COUNT + 1                                        0031
SET &LINE = &&SYSOUTLINE&COUNT                                       0032
SET &OUTDATA = &STR(&LINE)                                           0033
PUTFILE  OUTDATA                                                     0034
IF &COUNT < &ENDLINE  THEN  GOTO LOOP                                0035
CLOSFILE  OUTDATA                                                    0036
FREE FILE(OUTDATA)                                                   0037
WRITE                                                                0038
WRITE                                                                0039
WRITE    &ENDLINE LINES OF COMMAND OUTPUT HAVE BEEN                  0040
WRITE    PLACED IN '&SYSUID..COMMAND.OUTPUT'                         0041
WRITE                                                                0042
```

Line 35	This line tests the loop-counter variable &COUNT against the number of trapped output lines contained in variable &END-LINE. As long as the counter is less than the number of trapped lines, the GOTO statement will branch control back to the label LOOP.
Line 36	This line is only executed when the previous IF statement test fails. At that point, the loop counter and the number of lines of output are equal. That means that all output lines have been written to the data set. The CLOSFILE statement then closes the file.
Line 37	This line frees the file that was written to. The associated data set is also freed as a result.
Lines 38 through 42	These lines format a message at the end of the CLIST. That message details how many lines of output were written to the data set based upon the last-line variable &ENDLINE. The name of the data set containing the output records is also written to the screen so the user will know which data set to look at.

Debugging

Debugging is the process of isolating and correcting errors. Where CLIST code is concerned, this could mean that the expected results are not obtained, or even that the CLIST fails outright. It could be as subtle as an extra message that should have been suppressed or as dramatic as an abend that causes an early end to processing. Debugging is a normal part of the development process. It also may become necessary due to errors that surface from whatever production environment the CLIST was placed in.

While CLIST debugging shares some common elements with debugging in other languages, there are some significant differences as well. Even though there is no compile function, some CLIST errors will surface before execution begins. Others only become apparent as they are executed, and may even be data-dependent. Either of these is fairly easy to deal with when the error is conspicuous. This chapter will, therefore, concentrate on the more insidious, elusive errors that would otherwise go undetected. This includes making errors more conspicuous as well as monitoring CLIST execution.

RESOLVING PRE-EXECUTION ERRORS

Most pre-execution errors can be easily isolated using the line number that is included in the error message. This is typically the number of the line relative to the start of the data set. Some errors are more difficult to isolate because the error message does not indicate a line number. It is easy to see how this is possible when the error message is telling us, for example, that the end of the CLIST was reached before all DO groups were closed. This is where users hope that they have used consistent structured formatting in coding their DO groups. Proper indentation of related statements can make it much easier to search for unmatched DOs and ENDs or IFs and ELSEs.

When an examination of the code fails to reveal the error, a user might keep in mind a strategy that is often overlooked. This includes working with a copy of the code and removing portions of the code until the error disappears. The lines of code can be removed with the editor, or selected statements can be turned into comments. The trick, of course, is to remove code in such a way as to not introduce new errors. In the case of unmatched DO and END statements, this would mean removing only what is believed to be a complete DO group. When a portion of code is removed, and the problem goes away, that code is implicated in the problem.

Debugging code that is in development can take a different approach. Since users followed the instructions in Chap. 9 and saved their last working version of the code, they can return to a copy of that version and slowly add the new statements until the CLIST stops working. Statements can be added or removed until the problem is isolated. Whatever is learned can be applied to the latest version of the code. The fact that CLIST code does not have to be compiled, and runs in the foreground, makes this strategy easy to implement.

ENDLESS LOOP PROBLEMS

```
START:   +
SET &COUNT = &COUNT + 1
GOTO START
```

When providing for iterative or loop processing, it is possible to make a mistake like the one above. Unfortunately, most endless loops are not this simple. In fact, it is sometimes difficult to tell if the CLIST is stuck in a loop. The user is first alerted to the possibility of a loop when he or she realizes that the CLIST is taking longer to finish than it usually does. It could be that the CLIST is waiting for a resource. It might even be that the CLIST is the victim of poor response time. One of several products could be used to see if the session is accumulating CPU time. If it is, then the amount of CPU time consumed should be considered. Abnormally high consumption of CPU time hints at the possibility of loop problems.

Some products can provide information on data set contention.

When elapsed time is high, but consumed CPU time is low, this information should be checked. Another source of information that might discount the possibility of loop problems are messages that are written to the system log. In addition to resource contention, a needed volume may be off-line, and this information may be written to the system log.

It is very difficult to tell if an existing CLIST has loop problems. The one exception is when the loop contains some form of output processing. If the same message were written on screen after screen at the terminal, the user would probably suspect a loop problem. The same could be said if the user were to cancel the execution of his or her CLIST only to find the same line of data had been written 50,000 times to one of the output data sets. This, then, could serve as the basis for the debugging effort. Why not add WRITE or PUTFILE statements to the existing code to see if the output from the statement starts spilling out all over? It might also be advisable to reduce the size of the output disk data set so the CLIST can be stopped sooner. If the output data set is created with only a single track and no secondary extents, it would not take long to fill. When the data set is completely out of space, it causes a system abend and thereby stops the CLIST.

EXPLICIT MODE OF EXECUTION

The explicit mode of execution is helpful in debugging for two reasons. As we saw in Chap. 3, the explicit mode includes the data set name of the CLIST being executed. Pointing directly to a given CLIST helps to isolate the code being executed. With the ability to bring multiple CLIST libraries together in the SYSPROC file, mistakes are often caused by executing the wrong CLIST version. Explicit execution pinpoints the initial CLIST being invoked. Explicit execution also ensures that a like-named command is not being inadvertently invoked in place of the CLIST.

Explicit execution of a CLIST also allows the user to control LIST and PROMPT options without making changes to the CLIST itself. This would have the same effect as if the LIST and PROMPT parameters were coded inside the CLIST.

```
EX 'TS01234.CLIST(CALC)' LIST
```

The example above invokes a CLIST with the LIST option. The LIST option can be abbreviated with the letter L. The CLIST would execute and display each executed TSO command or subcommand at the terminal. The command is displayed before it executes, but after substitution of variable values has occurred. This allows the user to see the final syntax of the command, and trace what commands are being executed. It should be noted that while TSO commands and subcommands are listed, other CLIST statements are not. The listing of other CLIST statements will be discussed later in this chapter.

The PROMPT parameter is used to enable the CLIST user to receive system prompts for additional information. Both PROMPT and LIST can also be controlled with the CONTROL statement. The LIST and PROMPT options can also be turned off using the explicit form of the EXECUTE command. This would be effected by including NOLIST and NOPROMPT on the invoking EXECUTE statement.

CREATING DISPLAYS

Using options that display all executed statements can sometimes be overwhelming. They can be especially cumbersome when long-running loops are executed. There are times when debugging efforts can best be facilitated by the display of small amounts of information. This might include displaying return codes after a few key functions or displaying variable values at critical points in the CLIST. A simple way to display information like this is to add WRITE statements to the CLIST.

The following CLIST was introduced earlier. Its function is to convert an eight-character date in the format mm/dd/yy to a five-byte Julian date in the format yyddd.

```
PROC 1 DATE
SET &MM = &SUBSTR(1:2,&DATE)
SET &DD = &SUBSTR(4:5,&DATE)
SET &YY = &SUBSTR(7:8,&DATE)
IF (&YY // 4) EQ 0 THEN  SET &DAYS = &STR(313232332323)
ELSE SET &DAYS = &STR(303232332323)
SET &I = 1
DO WHILE &I LT &MM
  SET &DD = &DD + 28 + &EVAL(&SUBSTR(&I,&DAYS))
  WRITE INDEX IS &I MONTH IS &MM   DAY IS &DD
  SET &I = &I + 1
END
IF &LENGTH(&STR(&DD)) = 2  THEN  SET &DD = &STR(0&DD)
WRITE JULIAN DATE IS &YY.&DD
```

The only statement we have added to the original CLIST is a single WRITE statement. That statement is placed within the loop, and will display the variables &I, &MM, and &DD each time the loop is entered. When the CLIST is executed with the date 03/01/88 as the positional parameter, the following is displayed at the terminal.

```
INDEX IS 1  MONTH IS 03  DAY IS 32
INDEX IS 2  MONTH IS 03  DAY IS 61
JULIAN DATE IS 88.061
```

The loop is entered twice, and as a result, causes the first two lines to be displayed. The last line displayed is the normal output of the CLIST. Notice that it is easier to interpret the write-statement output if the variables are labeled in some fashion. Sometimes it is only necessary to show that a certain part of the CLIST code is being executed. In this case, the write statements may only need to contain literals that could uniquely identify positions within the CLIST.

DATA-DEPENDENT ERRORS

Data-dependent errors result from an incompatibility with the data and how it is used within the CLIST. Virtually every language, for example, would have trouble performing arithmetic calculations on nonnumeric data. This type of error may not surface immediately and it may not surface consistently. Another type of error can occur when the CLIST is not designed to handle certain data. This may be due, for example, to the range of data values or the CLIST's ability to handle missing data. To uncover these types of errors, it is wise to conditionally display errors.

```
IF &MONTH > 12 THEN WRITE THE MONTH VALUE IS &MONTH
```

or

```
IF &DATATYPE(&SUM) NE NUM THEN WRITE NON NUMERIC SUM IS &SUM
```

In the first example, the variable &MONTH is only displayed if it exceeds the normal expected value. In the second example, the variable &SUM is only displayed if it contains a nonnumeric value when the IF statement is executed. Obviously, if these were expected conditions, the CLIST would have been coded to account for those forms of data.

The drawback to adding WRITE statements to facilitate debugging is that the CLIST code is modified. Hopefully the individual is working with a copy of the code, and this would not constitute a problem. Otherwise, it would be a good idea to tag the debugging statements in a way that would make them easy to identify. For example, using the special character, $, in the text of the WRITE statement or in a comment on the same line would make the line easy to find later. Before returning the CLIST to a production mode, it would be easy to scan the code for dollar signs and remove those statements. The same thing applies to debugging as part of the development process or any time temporary statements are added to the CLIST code.

CONTROL LISTING OPTIONS

We have looked at various CONTROL statement options in previous chapters. One of the options, MSG/NOMSG, can be helpful in debugging CLIST code. This parameter controls the generation of messages. Message output is generated as a default, but is often turned off to make the CLIST less confusing to execute. The CLIST developer has typically determined which messages the CLIST user needs to see, and turned all other messages off. When an unexpected error arises, however, it may be necessary to turn the messages back on for the entire CLIST. Switching back to CONTROL MSG may provide enough information to resolve the existing problems.

Other CONTROL-statement parameters exist to list the CLIST statements as they execute. The list of statements could be considered a trace function. The default is for all such listing parameters to be turned off. These parameters, as well as the MSG/NOMSG parameter, can be turned on and off at various places in the CLIST. This allows the CLIST coder to pinpoint which sections of code are listed. If the error can be isolated to a particular section of code, there is no reason to list every executable statement.

The first of the listing parameters is invoked with the statement CONTROL LIST. This creates the same display of executed TSO commands and subcommands as when the LIST function is used during explicit execution. A second list parameter, CONLIST, will list CLIST statements as opposed to TSO commands or subcommands. It lists these statements after symbolic substitution of variables has occurred and before the statement is executed. This is extremely helpful in telling not only what statements are being executed, but what the variable values are.

The third list parameter, SYMLIST, is similar to the CONLIST option. It will list CLIST statements before symbolic substitution of variables has occurred and before the statement is executed. This then shows what the original statement looked like. Used in combination,

```
CONTROL SYMLIST CONLIST
```

it is possible to show the original statement format and the same statement with variable values inserted. In the above example, each CLIST statement executed would display on the screen twice. The following is an example of the date-conversion CLIST with the above statement added for debugging purposes

```
PROC 1 DATE
CONTROL SYMLIST CONLIST
SET &MM = &SUBSTR(1:2,&DATE)
SET &DD = &SUBSTR(4:5,&DATE)
SET &YY _ &SUBSTR(7:8,&DATE)
IF (&YY // 4) EQ 0 THEN  SET &DAYS = &STR(313232332323)
ELSE  SET &DAYS = &STR(303232332323)
SET &I = 1
DO WHILE &I LT &MM
   SET &DD = &DD + 28 + &EVAL(&SUBSTR(&I,&DAYS))
   SET &I = &I + 1
END
IF &LENGTH(&STR(&DD)) = 2  THEN  SET &DD = &STR(0&DD)
WRITE JULIAN DATE IS &YY.&DD
```

In the above example, the control options are added as the second statement of the CLIST. Those options (SYMLIST and CONLIST) are, by default, turned off until explicitly turned on. The CONTROL statement was added at the earliest possible location within the code. It is also possible to include other CONTROL parameters and to place the statement closer to where an error is expected. A statement could also be included later in the code to turn those same options off. Below is what the CLIST would now write to the terminal when executed with the date 03/01/88.

```
SET &MM = &SUBSTR(1:2,&DATE)
SET &MM = 03
SET &DD = &SUBSTR(4:5,&DATE)
SET &DD _ 01
SET &YY = &SUBSTR(7:8,&DATE)
SET &YY = 88
IF (&YY // 4) EQ 0 THEN
IF (88 // 4) EQ 0 THEN
SET &DAYS = &STR(313232332323)
SET &DAYS = 313232332323
SET &I = 1
SET &I = 1
DO WHILE &I LT &MM
```

```
DO WHILE 1 LT 03
  SET &DD = &DD + 28 + &EVAL(&SUBSTR(&I,&DAYS))
  SET &DD = 01 + 28 + 3
  SET &I = &I + 1
  SET &I = 1 + 1
END
END
DO WHILE &I LT &MM
DO WHILE 2 LT 3
  SET &DD = &DD + 28 + &EVAL(&SUBSTR(&I,&DAYS))
  SET &DD = 32 + 28 + 1
  SET &I = &I + 1
  SET &I = 2 + 1
END
END
DO WHILE &I LT &MM
DO WHILE 2 LT 03
IF &LENGTH(&STR(&DD)) = 2  THEN
IF 2 = 2  THEN
SET &DD = &STR(0&DD)
SET &DD = 061
WRITE JULIAN DATE IS &YY.&DD
WRITE JULIAN DATE IS 88061
JULIAN DATE IS 88061
```

With the before and after statements listed, it is fairly easy to follow the execution flow of the CLIST, and determine if it is functioning as designed. Because CONLIST and SYMLIST both list different types of statements than LIST, the user might want to use them with the LIST option as well.

It is also possible to code debugging flexibility into a CLIST. Obviously, LIST and PROMPT options can be controlled when using explicit execution. Adding code to the CLIST to check for execution parameters can facilitate the use of other debugging options. The following code, for example, could be added to the date-conversion CLIST.

```
PROC 1 DATE TRACE
IF &TRACE = TRACE  THEN  CONTROL SYMLIST CONLIST
SET &MM = &SUBSTR(1:2,&DATE)
    .
    .
    .
```

A modified keyword, TRACE, has been added to the PROC statement. Remember that a modified keyword is one that does not allow for different values. It is very similar to a switch that is on or off. In this case, the variable &TRACE either contains the value TRACE or it is blank. When the statement below is used to invoke the CLIST.

```
DATECONV 03/01/88 TRACE
```

the value TRACE is passed in the variable &TRACE. This would cause the first IF-statement test to follow the true path and execute the CONTROL statement to set the two listing options on. Since SYMLIST and CONLIST are turned off as a default, listing of executed statements would not occur if TRACE were omitted from the command that invokes the CLIST.

ERROR MESSAGES

In most cases, a message is issued after an error occurs. This message generally provides enough information to resolve the problem. If messages are not produced, a CONTROL MSG statement should be added to the code as described above. Some message output is withheld until requested by the user. When this occurs, the message that is presented will end with a plus sign. The "+" at the end of a message indicates that additional message text is available. To receive the additional messages, the user should type a question mark, "?", and press the ENTER key. Unless prohibited by the current execution mode, the additional messages will then be displayed.

Additional help with some messages can be obtained from vendor-supplied reference manuals. To facilitate finding these messages, it is often helpful to obtain the message-identification number. The message number for TSO messages is requested by changing the TSO profile with the following command.

```
PROFILE MSGID
```

When turned on in this fashion, the message-identification number will display in front of subsequent message text. That number can be located in the reference manual to obtain an expanded explanation. The following message contains the message-identification number.

```
IKJ56545I THIS STATEMENT HAS AN INVALID &SUBSTR RANGE OR
    EXIT CODE EXPRESSION
```

The message number IKJ56545I can be used to obtain a further explanation from the reference manual. The manual further describes this error as one where the built-in function &SUBSTR contains invalid data or invalid numbers in the substring range field. In this particular case and context, an example was even provided in the manual text. When the debugging effort is finished, the message numbers can be turned off with the following statement.

```
PROF NOMSGID
```

In the command above, we used the abbreviated form of the PROFILE command. Following the issuance of this command, messages will again display in their normal fashion, without the message identification number. Changes to the user's TSO profile would otherwise remain in effect across sessions.

DEBUGGING WITH ERROR ROUTINES

If messages are not produced, despite the presence of a CONTROL MSG statement, the ERROR statement can be added to the code. Including the ERROR statement without any other diagnostic statements will cause the statement that caused the error to display at the terminal. A more elaborate ERROR routine might be included to capture and display the return code of the errant statement. Even more sophisticated code can test for and distinguish between error codes that are acceptable and those that are not. The ERROR statement is discussed in Chap. 7.

REQUESTING A SYSTEM DUMP

Some problems involve other program products or seem to abend without providing any information. In cases such as this, or to have something tangible to hand over to system-support personnel, the user can request a *system dump*. This is a dump of memory at the time the abend occurred. To request a dump, the special file SYSUDUMP should be allocated to a SYSOUT file or to a data set.

```
ALLOC FILE(SYSUDUMP) SYSOUT(A)
```

Once allocated, any CLIST- or TSO-system abend information will be written to the designated resource. This dump facility will be retained until the TSO user leaves the TSO system or frees the SYSUDUMP file.

12

Release 3 Enhancements

This chapter deals exclusively with changes to the CLIST language that were made available with release 1.3 of TSO/E. This includes a way to obtain information about a data set, a string search facility, and new system variables. One of these variables will even indicate what level of TSO/E is installed, and can be the basis for determining if newer release features are available. First, we will examine the facility for obtaining data set information, LISTDSI.

LISTDSI FUNCTION

The *LISTDSI statement* can be used to obtain a substantial amount of information about a data set. This information is obtained from the system catalog and from the volume table of contents (VTOC) of the disk device that the data set is stored on. In addition, the return code issued by LISTDSI can be used to determine whether or not the data set is available. The LISTDSI statement should not be confused, however, with the older TSO command, LISTDS. While they both list data set information, LISTDSI has much more information available to it, and will function only in the context of a CLIST. LISTDS is a TSO command which can be invoked separately or within a CLIST. The format of the LISTDSI command is

```
LISTDSI data-set-name
```

Invoking the function within a CLIST will provide information in twenty-five standard variables. Each variable contains information about the data set, and can be accessed by the CLIST. The variables remain set within the current CLIST until the next use of the LISTDSI statement. Below is a summary of LISTDSI variables and the information they contain:

&SYSDSNAME   contains the fully qualified data set name (without quotes and without member name).

&SYSDSORG   contains the data set organization, including:
PO for partitioned organization
PS for physical sequential
DA for direct access
VS for Virtual Storage Access Methods (VSAM)
IS for Indexed Sequential Access Methos (ISAM)
Some of the data set organizations above can also contain the letter U to designate that the data set is unmoveable. In addition, the value of variable &SYSDSORG could be ???. This is indicative of a data set that does not yet have a data set organization. This is common for data sets allocated without the DSORG or DIRECTORY parameters before they are opened. Further definition of the data set characteristics may not occur until the data set is actually used.

&SYSRECFM   contains the data set record format, including the following basic formats:
F for fixed-length records
V for variable-length records
U for undefined-length records
which can be used in combination with the following:
B for blocked records (where multiple logical records make up a physical record or block)
S for spanned records (that are able to span from one block into another)
A for records that contain ASCII-designated print-control characters
M for records that contain machine-code print-control characters
T for records that may be written to overflow tracks
As with the data set organization, it is possible to have a value of ? when the data set has not yet been used in a way that would cause the record format to be defined.

&SYSLRECL   contains the data set record length.

&SYSBLKSIZE   contains the data set block size.

&SYSALLOC   contains the total amount of space currently allocated to the data set.

&SYSUSED   contains the amount of space currently used by the data set.

&SYSPRIMARY   contains the primary amount of space allocated to the data set.

&SYSSECONDS   contains the secondary space amount (if any) that is available to the data set.

&SYSVOLUME   contains the volume serial number of the disk that the data set resides on.

&SYSUNITS   contains the type of units that the data set was allocated in, either BLOCKS, TRACKS, or CYLINDERS.

&SYSEXTENTS   contains the number of extents used by the data set.

&SYSCREATE   contains the date that the data set was created (in the format yyyy/ddd).

&SYSREFDATE   contains the date that the data set was last referenced (in the format yyyy/ddd). The date is changed to reflect the current date when the data set is opened. This is true whether or not the data set itself was actually updated.

&SYSEXDATE   contains the expiration date (if any) of the data set (in the format yyyy/ddd).

&SYSPASSWORD   indicates whether or not the data set is password-protected. Variable values include:

> NONE when the data set is not password protected
> READ when a password is required to read the data set
>
> WRITE when a password is required to write to (update) the data set

&SYSRACFA   indicates whether or not the data set is RACF-protected. Variable values include:

> NONE when RACF protection is not available
> DISCRETE when the data set is RACF indicated, meaning that a flag byte in the VTOC would direct the search for a discrete profile
>
> GENERIC when the flag byte in the VTOC is turned off and the data set would be protected by a generic profile

&SYSUPDATED   indicates whether or not the change indicator is turned on. Valid values are YES and NO. The change indicator is typically used with programs that create backup copies of the data. When the indicator is on, it means that the data set has been changed, but not backed up. The program that backs up the data set would then turn the indicator off after the data is backed up.

&SYSTRKSCYL   contains the number of tracks per cylinder for the type of disk device that the data set is allocated on.

&SYSBLKSTRK   contains the number of blocks per track for the type of disk device that the data set is allocated on. This, of course, is also tied to the data set block size.

&SYSKEYLEN   contains the length of the keys in a keyed data set.

When the DIRECTORY parameter is added to the LISTDSI statement and the data set being referenced is partitioned, information is also available in the following variables:

&SYSADIRBLK   contains the number of directory blocks allocated to the data set, if the data set is a PDS.

&SYSUDIRBLK   contains the number of directory blocks used, if the data set is a PDS.

&SYSMEMBERS   contains the number of members in the data set, if the data set is a PDS.

Note that the directory parameter can be used routinely and will not cause problems when regular, sequential data sets are being utilized.

The return code issued after normal completion of the LISTDSI statement is 0. A return code of 16 indicates that the data set is not available. That does not necessarily mean that the data does not exist, which, of course, is one of the possibilities. Another possibility, however, is that the data set has been processed by some archival or migration system. Many installations have these installed to help conserve the disk space they use. They typically move data sets to cheaper storage media or compress the way that the data is stored. The RECALL parameter can be included on the LISTDSI statement to prompt a check of some of these archival systems. If the data set is available, this will typically cause it to be brought back from the archival system. The data set information would then be placed into the corresponding variables as normal. It should be noted, however, that the default is to not request retrieval from an archive system. This could, then, also be responsible for a return code of 16. If the data set is not retrieved, its data set information would not be available.

Three additional variables are available which do not directly list information about the data set. These variables describe the status of

LISTDSI processing, and are particularly useful when problems are encountered.

&SYSREASON   contains the last reason code. This reason code is like an extended-return code and when greater than zero, indicates a reason for less than complete processing. That reason might be that the data set does not reside on a mounted-disk volume, or that it has been archived and the RECALL parameter was not used.

&SYSMSGLVL1 and   contain first and second level error messages
&SYSMSGLVL2   respectively that the LISTDSI function might issue.

The following example shows how the LISTDSI statement can be used to obtain data set information and test for the presence of the data set.

```
LISTDSI 'TSO1234.PDS.DATA' DIRECTORY RECALL
IF &LASTCC = 16 THEN    +
  ALLOCATE DA('TSO1234.PDS.DATA') DIR(5) TRACK SP(3 2)   +
    RECFM(F B) LRECL(80) BLKSIZE(6160) CATALOG
ELSE    +
  DO
    IF &SYSDSORG NE PO  THEN  GOTO PDSERROR
    IF &SYSLRECL NE 80  THEN  GOTO LENERROR
  END
.
.
.
```

If the data set does not yet exist, a suitable data set is created. If the data set does exist, its characteristics are checked to make sure they are appropriate for whatever processing might follow. In particular, the data set organization is checked to be sure that the existing data set is partitioned, and the record length is checked for a value of 80. If either condition is not true, control branches to the relevant error code.

A volume parameter is available to reference data sets that are not cataloged. It is a keyword parameter used to specify the disk volume serial number that the data set resides on.

```
LISTDSI SEQUENTL.DATA RECALL VOLUME(TSO004)
```

The above example would cause the LISTDSI function to check disk volume TSO004 without first checking the system catalog. Notice, too, that the data set name specified is not fully qualified. A data set name that does not contain quotes is completed just like any TSO data set name. The VOLUME parameter can also be used to point to individual disk volume sections of a multivolume data set.

Additional uses of the LISTDSI function

LISTDSI can be used within a CLIST to derive a fully qualified data set name. This in itself is a very useful function that is often overlooked. The name specified to LISTDSI can be fully or partially qualified. When the data set is successfully located, the data set name that is returned in the variable &SYSDSNAME is fully qualified without quotes. As we will see later in this chapter, this makes the name contained in &SYSDSNAME ideally suited to pass to a JCL jobstream. Any member name is also removed from the data set name contained in &SYSDSNAME.

Below is an example of various forms of a data set name that could be input to the LISTDSI function and the value that is returned in the variable &SYSDSNAME.

Data Set Name Input To LISTDSI	Value Of &SYSDSNAME
'TS01234.PDS.DATA(MEMBERZ)'	TS01234.PDS.DATA
'TS01234.PDS.DATA'	TS01234.PDS.DATA
PDS.DATA(MEMBERZ)	TS01234.PDS.DATA
PDS.DATA	TS01234.PDS.DATA

Because each input data set name in the example above is a different form used to reference the same PDS, all values returned in the variable &SYSDSNAME are the same. Notice that the data set name is either completed or reduced to arrive at the final value.

The data set reference to the LISTDSI function can also be made indirectly using a file name. The file name must be one that is currently allocated to the TSO session and is designated using the FILE parameter. This is an effective way to determine what data set is allocated to a particular file. The example below specifies a file name of ISPPROF. The word FILE tells the LISTDSI function that it is a file name rather than a data set name.

```
LISTDSI ISPPROF FILE
```

Even if multiple data sets are allocated to the file specified, only the first such data set name is returned in the variable &SYSDSNAME. Below is a complete CLIST that accepts a file name as a positional parameter. That file name is used to find what data set is allocated to the file and that data set name is written to the terminal.

```
PROC 1 FILENAME
CONTROL END(ENDO)
LISTDSI &FILENAME FILE RECALL
IF &LASTCC = 16  THEN +
   DO
      WRITE FILE &FILENAME IS NOT CURRENTLY ALLOCATED
      END
   ENDO
WRITE THE FIRST DATA SET ALLOCATED TO FILE &FILENAME IS
WRITE        '&SYSDSNAME'
```

When the return code from LISTDSI is 16, that is an indication that the file specified is not currently allocated. In that particular case, an appropriate message is displayed and the CLIST is terminated. Remember, too, that only a single data set name is returned by the LISTDSI function. When multiple data sets are allocated to a file, only the name of the first such data set is returned, and the message at the end of this CLIST is worded to reflect this.

The LISTDSI function can also be used to assist with data-management functions. In the example below, LISTDSI variables are used to gauge the amount of space left in the data set before the data set is allocated for output processing. If the data set is determined to be partitioned and its space limited, a compress CLIST is invoked to maximize the space available.

```
.
.
CONTROL END(ENDO)
LISTDSI &DSN RECALL
IF &LASTCC = 16 THEN +
   DO
      WRITE DATA SET  &DSN  CANNOT BE FOUND
      END
   ENDO
IF &SYSEXTENTS > 12 AND (&SYSALLOC - &SYSUSED) < 5 +
   AND &SYSDSORG = PO  THEN +
   COMPRESS '&SYSDSNAME'
ALLOCATE FILE(SYSUT2) DA(&DSN) OLD
.
.
```

When the return code is 16, the data set is unavailable, and the CLIST is terminated. When the number of data set space extents exceeds 12 and the number of space units (blocks, tracks, or cylinders—depending on how the data set was allocated) left is less than 5, a compress CLIST is executed supplying the data set name as a positional parameter. Part of the qualifying test is to ensure that the data set in question is partitioned. As a partitioned data set, the data set name (contained in variable &DSN) could contain a member name. Using the name that is returned in variable &SYSDSNAME, we can be assured that it is appropriate to pass to the compress CLIST since the member name would have been removed.

CHARACTER STRING SEARCH

&SYSINDEX is a built-in function that can be used to search for character strings. In using the function, it is necessary to specify a string that the user is searching for as well as one that will be searched. The function will return the starting position of the search string within the string searched. If that string cannot be found within the searched string, a value of zero is returned. In the example below, an attempt is made to locate the string HIDDEN within the string LOOK FOR THE HIDDEN STRING.

```
&SYSINDEX(HIDDEN,LOOK FOR THE HIDDEN STRING)
```

The result of the above search is the value 14, since the string HIDDEN starts in the fourteenth position of the string being searched. Either or both strings can be represented using variables.

```
&SYSINDEX(&SEARCH_STRING,&SEARCHED_STRING)
```

Notice that the string being searched for is always specified first and is always separated from the string being searched by a comma. The result of the &SYSINDEX function can be tested directly as in the next sample.

```
IF  &SYSINDEX(&SEARCH_STRING,&SEARCHED_STRING) > 0  THEN  +
    WRITE  STRING  &SEARCH_STRING  HAS BEEN LOCATED.
```

or the value can be saved in a variable, as demonstrated below.

```
SET &RESULT = &SYSINDEX(&SEARCH_STRING,&SEARCHED_STRING)
IF    &RESULT >0  THEN  +
    WRITE  STRING  &SEARCH_STRING  HAS BEEN LOCATED.
```

Below is a complete CLIST that was shown in Chap. 10. The CLIST searches for the first period in a fully qualified data set name and then uses the &SUBSTR function to extract the data set name high-level qualifier. The &SYSINDEX function has been inserted into that code and is highlighted. That code is used to replace a loop that checked each character in turn, looking for a period.

```
PROC 1 DSN
CONTROL END(ENDO)
SET &INDEX = &SYSINDEX(.,&DSN)
IF &INDEX = 0 THEN +
  DO
    WRITE
    WRITE THE DATA SET NAME PROVIDED DOES NOT CONTAIN
    WRITE VALID MULTIPLE QUALIFIERS.
    WRITE
    END
  ENDO
SET &TO = &INDEX - 1
SET &QUAL = &SUBSTR(1:&TO,&DSN)
WRITE THE DATA SET FIRST QUALIFIER IS &QUAL
```

There are times when it is not possible to include a particular character string directly. This is generally because some special character in the string would be confused with the statement syntax itself. In a case such as this, it should be possible to place the string in a variable and use the variable within the &SYSINDEX built-in function.

```
SET &PAREN = )
IF &SYSINDEX (&PAREN,&DSN) > 0 THEN . . .
```

The code above might be used, for example, to determine whether or not a member name (enclosed within parentheses) is included in the data set name contained within the variable being searched, &DSN. It is also possible to use the &STR function within the &SYSINDEX function. The example below searches for a comma within a variable.

```
SET &STRING = A,STRING,WITH,COMMAS
SET &TEST = &SYSINDEX(&STR(,),&STR(&STRING))
IF &TEST > 0 THEN  WRITE   THE STRING CONTAINS COMMAS
ELSE  WRITE   THE STRING DOES  NOT  CONTAIN COMMAS
```

The &STR function is used for both &SYSINDEX parameters. The commas in either parameter would otherwise have caused a syntax error.

The &SYSINDEX function also has an optional third parameter that can be used to specify a start position. That parameter is used to indicate where the search is to start. Strings occurring before that start position are essentially ignored. Below is part of the previous example with a start position of 5 specified.

```
SET &STRING = A,STRING,WITH,COMMAS
SET &TEST = &SYSINDEX(&STR(,),&STR(&STRING),5)
```

Coded in this fashion, the result placed in variable &TEST is 9 rather than 2, since the search started in the fifth position. The code in the last two examples could be changed to locate all of the commas in the string. Below is what that code might look like.

```
CONTROL END(ENDO)
SET &STRING = A,STRING,WITH,COMMAS
SET &TEST = 1
DO WHILE &TEST > 0
SET &TEST = &SYSINDEX(&STR(,),&STR(&STRING),&TEST)
IF  &TEST > 0 THEN +
  DO
    WRITE   POSITION &TEST OF THE STRING CONTAINS A COMMA
    SET &TEST = &TEST + 1
  ENDO
ENDO
```

In this case, a variable is used to indicate the starting position for the string search. That variable starts at a value of one and is reset each time the string is successfully located. The value in variable &TEST is then incremented by 1 so the search can be continued just past the current position. A failure to locate the string in any iteration of the loop will set &TEST to zero, and subsequently stop loop processing. When the above CLIST is executed, the following text is displayed at the terminal.

```
POSITION 2 OF THE STRING CONTAINS A COMMA
POSITION 9 OF THE STRING CONTAINS A COMMA
POSITION 14 OF THE STRING CONTAINS A COMMA
```

Below is a section of code that combines the LISTDSI and &SYSINDEX functions to make certain checks before allocating an existing data set to the SYSUT1 file of the utility program IEBGENER.

```
    .

    .

CONTROL END(ENDO)
LISTDSI &DSN DIRECTORY RECALL
```

```
IF &LASTCC = 16   THEN +
  DO
    WRITE DATA SET   &DSN
    WRITE DOES NOT EXIST AND CANNOT BE ALLOCATED
    END
  ENDO
IF &SYSDSORG = PO   THEN +
  DO
    SET &MEMTEST = &SYSINDEX((,&DSN)
    IF &MEMTEST = 0   THEN +
      DO
        WRITE MEMBER NAME REQUIRED BUT NOT SPECIFIED FOR DATA SET
        WRITE     &DSN
        END
      ENDO
    IF &SYSDSN(&DSN) = MEMBER NOT FOUND   THEN +
      DO
        WRITE MEMBER NAME SPECIFIED DOES NOT EXIST IN DATA SET
        WRITE     &DSN
        END
      ENDO
  ENDO
ELSE +
IF &SYSDSORG = PS   THEN +
  DO
    SET &MEMTEST = &SYSINDEX((,&DSN)
    IF &MEMTEST > 0   THEN +
      DO
        WRITE MEMBER NAME CANNOT BE SPECIFIED FOR DATA SET
        WRITE     &DSN
        END
      ENDO
  ENDO
ELSE +
  DO
    WRITE INVALID DATA SET ORGANIZATION &SYSDSORG FOR DATA SET
    WRITE     &DSN
    END
  ENDO
ALLOC F(SYSUT1) DA(&DSN) SHR REUSE
CALL 'SYS1.LINKLIB(IEBGENER)'
  .
  .
```

The data set name is contained in the variable &DSN and must represent a regular sequential data set or a member of a PDS. Checks are, therefore, made for (1) the existence of the data set, (2) the proper data set organization, and (3) agreement between the data set organization and whether or not a member name is specified.

OTHER BUILT-IN FUNCTIONS

There are two built-in functions that provide for case translation of character data. The &SYSCAPS *function* can be used to translate data to uppercase characters. Conversely, the &SYSLC *function* can be used to translate data to lowercase characters. Both work on alphabetic characters only and will not change numbers or special characters. The following statement illustrates how to change the data in variable &IN_DATA to uppercase characters.

```
SET &IN_DATA = &SYSCAPS(&IN_DATA)
```

The &SYSCAPS and &SYSLC functions should be coordinated with the default or stated setting for capitalization. The default is to have data translated to uppercase. This includes data read from the terminal or from a data set. To keep data from being translated to uppercase, the CONTROL statement options ASIS or NOCAPS can be used. These options were available prior to release 1.3 of TSO/E and might be coded as in the example below.

```
CONTROL ASIS
```

Neither of these options cause data to be translated to lowercase. They merely allow data to remain in lowercase. Data entered with a mixture of upper- and lowercase characters would be be maintained that way. A CONTROL statement with the CAPS parameter can be executed to return to the default of translating alphabetic data to uppercase.

Another built-in function, &SYSNSUB, controls the levels of substitution of symbolic variables and expressions. The levels, or number of times substitution takes place, can be set at 0 through 99 inclusive. The literal or variable specifying the level is separated from the expression with a comma. The CLIST below demonstrates the effect that different levels of substitution can have. It sets the variable &VAR3 to the value START. It does this using two intermediate variables, &VAR1 and &VAR2. The WRITE statements that follow display the value of &VAR3 while using the &SYSNSUB function to limit symbolic substitution.

```
SET &VAR1 = START
```

```
SET &VAR2 = &&VAR1
SET &VAR3 = &&VAR2
WRITE &SYSNSUB(0,&VAR3)
WRITE &SYSNSUB(1,&VAR3)
WRITE &SYSNSUB(2,&VAR3)
WRITE &SYSNSUB(3,&VAR3)
```

When the above CLIST is executed, the following display is produced by the WRITE statements.

```
&VAR3
&VAR2
&VAR1
START
```

Under normal circumstances, symbolic substitution would be complete and the variable &VAR3 would contain the character string START. That is, in fact, the value that is displayed from the final WRITE statement where three levels of substitution are specified. The initial value shows the opposite extreme, where no substitution was allowed to take place. The value displayed is the variable name itself. Displayed between those two values are the results of partial substitution which, of course, are the intermediate variables that were used to supply the value to variable &VAR3.

The &SYSNSUB function can also be used to maintain natural occurrences of a double ampersand. A double ampersand, for example, is fairly common in JCL where it is one way to designate a temporary data set. Below is an example of a JCL DD statement that is stored in a variable to be written to a file.

```
SET &JCLOUT = &SYSNSUB(0,//TEMPFILE DD DSN=&&TEMP1,DISP=(,PASS),)
PUTFILE JCLOUT
```

The string &&TEMP1 represents a temporary data set name within the JCL DD statement. The &SYSNSUB function is used with a value of zero to indicate that no substitution is to take place within the character string that follows. To display the same variable contents at the terminal, the following statement can be used.

```
WRITE &SYSNSUB(1,&JCLOUT)
```

Allowing only a single level of substitution allows the variable contents to be written to the screen without further substitution which would try to further resolve &&TEMP.

SYSTEM VARIABLES

Several new variables are available with release 1.3 of TSO/E. These center around providing additional information about the environment. Many of the new variables indicate whether or not a particular program product is available or indicate the version and release of a product. This can be used within a CLIST to determine what program product services are available and help in creating code that is portable to other systems that may be at different product-maintenance levels. Below are the system variables that are added with release 1.3.

Variables containing date and time information

&SYSSDATE   This variable contains the current date value in the format yy/mm/dd. The format of this date variable was made different from the mm/dd/yy format of variable &SYSDATE. This was done to allow data containing the changed format (yy/mm/dd) to be sorted and therefore more easily be rearranged in chronological order. This would also make comparisons against other data values in the same format much more practical.

&SYSJDATE   This variable contains the current date value in Julian format. That format presents the date information as yy.ddd, where ddd is the day of the year relative to January 1. The last day of the year then is 365 except in a leap year when it is 366. This format, like that of &SYSSDATE, is easier to sort and use in comparisons than the standard numeric date.

&SYSSTIME   This variable contains the current time as set in the computer's time-of-day clock. The time information is in twenty-four–hour format stored as hh:mm. This is a shorter version of the time information in variable &SYSTIME, which also contains a two-digit representation of the seconds.

Variables used to monitor CLIST performance

&SYSSRV   This variable contains the number of service units used in the current TSO session. This is a standard of measurement for services provided by the operating system System Resource Manager component.

&SYSCPU   This variable contains the number of processor seconds used in the current TSO session. The value is presented in seconds.hundredths format. This and the previous variable can be used to measure the performance of a given CLIST by capturing the variable values at the beginning of the CLIST, and comparing them to the variable values at the end (or other significant points) of the CLIST.

Variables describing the environment

&SYSTSOE   This variable contains the version, *release,* and modification level of the TSO/E product that is installed on the user's system. All of the features in this chapter, for example, are first available with version 1, release 3 of the product. This would be represented with the value 1030 in the variable &SYSTSOE. The release number is the middle two digits and is much more likely to change than the version number. The next chapter contains significant changes only available to the language starting with release 4. This variable can be tested to see what release of TSO/E is installed, and therefore, what statements are available. Those statements that are only available with a particular release can be conditionally executed once the level of the product is determined. This is a significant benefit when designing code that would need to be portable across computer installations.

The variable &SYSTSOE would have a null value if tested on a system where the release of the TSO/E product was prior to release 1.3. The following is an example of how the release level can be tested.

```
IF &DATATYPE(&SYSTSOE) = NUM
  IF &SYSTSOE GE 1030 THEN +
    LISTDSI `TSO1234.SEQ.DATA' RECALL
```

In the above example, the LISTDSI command (to obtain data set information) is only executed if the TSO/E product is at release 1.3 or greater. The alternative might be to prompt the user to supply data set information. Note that the above example could also be conducted as a simple character compare.

&SYSISPF   This variable indicates whether or not ISPF is active. If the ISPF product is installed, and the currently executing CLIST was invoked from within the ISPF environment, the variable will contain the value ACTIVE. This would mean that the CLIST would have access to the various dialog manager services. In the opposite condition, as when a CLIST is invoked from native TSO mode, the variable &SYSISPF contains the value NOT ACTIVE.

&SYSENV   This variable contains an indication of the environment under which the CLIST is run. The valid values for this variable are FORE when invoked in the foreground, and BACK when invoked from the background, using JCL. The latter process is described in Chap. 9.

&SYSRACF   This variable indicates whether or not the RACF security product is installed, and if it is available. The three possible variable values are AVAILABLE, NOT AVAILABLE, and NOT INSTALLED.

&SYSLRACF   If the RACF security product is installed, this variable contains the version and release levels. For example, if version 1 release 8 of the RACF product was installed, the variable &SYSLRACF would contain the value 1080. Like the variable &SYSTSOE that was mentioned earlier, this variable will contain a null value when tested on a system that has a release prior to 1.3 of the TSO/E product installed.

Variables containing terminal characteristics

&SYSWTERM   This variable contains the screen width as the number of columns available at the terminal being used.

&SYSLTERM   This variable contains the screen length as the number of lines available at the terminal being used.

NEW AND CHANGED TSO COMMANDS

Changes to the ALLOCATE command

The ALLOCATE command is fundamental to most CLIST processing. Release 1.3 of the TSO/E product brought with it enhancements to the processing of SYSOUT data. These were mentioned in Chap. 5 and include the ability to specify multiple copies of print data as well as the print characteristics. The former is specified with the COPIES keyword while the later is specified with the FCB keyword. The keyword names and functions are identical to those that are found in JCL.

In addition to the availability of data set information provided by the LISTDSI command, information about an existing data set is also available via the ALLOCATE statement LIKE parameter. This is a convenient way to model one data set after the characteristics of another, and will be examined next.

Modeling data set characteristics

The data set information provided by the LIKE parameter is not available in separate variables the way it is with the LISTDSI statement. Instead, the characteristics of an existing data set referenced by the LIKE parameter, are automatically incorporated into a data set that is being created. Various characteristics can also be overridden by including the appropriate ALLOCATE statement parameter.

In an earlier example, a new CLIST library was created and put in place of any of the standard system libraries that were allocated to the SYSPROC file. We would more likely want to add our private CLIST library to those that are already allocated to the SYSPROC file. To help ensure that our CLIST library is created with compatible characteristics that would allow it to be concatenated with other libraries, we can use the LIKE parameter. Below is what such an ALLOCATE command might look like using the LIKE parameter.

```
ALLOCATE DATASET('TSO1234.CLIST') +
LIKE('SYS1.CLIST') TRACKS SPACE(3 1) DIR(15)
```

The LIKE parameter makes reference to an existing data set, SYS1.CLIST, and uses that data set's characteristics when the new data set, TSO1234.CLIST, is created. The characteristics that are normally modeled are the space attributes and those that describe the data set characteristics. With the LIKE parameter, we were able to omit the DSCB parameters like DSORG, RECFM, LRECL, and BLK-SIZE. These parameters are of primary concern to data set compatibility, but can be obtained automatically from the modeled data set and thus help to insure compatibility with it.

Certain space-related parameters are specified in the above ALLO-CATE command so they will not be copied from the model data set. The various space parameters TRACKS, SPACE, and DIR were included because the data set we are creating for our own use need not be as large as the system data set we are modeling from. These three parameters could have otherwise been omitted, and their characteristics would also have been modeled from the data set specified in the LIKE parameter.

The same ALLOCATE command modeled after another private CLIST library would be even more simplified as in the example below.

```
ALLOCATE DATASET('TSO1234.CLIST') +
LIKE('TSO9872.FOCUS.CLIST')
```

With more appropriate overall characteristics, there is less need to override parameters. In fact, in the above example, none of the modeled characteristics are overridden.

Freeing all dynamic allocations

With release 1.3 of the TSO/E product, the ALL parameter has been added to the FREE command. The FREE command is used to free or deallocate a particular resource. That resource can be a file, data set, or attribute list. The ALL parameter extends the scope of the command to all resources that were dynamically allocated and are not currently in use.

The term *dynamic,* in reference to allocation, refers to resources that were attached after the execution of the initial logon procedure. The ALL parameter should be used with caution since it is common practice to reallocate standard TSO and ISPF files during a TSO session. The circumstances under which the FREE ALL is invoked may see some of these files as not in use and cause them to be freed. This could cause the deallocation of important ISPF files and even happen to the SYSPROC file if its allocations have been changed after LOGON.

FREE ALL is a powerful function and can be used to clean up file allocations very quickly. Its routine use is not advised, however, due to the potential disruption it can cause. As discussed in Chap. 5, directed use of the FREE command to clean up each resource after it is used is preferable. This usually avoids the sort of situation where allocations are building up that makes the use of FREE ALL so attractive.

Instream submit function

The *SUBMIT* command has traditionally operated with one or more data sets to read them into the job entry subsystem for background execution. With release 1.3 of TSO/E, the SUBMIT command has been modified to accept instream data. When used in a CLIST, it becomes a convenient way to incorporate variable data into a JCL jobstream. Below is a very simple example of a background print job.

```
PROC 1 DSN CLASS(A)
SUBMIT *
//&SYSUID.M JOB '0','SUBMIT EXAMPLE',CLASS=A.
// MSGCLASS=A,NOTIFY=&SYSUID
//STEP1   EXEC PGM=IEBGENER
//SYSPRINT DD SYSOUT=&CLASS
//SYSUT1   DD DISP=SHR,DSN=&DSN
//SYSUT2   DD SYSOUT=&CLASS
//SYSIN    DD DUMMY,DCB=BLKSIZE=80
&NULL
```

Assuming that the CLIST name is BATCHPRT, it can be invoked in the following fashion.

```
BATCHPRT TSO12345.TRANSACT.DATA CLASS(J)
```

Required and optional information is communicated to the CLIST by way of PROC statement variables. This includes a fully qualified data set name without quotes and the optional output print class. Another alternative would be to prompt the CLIST user using READ and WRITE statements. Whether specified (as in the example) or left to default to the value A the variable CLASS is used in two different places within the JCL. The system variable &SYSUID is also used in two separate places within the JCL, but was automatically available.

The null statement that ends the CLIST is created using a variable with a null value. It serves to delimit the end of the jobstream and suppress any prompts the SUBMIT command would otherwise issue. Other delimiters can be established using the SUBMIT command END keyword. This keyword allows the user to specify a one- or two-character delimiter that would be used to mark the end of the jobstream.

Data set and message transmission

A set of commands was created that can be used to transmit or send a disk data set or messages to the same or a different system within a given communication network. A recipient within the target system or node is also designated. The data is transformed into spool data for transmission, and appropriately reformatted at the other end of the process.

Separate commands initiate the processing at each end. The TRANSMIT command is used to send the data set and full screen message. The command can also be abbreviated XMIT. The RECEIVE command is used at the target destination to transform the data back into its original format. Logging of data sent and received is also possible at both the point of origin and the ultimate destination.

Establishing an authorized environment

There are some cases where a command or program will fail because it is running in an environment where it is not authorized to run. The *TSOEXEC command* can be used to try to establish an environment that will support the command or program. To utilize the TSOEXEC command, it is merely placed in front of some other command. Where program execution is involved, that would be the CALL statement.

```
TSOEXEC CALL 'SYS1.LINKLIB(IEBCOPY)'
```

The above statement might be required, for example, if the utility program IEBCOPY were authorized for background use but not for foreground execution. The TSOEXEC command should only be used when it resolves a problem like the one just described.

RELEASE 3 EXAMPLE

The following example brings together several of the functions introduced in this chapter. These include the LISTDSI, &SYSINDEX, and
instream SUBMIT functions. The previous instream SUBMIT example is repeated here with additional statements (in bold print) added
to validate the data set and print-class information.

The added code allows the CLIST user to specify a data set name
that is either fully or partially qualified. The LISTDSI function will be
used to arrive at a fully qualified data set name that is appropriate for
use in JCL statements. It will also be used to indicate whether or not
the data set exists, and to supply the data set organization. The data
set organization will then be used to determine whether or not a
member name should be included.

When a member name is specified and the data set is partitioned,
the &SYSDSN function is used to determine whether or not the member actually exists. Finally, the &SYSINDEX function is used to validate the print class against a list of acceptable values. Prompts are
issued for missing or incorrect member names as well as an invalid
print class. The CLIST is terminated when the data set name specified cannot be found or the data set organization cannot be printed
with the utility IEBGENER.

```
PROC 1 DSN CLASS(A)                                        0001
CONTROL NOFLUSH                                            0002
LISTDSI &DSN RECALL DIR                                    0003
IF &LASTCC = 16  THEN +                                    0004
  DO                                                       0005
    WRITE DATA SET  &DSN  NOT FOUND                        0006
    WRITE RE EXECUTE SPECIFYING A DIFFERENT DATA SET NAME  0007
    WRITE CLIST HAS TERMINATED                             0008
    EXIT                                                   0009
  END                                                      0010
IF &SYSDSORG = PO THEN +                                   0011
  DO                                                       0012
    SET &TEST1 = &SYSINDEX((,&DSN)                         0013
  IF &TEST1   = 0 THEN +                                   0014
    DO                                                     0015
      WRITE DATA SET TO BE PRINTED IS PARTITIONED          0016
      WRITE ENTER THE NAME OF THE MEMBER TO BE PRINTED     0017
      WRITE OR ENTER A BLANK TO TERMINATE ===>             0018
```

Line 1
This line is a PROC statement that defines two variables. The first variable, DSN, is positional. That means that the variable value must be specified for execution to proceed. The variable will be used to convey the name of the data set to be printed. That data set name can be either fully or partially qualified. The second variable, CLASS, is a keyword. The CLIST user can use it to supply an output print class other than the default A.

Line 2
This line uses the CONTROL statement to prevent the command stack from being flushed in the event of an error.

Line 3
This line invokes the LISTDSI function using the data set name contained in variable &DSN. The variable contents are in whatever format the terminal user choses to enter. Any standard TSO format data set name is acceptable. Data set names that are entered with invalid syntax or that do not match an entry in the system catalog will cause this statement to issue a high-return code that will prematurely terminate the CLIST. The RECALL and DIRECTORY parameters are included to bring the data set to active disk from various forms of archive storage and to make PDS directory information available respectively.

Line 4
This line tests the condition code returned from the LISTDSI function. A condition code of 16 indicates that the data set could not be found.

Lines 5 through 10
These lines form a DO group that is executed in the true path of the IF statement test (line 4). These statements display a three-line message at the terminal and terminate the CLIST with the EXIT statement. The message indicates that the data set specified by the user when the CLIST was invoked could not be found. This is determined early in the CLIST so the user can locate the correct data set name and restart the CLIST.

Line 11
At this point of the CLIST, it has been determined that the data set exists. This statement tests the data set organization value provided by the LISTDSI function. That value is contained in variable &SYSDSORG and is tested against the string PO to see if the data set is partitioned.

Lines 12 through 40
These lines form a DO group that contains logic that is specific to the processing of partitioned data sets. Line 12 marks the start of that DO group.

Line 13
This line uses the &SYSINDEX function to search for a left parenthesis in the data set name contained in variable &DSN. The numeric value representing the position of that symbol within the data set name will be placed in variable &TEST1. This value will be used to determine whether or not the CLIST user attempted to code a member name (enclosed in parentheses) within the data set name value.

RELEASE 3 EXAMPLE *(Continued)*

```
IF &SYSDSORG = PO THEN +                                        0011
 DO                                                             0012
  SET &TEST1 = &SYSINDEX((,&DSN)                                0013
  IF &TEST1   = 0 THEN +                                        0014
   DO                                                           0015
    WRITE DATA SET TO BE PRINTED IS PARTITIONED                 0016
    WRITE ENTER THE NAME OF THE MEMBER TO BE PRINTED            0017
    WRITE OR ENTER A BLANK TO TERMINATE ===>                    0018
    READ &MEMBER                                                0019
    IF &MEMBER =  THEN EXIT                                     0020
   END                                                          0021
  ELSE +                                                        0022
   DO                                                           0023
    SET &PAREN = )                                              0024
    SET &END = &SYSINDEX(&PAREN,&DSN)                           0025
    SET &MEMBER = &SUBSTR(&TEST1 + 1:&END - 1,&DSN)             0026
   END                                                          0027
CHECK2: +                                                       0028
  SET &TEST2 = &SYSDSN('&SYSDSNAME(&MEMBER)')                   0029
  IF &TEST2 = &STR(MEMEBER NOT FOUND) THEN +                    0030
   DO                                                           0031
    WRITE THE MEMBER NAME SPECIFIED DOES NOT EXIST              0032
    WRITE IN DATA SET  &SYSDSNAME  , RE ENTER THE MEMBER        0033
    WRITENR NAME OR A BLANK TO TERMINATE ===>                   0034
    READ &MEMBER                                                0035
    IF &MEMBER =  THEN EXIT                                     0036
    GOTO CHECK2                                                 0037
   END                                                          0038
  SET &DSN = &SYSDSNAME(&MEMBER)                                0039
 END                                                            0040
IF &SUBSTR(1:1,&SYSDSORG) = P THEN +                            0041
 IF &SYSDSORG = PS THEN SET &DSN = &SYSDSNAME                   0042
 ELSE                                                           0043
ELSE +                                                          0044
 DO                                                             0045
  WRITE DATA SET  &DSN  CANNOT BE PRINTED                       0046
  WRITE DUE TO  &SYSDSORG  DATA SET ORGANIZATION                0047
  WRITE CLIST HAS TERMINATED                                    0048
  EXIT                                                          0049
 END                                                            0050
```

Line 14	This line tests the variable that was set in the previous statement. A value of 0 indicates that no member name is included in the data set name.
Lines 15 through 21	These lines form a DO group that represent the true path of the previous IF statement test (line 14). These statements display a three-line message at the terminal. The message indicates that the data set has been determined to be partitioned, but the member name has been omitted. The CLIST user is then prompted to enter a member name which is read into variable &MEMBER. The CLIST user also has the option of terminating the CLIST by entering a null value. Line 20 tests the member name read from the screen. When a null value is detected, the CLIST is terminated.
Line 22	This line represents the start of the false path of the previous IF statement test (line 14). The false path code is executed if the user attempted to code a member name within the data set name supplied.
Lines 23 through 27	These lines form a DO group that will be used to extract the member name from the rest of the data set name. Line 23 represents the start of that DO group.
Line 24	This line sets the variable &PAREN to a value of). This variable will be used in the &SYSINDEX function to avoid getting a syntax error.
Line 25	This line uses the &SYSINDEX function to determine which byte of the data set name contains the right parenthesis. The numeric value for the position number is stored in variable &END.
Line 26	This line extracts the member name from the data set name and places it in variable &MEMBER. The &SUBSTR function is used to reference only the member name by offsetting one byte more than the left parenthesis (represented by the value in variable &TEST1) and one byte less than the right parenthesis (represented by the value in variable &END).
Line 27	This line marks the end of the DO group to extract the member name from the data set name.
Line 28	This line is a label followed by a continuation character. The continuation character is required because there is no executable code on this particular line. Control will branch to this label when it is necessary to recheck the presence of a member within the data set.
Line 29	This line uses the &SYSDSN function to check for the presence of a member. The member name was extracted from the originally entered data set name or obtained by prompting the CLIST user. It is combined with the fully qualified data set name contained in the LISTDSI variable &SYSDSNAME. The result of the &SYSDSN function is stored in the variable &TEST2.

RELEASE 3 EXAMPLE *(Continued)*

```
        ELSE +                                                    0022
          DO                                                      0023
            SET &PAREN = )                                        0024
            SET &END = &SYSINDEX(&PAREN,&DSN)                     0025
            SET &MEMBER = &SUBSTR(&TEST1 + 1:&END - 1,&DSN)       0026
          END                                                     0027
  CHECK2: +                                                       0028
      SET &TEST2 = &SYSDSN('&SYSDSNAME(&MEMBER)')                 0029
      IF &TEST2 = &STR(MEMEBER NOT FOUND) THEN +                  0030
        DO                                                        0031
          WRITE THE MEMBER NAME SPECIFIED DOES NOT EXIST          0032
          WRITE IN DATA SET  &SYSDSNAME  , RE ENTER THE MEMBER    0033
          WRITENR NAME OR A BLANK TO TERMINATE ===>               0034
          READ &MEMBER                                            0035
          IF &MEMBER =  THEN EXIT                                 0036
          GOTO CHECK2                                             0037
        END                                                       0038
      SET &DSN = &SYSDSNAME(&MEMBER)                              0039
    END                                                           0040
  IF &SUBSTR(1:1,&SYSDSORG) = P THEN +                            0041
    IF &SYSDSORG = PS THEN SET &DSN = &SYSDSNAME                  0042
    ELSE                                                          0043
  ELSE +                                                          0044
    DO                                                            0045
      WRITE DATA SET  &DSN  CANNOT BE PRINTED                     0046
      WRITE DUE TO  &SYSDSORG  DATA SET ORGANIZATION              0047
      WRITE CLIST HAS TERMINATED                                  0048
      EXIT                                                        0049
    END                                                           0050
  SET &CLASSES = &STR(ABCDEFGLMNO23478)                           0051
  CHECK3:  IF &SYSINDEX(&CLASS,&CLASSES) = 0  THEN +              0052
    DO                                                            0053
      WRITE THE PRINT CLASS SPECIFIED IS INVALID, VALID CLASSES   0054
      WRITE INCLUDE A B C D E F G L M N 0 2 3 4 7 AND 8           0055
      WRITE RE ENTER THE PRINT CLASS OR                           0056
      WRITENR ENTER A BLANK TO TERMINATE ===>                     0057
      READ &CLASS                                                 0058
      IF   &CLASS =  THEN EXIT                                    0059
      GOTO CHECK3                                                 0060
    END                                                           0061
```

Line 30   This line tests the &SYSDSN function result (stored in variable &TEST2) against the string MEMBER NOT FOUND. When the IF statement condition test is true, it means that the member could not be found in the indicated data set.

Lines 31   These lines form the true path of the last IF statement test
through 38   and reflect a situation where the member that has been specified cannot be found. A three-line message is written to the terminal describing the situation, prompting the CLIST user to enter a new member-name value. The entered value is read into variable &MEMBER and tested for a null value. When the value is null, it is an indication that the CLIST user is trying to halt processing, and the CLIST is terminated using the EXIT statement. When the value is not null, the GOTO statement directs processing back to the label CHECK2, to recheck for the member presence.

Line 39   As the last executable statement in the DO group for PDS data sets, line 39 resets the variable &DSN to the fully qualified data set name plus the tested member name. Even though the name is fully qualified, quotes are omitted because the name will be used in a JCL statement where quotes are not appropriate.

Line 40   This line ends the DO group for PDS processing.

Line 41   This line tests the first byte of the LISTDSI variable for a value of *P*. The intent is to isolate sequential (PS) and partitioned (PO) data sets from all other data set organizations. The &SUBSTR function is used to reference the first byte of the variable &SYSDSORG.

Line 42   This line tests specifically for sequential data sets (further refining the previous test) and when found, sets the variable &DSN to the value contained in the LISTDSI variable &SYSDSNAME. The variable &SYSDSNAME contains the fully qualified data set name. The advantage to placing its value in &DSN is that it will (1) ensure that the data set name is fully qualified, (2) ensure that the data set name does not contain quotes, and (3) remove any member name that may have been entered with the initial data set name value. These features are required of the sequential data set name that will be included in the JCL jobstream.

RELEASE 3 EXAMPLE *(Continued)*

```
   IF &TEST2 = &STR(MEMEBER NOT FOUND) THEN +              0030
     DO                                                    0031
        WRITE THE MEMBER NAME SPECIFIED DOES NOT EXIST     0032
        WRITE IN DATA SET  &SYSDSNAME  , RE ENTER THE MEMBER  0033
        WRITENR NAME OR A BLANK TO TERMINATE ===>          0034
        READ &MEMBER                                       0035
        IF &MEMBER =  THEN EXIT                            0036
        GOTO CHECK2                                        0037
     END                                                   0038
     SET &DSN = &SYSDSNAME(&MEMBER)                         0039
   END                                                     0040
IF &SUBSTR(1:1,&SYSDSORG) = P THEN +                       0041
   IF &SYSDSORG = PS THEN SET &DSN = &SYSDSNAME            0042
   ELSE                                                    0043
ELSE +                                                     0044
   DO                                                      0045
      WRITE DATA SET  &DSN  CANNOT BE PRINTED              0046
      WRITE DUE TO  &SYSDSORG  DATA SET ORGANIZATION       0047
      WRITE CLIST HAS TERMINATED                           0048
      EXIT                                                 0049
   END                                                     0050
SET &CLASSES = &STR(ABCDEFGLMNO23478)                      0051
CHECK3:  IF &SYSINDEX(&CLASS,&CLASSES) = 0  THEN +         0052
   DO                                                      0053
      WRITE THE PRINT CLASS SPECIFIED IS INVALID, VALID CLASSES  0054
      WRITE INCLUDE A B C D E F G L M N O 2 3 4 7 AND 8    0055
      WRITE RE ENTER THE PRINT CLASS OR                    0056
      WRITENR ENTER A BLANK TO TERMINATE ===>              0057
      READ &CLASS                                          0058
      IF   &CLASS =  THEN EXIT                             0059
      GOTO CHECK3                                          0060
   END                                                     0061
SUBMIT*                                                    0062
//&SYSUID.M JOB '0','SUBMIT EXAMPLE',CLASS=A,              0063
//  MSGCLASS=A,NOTIFY=&SYSUID                              0064
//STEP1 EXEC PGM=IEBGENER                                  0065
//SYSPRINT DD SYSOUT=&CLASS                                0066
//SYSUT1   DD DISP=SHR,DSN=&DSN                            0067
//SYSUT2   DD SYSOUT=&CLASS                                0068
//SYSIN    DD DUMMY,DCB=BLKSIZE=80                         0069
&NULL                                                      0070
```

Line 43

This line is a null ELSE because there is nothing to execute when the data set is not sequential (partitioned data set processing has already taken place). The null ELSE is required here to maintain the proper IF-ELSE pairing for the following ELSE statement.

Lines 43 through 50

These lines form the false path for when the first byte of the data set organization variable &SYSDSORG is not equal to the letter P. When this point is reached, the data set is determined to have an invalid data set organization (not PO or PS) for this particular print function. A three-line message is written to the screen to describe the circumstance and the CLIST is terminated using the EXIT statement.

Line 51

This line places a string of letters and numbers in the variable &CLASSES. These characters each represent a valid output print class which will be used in a later comparison.

Line 52

This line uses the &SYSINDEX function to determine whether or not the value in variable &CLASS is also contained in the variable containing valid print classes &CLASSES. When the value obtained from the function is zero, the print class is invalid because it cannot be found among the list of valid classes. The label CHECK3 is used to return to the statement where the CLIST user enters a new print class value. That allows the same statement to test either the initial or changed class value.

Lines 53 through 61

These lines form the true path of the previous IF statement test. This code is executed when the print class is determined to be invalid. Valid print classes are displayed within the text that is written to the terminal. Again, the CLIST user can terminate the CLIST by entering a null value; otherwise, control is directed back to the label CHECK3. This allows the new class value to be validated.

Lines 62 through 70

These lines implement an instream submit of a print jobstream using the TSO SUBMIT command. Lines 63 through 69 contain the jobstream which includes three variables (excluding &NULL). The values for two of the three variables is set and validated within the CLIST. The third variable, &SYSUID, is a system variable containing the CLIST user's user-ID. The variable &NULL is not initialized and serves to suppress prompting by the SUBMIT command.

13

Release 4 Enhancements

Among the release 4 enhancements are several looping structures. This includes a *DO UNTIL structure,* an *iterative DO structure* that automatically increments loop controlling variables, and a *compound DO structure* that combines other loop types. This release also includes a new selection structure that is based upon condition tests and a facility for executing subprocedure code. The discussion of release 4 enhancements will start with the SELECT statement.

THE SELECT STATEMENT

The *SELECT statement* can be used to execute one of a finite set of alternatives. Conditional tests are performed to determine which alternative to select. If no alternative is selected, a catchall section of code can be invoked or the SELECT structure can merely be exited. Before the SELECT statement became available, this type of function was usually performed by a long series of IF-THEN-ELSE condition tests. After an alternative is executed, control falls to the end of the SELECT structure just as it would with a properly coded series of IF-THEN-ELSE condition tests.

The SELECT statement is based upon some number of WHEN expressions. These WHEN expressions test conditions and direct other statement execution when the condition is true. This can also include a null action. Only one of the WHEN condition actions (the first to be satisfied) will be executed. If none of the WHEN conditions is satisfied, the actions of an OTHERWISE section can be executed. Below is an example of a SELECT structure that contains an OTHERWISE section.

```
PROC 1 CMD
CONTROL END(ENDO)
.
.
SELECT
WHEN (&CMD = L) +
  DO
    WRITE THIS IS THE LIST FUNCTION
    .
    .
  ENDO
WHEN (&CMD = R) +
  DO
    WRITE THIS IS THE RENAME FUNCTION
    .
    .
  ENDO
WHEN (&CMD = D) +
  DO
    WRITE THIS IS THE DELETE FUNCTION
    .
    .
  ENDO
OTHERWISE +
  DO
    WRITE AN INVALID OPTION HAS BEEN SPECIFIED
    .
    .
  ENDO
ENDO
.
.
```

In the example above, one of three sections of code is executed depending on the value contained in variable &CMD. DO groups are used so that more than a single statement can be executed when a WHEN clause condition is true. After that, the SELECT structure is exited at the final ENDO statement (since a CONTROL statement was added to change END to ENDO). If the value of &CMD does not cause any of the expressions to be true, the code following the OTHERWISE clause will be executed. In the latter case, if the OTHERWISE clause had not been included, none of the sections of the SELECT statement would have been executed.

Because of its format, the above example represents a simple SELECT statement. In this case, the same variable is tested for mutually exclusive values. The WHEN statement tests, however, do not need to test the same variable or expression. When the conditions tested are not mutually exclusive, however, their order becomes more important. The reason for this is that while it is possible to have more than one true condition in a SELECT statement, only a single section of code can be executed. The most important conditions, therefore, should be placed before those of lesser importance.

THE COMPOUND SELECT STATEMENT

There is a second form of the SELECT statement, the *compound SELECT*. This form is distinguished from the other by a single test expression which is included on the SELECT portion of the statement. With this second form, WHEN values are then compared to the value of that previous test expression. Below is the previous example changed to the compound SELECT statement format.

```
PROC 1 CMD
CONTROL END(ENDO)
.

.
SELECT &CMD
WHEN (L) +
  DO
    WRITE THIS IS THE LIST FUNCTION
    .

    .
  ENDO
WHEN (R) +
  DO
    WRITE THIS IS THE RENAME FUNCTION
    .

    .
  ENDO
WHEN (D) +
  DO
    WRITE THIS IS THE DELETE FUNCTION
```

```
        .
        .
        .
   ENDO
   OTHERWISE +
   DO
      WRITE AN INVALID OPTION HAS BEEN SPECIFIED
        .
        .
      ENDO
   ENDO
        .
        .
```

The overall effect of this code is the same as the previous example.
With the compound format, it is also possible to combine values in a
single WHEN test as well as specifying a range or ranges of values.
Below is an example of testing for multiple values. The expression is
again a single-variable value.

```
        .
        .
   CALL MYPROG(UPDATE)
   SET &RET_CODE = &LASTCC
   SELECT &RET_CODE
   WHEN (0) +
      WRITE RETURN CODE INDICATES NORMAL COMPLETION (&RET_CODE)
   WHEN (100:199) +
      WRITE AN INFORMATION CODE HAS BEEN ISSUED (&RET_CODE)
   WHEN (200:299) +
      WRITE A WARNING CODE HAS BEEN ISSUED (&RET_CODE)
   WHEN (312 OR 323 OR 527 OR 613) +
      WRITE PROBLEM WITH FILE OPEN OR CLOSE (&RET_CODE)
   WHEN (300:799) +
      WRITE A CONDITIONAL WARNING CODE HAS BEEN ISSUED (&RET_CODE)
   WHEN (997 OR 999) +
      WRITE A FATAL ERROR HAS BEEN DETECTED (&RET_CODE)
   OTHERWISE +
      WRITE THE RETURN CODE CANNOT BE INTERPRETED (&RET_CODE)
   END
```

The return code from the user program UPDATE is tested for certain ranges of values. These were apparently designed to reflect the
severity level of any messages that the program would have issued.

WHEN statements are used to categorize the type of message by defining ranges of return code values. The above example contains tests for:

a single value

```
WHEN (0)
```

multiple values

```
WHEN (312 OR 323 OR 527 OR 613)
```

and a range of values

```
WHEN (300:799)
```

Where nonmutually exclusive conditions are tested, the more important (and in this case more specific) test is placed in advance of the other.

```
WHEN (312 OR 323 OR 527 OR 613) . . .
WHEN (300:799) . . .
```

ADDITIONAL LOOPING STRUCTURES

In Chap. 6 we saw that a loop could be created using the GOTO statement to branch to a label, or by using the DO WHILE statement. With release 4, additional iterative structures are added that make repetitive processing easier to code and give it more flexibility. We will now direct our attention to those structures.

Iterative DO

The *iterative DO structure* controls loop execution by way of a numeric variable. The variable is specified with a starting and ending value. These are the "FROM" and TO values. Optionally, a BY value may be specified to determine the amount that the control variable is incremented each time that the loop is executed. When omitted, this value defaults to one. The starting, ending, and increment values are specified by literal numeric value, numeric variable value, or numeric expression. Below is an example that includes all three statement values.

```
        .

        .

DO &LOOP_VAR = 10 TO 100 BY 10
```

.
.

END

.
.

In the example, the loop is controlled by the variable &LOOP_VAR. Its initial or "FROM" value is 10 and is set using the equal sign. Each time through the loop, that variable is incremented by the BY value which is also 10. The loop will execute 10 times to reach the TO value of 100.

The iterative DO structure has an advantage over previous looping techniques. The variable that controls the loop is automatically initialized based upon the "FROM" value and is automatically incremented at the end of the loop. When the TO range is exceeded, the loop is stopped, and the next sequential instruction, if any, is executed. Below is code that was used to demonstrate other loop structures. The iterative DO statement has been inserted into the example, and is highlighted.

```
SET &ANSWER = 2
WRITE &ANSWER
DO &COUNT = 1 TO 25
    SET &ANSWER = &ANSWER ** 2
    WRITE &ANSWER
END
```

In the example, the control variable &COUNT is initially set to one. Each time through the loop, its value is incremented by 1 until it reaches a value of 25. Each time through the loop, the CLIST writes the next power of two to the terminal. When the TO value specified is less than the start value of the control variable, the BY value becomes the value by which to decrement the "FROM" value.

Nested DO

Any type of loop structure can be *nested* within another loop. That includes the loop structures that were introduced with release 4. None of these is any easier to use in this fashion than the iterative DO structure. The reason for this is that the variables that control loop processing (and that might be used within the loops themselves) are incremented automatically. Below is a nested DO structure that accounts for processing twelve months within a two-year period.

```
DO &YEAR = 90 TO 91
  DO &MONTH = 1 TO 12
    WRITE &YEAR &MONTH
  END
END
```

Because the iterative DO sequence is used, the variables are automatically controlled, and the code is very much simplified.

DO UNTIL

The *DO UNTIL structure* is very much like the DO WHILE structure. In both, variables must be explicitly set or incremented. The DO UNTIL structure, however, will always execute at least once, because the condition test is conducted at the end of the loop. The expression tested may be a compound expression, and, as in the following example, DO UNTIL structures may be nested.

```
SET &YEAR = 90
DO UNTIL &YEAR = 92
  SET &MONTH = 1
  DO UNTIL &MONTH = 13
    WRITE &YEAR &MONTH
    SET &MONTH = &MONTH + 1
  END
  SET &YEAR = &YEAR + 1
END
```

This is the same example used to demonstrate nested DO WHILE structures. The variable controlling the outer loop is incremented upon completion of the inner loop. Condition expressions here test against an equal condition as opposed to the DO WHILE which tested for a less than condition to obtain the same result.

Compound DO

The last iterative structure to be discussed here is the compound DO structure. It is a combination of the previously discussed forms of loop processing. The example below adds to the previous examples that process monthly data over a two-year period.

```
SET &TOTAL = 0
SET &YEAR = 90
DO &MONTH = 2 TO 12 BY 2 +
```

```
UNTIL &YEAR = 92
WHILE &DATATYPE(&TOTAL) = NUM
  GETFILE TOTAL
  WRITE &YEAR &MONTH &TOTAL
  IF &MONTH = 12 THEN +
    DO
      SET &MONTH = 0
      SET &YEAR = &YEAR + 1
    END
END
```

In the example, the month variable &MONTH is automatically incremented. Rather than use the default, a value of 2 is specified as the increment value. The year variable &YEAR is initialized before the iterative structure to provide a valid starting point. It is incremented using a SET statement within the loop. A third variable, &TOTAL, will have its value supplied during loop processing too, by way of the GETFILE statement. It is given an initial value of zero before entering the loop for the first time. This allows the variable to pass a test for numeric value which is part of the loop condition. If nonnumeric data is subsequently read into the variable, the loop will terminate. Otherwise, the month variable values will be even numbers from 2 to 12 inclusive within year values of 90 and 91. The month variable is reset using the SET statement when the year variable is incremented.

PERFORMED SUBPROCEDURES

In Chap. 6, we saw how a CLIST can invoke another CLIST. A similar facility is available with *performed subprocedures*. The difference is that with subprocedures, all CLIST code is contained within a single CLIST. In addition, invoking subprocedure code can be much more efficient, in terms of execution time, than invoking an external CLIST. The more often the subprocedure code is invoked, the more dramatic the difference.

As with modular programming, the advantage in using subprocedures is seen when code that is relevant to several points in a given CLIST can be extracted and placed in a single section. The code in that section is then accessed from various points in the CLIST with control automatically brought back to the next sequential instruction. This can greatly simplify the CLIST code, and make it easier to maintain. When a change to the code is required, it can be made in a single place rather than replicated throughout the CLIST.

There is an additional advantage to invoking a subroutine over an external CLIST. Because subprocedure code is self-contained, there are less likely to be changes made that make the code incompatible with main procedure code. It is very difficult to tie external CLIST code with other code that may invoke it. The advantage of invoking a subroutine over normal (GOTO) branching to a labeled section of code is that return is automatic. Using subprocedures, however, the communication of variable information is no longer automatic. As we look at subroutines in more detail, we will look at various methods of how information can be communicated.

Subprocedures are implemented in much the same way that multiple CLISTs are. The SYSCALL statement is used rather than an implicit or explicit EXEC. Another difference is that a label is added to the PROC statement of code that serves as a subprocedure, and as we just noted, all such code is contained within a single CLIST data set. The PROC statement of a subprocedure is required, and still uses the positional specification parameter to define how many positional parameters it contains. The statement would also list the names of the positional variables as well as any keywords and their default values. The end of the subprocedure code must be delimited with the END statement or the equivalent as defined on a CONTROL statement. This is true even if the subprocedure code also represents the physical end of the CLIST anyway.

As with external CLISTs, the flow of variable information is unidirectional from main CLIST to subprocedure. The subprocedure can, however, set and return an exit code to be used by the main CLIST. That information would be available following the SYSCALL statement in the system variable provided for that purpose, &LASTCC. More complete forms of variable information communication will be discussed later in this chapter.

The following example uses code from the previous chapter. That code is used to make certain checks against an existing data set before the data set is allocated to a file. Because it is necessary to do this for several data sets, it is prudent to isolate the code in a subroutine and access it from various points in the main CLIST code.

```
   .
   .
SYSCALL MYALLOC &FILE#1 &DSN#1
IF &LASTCC > 0  THEN WRITE DATA SET &DSN#1 NOT ALLOCATED
SYSCALL MYALLOC &FILE#2 &DSN#2
IF &LASTCC > 0  THEN WRITE DATA SET &DSN#2 NOT ALLOCATED
SYSCALL MYALLOC &FILE#3 &DSN#3
```

```
IF &LASTCC > 0  THEN WRITE DATA SET &DSN#3 NOT ALLOCATED
 .
 .
 .
MYALLOC: PROC 2 FILE DSN
CONTROL END(ENDO)
LISTDSI &DSN DIRECTORY RECALL
IF &LASTCC = 16  THEN RETURN CODE(16)
IF &SYSDSORG = PO  THEN +
  DO
    SET &MEMTEST = &SYSINDEX((,&DSN)
    IF &MEMTEST = 0  THEN +
      DO
        WRITE MEMBER NAME REQUIRED BUT NOT SPECIFIED FOR DATA SET
        WRITE    &DSN
        RETURN CODE(12)
      ENDO
    IF &SYSDSN(&DSN) = MEMBER NOT FOUND  THEN +
      DO
        WRITE MEMBER NAME SPECIFIED DOES NOT EXIST IN DATA SET
        WRITE    &DSN
        RETURN CODE(12)
      ENDO
  ENDO
ELSE +
  DO
    SET &MEMTEST = &SYSINDEX((,&DSN)
    IF &MEMTEST > 0  THEN +
      DO
        WRITE MEMBER NAME CANNOT BE SPECIFIED FOR DATA SET
        WRITE    &DSN
        RETURN CODE(12)
      ENDO
  ENDO
ALLOC F(&FILE) DA(&DSN) SHR REUSE
RETURN CODE(&LASTCC)
ENDO
```

Notice that the variable names used in the main CLIST keep changing and do not match the names used in the subprocedure. This is possible because variable communication is by position rather than variable name. Each set of variables contains a different combination of
file name and data set name which the subprocedure allocates. A
return code is then passed back to the main CLIST from one of several

places within the subprocedure. Detectable errors pass back a return code of 12 or 16 using the RETURN statement. The main CLIST is then able to test or capture that code using the system variable &LASTCC immediately following any SYSCALL statement.

SYSREF VARIABLES

Other variable information can be returned from a subprocedure by defining those variables with the *SYSREF statement*. This allows variables referenced on the SYSCALL statement to be modified within the subprocedure and their changed values returned to the main CLIST. Variables used in this fashion are coded differently on the SYSCALL statement. The difference is that the variable name is passed rather than the variable itself. That is illustrated in the following SYSCALL statement.

```
SYSCALL SUBPROC1 &VARIABLE VARNAME
```

On this statement, two variables are passed to the subprocedure SUBPROC. The first (&VARIABLE) is an actual variable, while the second (VARNAME) has had the ampersand removed so that it now represents a variable name rather than the variable itself. This is required for use as a SYSREF variable. The SYSREF statement is included in the subprocedure in the manner shown below.

```
SUBPROC1: PROC 2 SUBVAR1 SUBVAR2
SYSREF &SUBVAR2
```

Of the two variables passed to the subprocedure, only the second was included on the SYSREF statement. The ampersand used with the variable name is optional on the SYSREF statement. Having been defined in this fashion, the variable value can be passed back from the subprocedure to the main CLIST. The example below shows similar statements in a larger context where a literal, a variable, and a variable name are passed to a subprocedure.

```
SET &VARIABLE = MAIN#1
SET &VARNAME  = MAIN#2
SYSCALL SUBPROC2 LITERAL &VARIABLE VARNAME
WRITE LITERAL    &VARIABLE    VARNAME
SUBPROC2: PROC 3 SUBLIT SUBVAR1 SUBVAR2
SYSREF &SUBVAR2
WRITE &SUBLIT    &SUBVAR1    &SUBVAR2
```

```
SET &SUBVAR1 = SUB VALUE 1
SET &SUBVAR2 = SUB VALUE 2
END
```

The passed variable name SUBVAR2 can be distinguished from a literal by its inclusion on the SYSREF statement. It can be traced back to the PROC statement parameter of the same name as well the SYSCALL parameter of the same relative position. The first WRITE statement executed is in the subprocedure. It displays the following values

```
LITERAL   MAIN#1   MAIN#2
```

representing the passed literal, variable, and variable name. Both variable values are then updated in the subprocedure under the changed variable names &SUBVAR1 and &SUBVAR2. The second WRITE statement is executed after control is returned from the subprocedure. It displays the same three values using their original names.

```
LITERAL   MAIN#1   SUB VALUE 2
```

The literal, of course, will not change. Of the two variables, only the changed value of the variable defined on the SYSREF statement is available in the main CLIST code.

NAMED GLOBAL VARIABLES

Named global variables are variables that are available to the main CLIST and all of its subprocedures. They further remove the limitations of one-way communication of variable information. The variables are made available to the subroutines when they are defined on an NGLOBAL statement. The following statement, for example, makes two variables, &NUM_DATE and &JUL_DATE, available to any subprocedure.

```
NGLOBAL &NUM_DATE &JUL_DATE
```

Unlike variables defined with the GLOBAL statement, NGLOBAL variables work by name rather than position. This means that the name of a variable must be consistent throughout its use. Named global variables only work within a CLIST which further differentiates them from GLOBAL variables. NGLOBAL variables have a distinct advantage, however. Because they function through a consistent variable name, they need not be specified as SYSCALL statement arguments. That also allows the variables to be omitted from the subprocedure PROC statement.

The following is a complete CLIST example using NGLOBAL to communicate variable values. It uses the date routine presented earlier as a subprocedure to convert numeric dates into Julian dates. Records are read into the CLIST from an external file. A date is extracted from a fixed position within the record. That date is converted and compared to the previously converted system date. When the input-record date is less than the current date, the entire record is written to a separate external data set. This is repeated for each record obtained from the input file. The DATECONV subprocedure is, therefore, invoked every time a record is read into the CLIST.

```
CONTROL NOFLUSH
ALLOC F(INPUT) DA(SHIPMENT.DATA) SHR REUSE
ALLOC F(OVERDUE) DA(OVERDUE.DATA) MOD REUSE
OPENFILE INPUT
OPENFILE OVERDUE OUTPUT
NGLOBAL &NUM_DATE &JUL_DATE
SET &NUM_DATE = &STR(&SYSDATE)
SYSCALL DATECONV
SET &TODAY = &JUL_DATE
DO WHILE &RETCODE NE 400
  GETFILE INPUT
  SET &NUM_DATE = &SUBSTR(20:27,&INPUT)
  SYSCALL DATECONV
  IF &JUL_DATE < &TODAY  THEN +
    DO
      SET &OVERDUE = &STR(&INPUT)
      PUTFILE OVERDUE
    END
  ERROR +
    DO
      SET &RETCODE = &LASTCC
    END
  END
CLOSFILE INPUT
CLOSFILE OVERDUE
FREE F(INPUT OVERDUE)
DATECONV: PROC 0
SET &MM = &SUBSTR(1:2,&NUM_DATE)
SET &DD = &SUBSTR(4:5,&NUM_DATE)
SET &YY = &SUBSTR(7:8,&NUM_DATE)
```

```
IF (&YY // 4) EQ 0 THEN  SET &DAYS = &STR(313232332323)
ELSE SET &DAYS = &STR(303232332323)
SET &I = 1
DO WHILE &I LT &MM
  SET &DD = &DD + 28 + &EVAL(&SUBSTR(&I,&DAYS))
  SET &I = &I + 1
END
IF &LENGTH(&STR(&DD)) = 2  THEN  SET &DD = &STR(0&DD)
SET &JUL_DATE = &STR(&YY.&DD)
END
```

Notice that two variables, &NUM_DATE and &JUL_DATE, are established in the NGLOBAL statement before the first SYSCALL statement that references them. Notice too, that the variable names shared by the main CLIST and the subprocedure are the same. The variable names within the date-conversion subprocedure were changed to match those used in the main CLIST logic. This allows the variables to be omitted from the SYSCALL statement and the subprocedure PROC statement.

CONTROL VARIABLES

We have discussed several CONTROL statement parameters at various times in the preceding chapters. With release 1.4 of the TSO/E product, these parameters can also be controlled using system variables. These variables can be tested to determine what options are currently in effect, and they can be updated to set or change options. The following statement, using the variable &SYSCONLIST,

```
SET &SYSCONLIST = ON
```

is equivalent to the traditional style CONTROL statement.

```
CONTROL CONLIST
```

Both of the statements above cause the CLIST to display statements after symbolic substitution has occurred and just before the statement is executed. When the variable is set to the value OFF, as when CONTROL NOCONLIST is specified, the executing statements are not displayed. Below are the other variables that affect CONTROL statement options.

&SYSPROMPT   This variable controls whether or not TSO commands can prompt for input from the terminal. The value of ON corresponds to CONTROL PROMPT and allows for prompting. The value of OFF corresponds to CONTROL NOPROMPT and prevents the commands from prompting.

&SYSSYMLIST   This variable controls whether or not CLIST statements are listed at the terminal. The listing, if produced, would be of the statements before symbolic substitution takes place. The value of ON corresponds to CONTROL SYMLIST and causes the statements to be listed at the terminal. The value of OFF corresponds to CONTROL NOSYMLIST and prevents the statements from being listed.

&SYSLIST   This variable controls whether or not TSO commands and subcommands are listed at the terminal. The value of ON corresponds to CONTROL LIST and causes commands and subcommands to be listed at the terminal. The value of OFF corresponds to CONTROL NOLIST and prevents the commands and subcommands from being listed.

&SYSASIS   This variable controls whether or not lowercase letters are converted to uppercase. The value of ON corresponds to CONTROL ASIS and prevents conversion to uppercase. The value of OFF corresponds to CONTROL CAPS and allows the conversion to uppercase letters.

&SYSMSG   This variable controls whether or not messages are displayed at the terminal. The value of ON corresponds to CONTROL MSG and causes messages to be displayed at the terminal. The value of OFF corresponds to CONTROL NOMSG and prevents the messages from displaying.

&SYSFLUSH   This variable controls whether or not the command stack can be flushed or terminated. The value of ON corresponds to CONTROL FLUSH and allows the command stack to be flushed. The value of OFF corresponds to CONTROL NOFLUSH and prevents the command stack from being flushed.

While both forms of setting control options are easy to use, the use of variables to supply control options can facilitate obtaining option information from other sources. For example, the information to control these variables can be stored in a data set. The variable values can be read from the data set into the appropriate variables. This would then serve to control the options for any CLIST that contained code similar to the following.

```
CONTROL NOFLUSH
ALLOC FILE(CONTROLS) DA('TSO1234.EXECUTE.OPTIONS') SHR REUSE
IF &LASTCC = 0  THEN  +
  DO
    OPENFILE CONTROLS
    GETFILE CONTROLS
    CLOSFILE CONTROLS
    FREE F(CONTROLS)
    SET &SYSDVAL = &STR(&CONTROLS)
    READDVAL &SYSLIST &SYSSYMLIST &SYSCONLIST +
      &SYSMSG &SYSFLUSH &SYSPROMPT &SYSASIS
  END
.
.
```

In the example above, the variable values are distributed by first placing them in the &SYSDVAL variable and then using the READDVAL function to distribute them to the various system-control variables. It should also be noted that if the options data set does not exist, the DO group is bypassed, and default options are left to apply. The data read into the CLIST could be formatted like the data shown below.

```
ON        ON         ON          ON        OFF       OFF         OFF
SYSLIST SYSSYMLIST SYSCONLIST SYSMSG SYSFLUSH SYSPROMPT SYSASIS
```

The CLIST user could edit the data set and tailor the options before running a given CLIST. The CLIST itself only reads the first data line. The second line of data lists the variable names to help the user remember which variable value is which when read into the CLIST. If a given CLIST gives the user the ability to change the control options, the data set can instead be opened for UPDATE. At the end of the CLIST, the changed variable values can then be written back to the data set. .

Those who are familiar with the ISPF Dialog Management function can easily see how these control variables could be stored as dialog variables in the profile-variable pool. Simple VGET and VPUT statements can copy the variable values to and from the CLIST respectively.

PRINTDS COMMAND

The *PRINTDS command* can be used to print regular sequential or partitioned data sets. Alternately, the PRINTDS command can reference a file name and print the data set or data sets that are allocated to that particular file. When a PDS is printed, the member contents, or the member name list, or both can be printed. The mutually exclusive parameters for those options are MEMBERS, DIRECTORY, and ALL, respectively. Selected members can be printed, or, by default, all members of the PDS will be printed. The ability to automatically print all of the members of a PDS makes this a very useful command.

Titles are added, by default, to the data that is printed. An exception to this is when a data set is printed that contains carriage-control characters. In this latter case, an assumption is made that the data is already formatted into an acceptable print format. Titles are also omitted when the parameter NOTITLES is included when the command is invoked. Conversely, titles can be forced to print by including the TITLES parameter. The title created by PRINTDS contains the data set name, member name (if any), date, time, and page number.

```
PRINTDS DATASET(REPORT.PDS) CLASS(A) DEST(R17) FCB(STD4)
```

The example above shows the PRINTDS command used to print an entire PDS. Keyword parameters are used to specify the print class (CLASS), the print characteristics (FCB), and the location of the printer (DEST). Some of the other print option parameters are specified below:

TODATASET   This keyword allows the data set contents to be written to another data set. This is particularly useful to unload a partitioned data set into a sequential data set. If the data set referenced in the TODATASET keyword does not already exist, the PRINTDS command will create it. Below is an example of how an entire PDS can be unloaded into a sequential data set.

```
PRINTDS DATASET(REPORT.PDS) TODATASET(NEW.REPORT)
```

The member contents of the PDS, REPORT.PDS, will be unloaded into the sequential data set NEW.REPORT. If the data set NEW.REPORT does not already exist, the PRINTDS command will create it based upon the characteristics of REPORT.PDS. The keyword TODSNAME can also be used in place of the keyword TODATASET.

FILE

This keyword allows data to be printed by file name. When the FILE keyword is used in place of the DATASET keyword, the data set currently allocated to the file specified will be printed. If more than one data set is concatenated to the file, all of those data sets will be printed. The keyword DDNAME can be used in place of the keyword FILE.

COLUMNS

This keyword allows particular columns of the data to be printed. The columns are specified by start and end column separated by a colon. Multiple-column specifications are separated by blanks or commas. This keyword can, therefore, be used to print only selected parts of a line of data, or it can be used to change the order of the data within the line as it is written out. The example below does both, using the abbreviation for the command PR and an abbreviation for the DATASET keyword DA.

```
PR DA(SEQUENTL.DATA) CLASS(A) +
   COLUMNS(1:10 37:43 60:80 15:20)
```

LINES

The LINES keyword allows specific lines of the data set to be printed. Both starting line number, and optionally, ending line number can be specified. If both line numbers are specified, they are separated by a colon.

TRUNCATE

This keyword will cause the print output to be truncated at the column value specified with this parameter. When used, no data beyond the column value specified will be printed.

FOLD

This keyword is used to cause the data to wrap at the column specified. Subsequent data is written on successive lines. This can be used when the data is longer than the print characteristic can print on a single line of output.

PAGELEN

This keyword specifies the number of lines to be printed on each page. This would be used to change the default value from 60 lines per page where a data set was not already using carriage control characters.

LMARGIN

This keyword specifies the left margin to be maintained when printing the data set. The value is specified in column positions.

TMARGIN

This keyword specifies the top margin to be maintained

when printing the data set. The value is specified in number of lines.

BMARGIN   This keyword specifies the bottom margin to be maintained when printing the data set. The value is also specified in number of lines.

RELEASE 4 EXAMPLE

The following CLIST serves as an interface to the PRINTDS command, and is intended to facilitate the entering of specific print columns to be extracted from the data. The &SYSDSN function is used to validate the data set and member names entered by the CLIST user, while error logic is directed using a SELECT statement. A DO UNTIL loop is used to prompt the CLIST user to enter start and end positions for columns of data to be printed. The loop is repeated until a blank value is entered. The information is strung together and used within the PRINTDS command.

```
PROC 1 DSN CLASS(A)                                      0001
CONTROL END(ENDO) NOMSG                                  0002
DSNCHECK: SET &DSNTEST = &SYSDSN(&DSN)                   0003
SELECT &DSNTEST                                          0004
WHEN (OK)                                                0005
WHEN (DATA SET NOT FOUND) +                              0006
  DO                                                     0007
    WRITE THE DATA SET SPECIFIED DOES NOT EXIST          0008
    WRITE RE ENTER THE DATA SET NAME OR A BLANK          0009
    WRITENR TO TERMINATE ===>                            0010
    READ                                                 0011
    IF &SYSDVAL =  THEN EXIT                             0012
    SET &DSN = &STR(&SYSDVAL)                            0013
    GOTO DSNCHECK                                        0014
  ENDO                                                   0015
WHEN (MEMBER NOT FOUND) +                                0016
  DO                                                     0017
    WRITE THE MEMBER NAME SPECIFIED DOES NOT EXIST       0018
    WRITE RE ENTER THE DATA SET NAME                     0019
    WRITE AND MEMBER NAME (IF ANY) OR A BLANK            0020
    WRITENR TO TERMINATE ===>                            0021
    READ                                                 0022
    IF &SYSDVAL = THEN EXIT                              0023
    SET &DSN = &STR(&SYSDVAL)                            0024
    GOTO DSNCHECK                                        0025
  ENDO                                                   0026
WHEN (INVALID DATA SET NAME, &DSN) +                     0027
  DO                                                     0028
    WRITE THE DATA SET NAME IS INVALID AS SPECIFIED.     0029
    WRITE RE ENTER THE DATA SET NAME OR A BLANK          0030
```

Line 1   This line includes a PROC statement that is used to convey two variable values. The first variable, &DSN, is a positional parameter that will include the name of the data set that is to be printed. This information is required for the CLIST to execute. The second variable contains the hardcopy print class. This keyword can optionally be specified when the CLIST is invoked if other than the default (supplied on the PROC statement) print class of A is desired.

Line 2   This line includes a CONTROL statement that is used to set processing options. The statement turns message output off, and substitutes the string ENDO for END in ending DO groups.

Line 3   This line uses the &SYSDSN function to test for the presence of the data set (and member if included) that was specified using the positional parameter variable &DSN. The message text from the &SYSDSN function is placed in variable &DSNCHECK. That message text will become part of the condition testing of the SELECT structure that follows. The SET statement on this line is preceded by the label DSNCHECK. That label will allow control to be directed back to this statement when new data set name information is entered and must again be checked.

Line 4   This line includes the SELECT statement and the variable that was set in the preceding statement. All subsequent WHEN statements will then be tested against this variable value (which reflects the status of the data set).

Line 5   This line is the first WHEN statement of the SELECT structure and it tests for a variable value of OK. It was placed first with the expectation that this condition would occur most often. This maximizes the efficiency of the SELECT structure just as it would a series of mutually exclusive IF-THEN-ELSE condition tests. When the value of variable &DSNTEST is equal to OK, it indicates that the data set, and optionally member, was located and is available. This WHEN test does not execute any statements. Control merely falls to the end of the SELECT structure.

Lines 6 through 15   These lines create the second of five WHEN conditions and includes logic for dealing with a situation where the data set name specified or reentered cannot be found.

Line 6   This line is the second of five WHEN statements. It tests for a variable value of DATASET NOT FOUND.

Line 7   This line starts a DO group that will be executed when the WHEN condition is true.

Lines 8 through 10   These lines write a message to the terminal that describe the error that has been detected as well as how the CLIST user can terminate the CLIST. The last of these statements uses WRITENR to retain the cursor on the last display line.

RELEASE 4 EXAMPLE *(Continued)*

```
      WRITE RE ENTER THE DATA SET NAME OR A BLANK                      0009
      WRITENR TO TERMINATE ===>                                        0010
      READ                                                             0011
      IF &SYSDVAL =  THEN EXIT                                         0012
      SET &DSN = &STR(&SYSDVAL)                                        0013
      GOTO DSNCHECK                                                    0014
    ENDO                                                               0015
  WHEN (MEMBER NOT FOUND) +                                            0016
    DO                                                                 0017
      WRITE THE MEMBER NAME SPECIFIED DOES NOT EXIST                   0018
      WRITE RE ENTER THE DATA SET NAME                                 0019
      WRITE AND MEMBER NAME (IF ANY) OR A BLANK                        0020
      WRITENR TO TERMINATE ===>                                        0021
      READ                                                             0022
      IF &SYSDVAL = THEN EXIT                                          0023
      SET &DSN = &STR(&SYSDVAL)                                        0024
      GOTO DSNCHECK                                                    0025
    ENDO                                                               0026
  WHEN (INVALID DATA SET NAME, &DSN) +                                 0027
    DO                                                                 0028
      WRITE THE DATA SET NAME IS INVALID AS SPECIFIED.                 0029
      WRITE RE ENTER THE DATA SET NAME OR A BLANK                      0030
      WRITENR TO TERMINATE ===>                                        0031
      READ                                                             0032
      IF &SYSDVAL = THEN EXIT                                          0033
      SET &DSN = &STR(&SYSDVAL)                                        0034
      GOTO DSNCHECK                                                    0035
    ENDO                                                               0036
  WHEN (MEMBER SPECIFIED, BUT DATA SET IS NOT PARTITIONED) +           0037
    DO                                                                 0038
      WRITE THE DATA SET SPECIFIED IS NOT A PDS                        0039
      WRITE AND CANNOT BE SPECIFIED WITH A MEMBER NAME                 0040
      WRITE RE ENTER THE DATA SET NAME OR A BLANK                      0041
      WRITENR TO TERMINATE ===>                                        0042
      READ                                                             0043
      IF &SYSDVAL =  THEN EXIT                                         0044
      SET &DSN = &STR(&SYSDVAL)                                        0045
      GOTO DSNCHECK                                                    0046
    ENDO                                                               0047
```

Line 11	This line reads user-supplied input. In this instance, the user is expected to enter a new data set name. The system variable &SYSDVAL will be used to handle the data set name entered in case it contains quotes.
Line 12	This line tests the value read from the terminal. If nothing was entered, the CLIST is terminated using the EXIT statement.
Line 13	This line places the newly entered data set name in the variable &DSN. This is the same variable that was used as a positional parameter to convey the data set name when the CLIST was first invoked.
Line 14	This line uses the GOTO statement to transfer control to the top of the CLIST where the data set name information just entered can be rechecked.
Line 15	This line ends the DO group statements that deal with a data set-not-found condition.
Lines 16 through 26	These lines create the third of five WHEN conditions and includes logic for dealing with a situation where the member name entered cannot be found in the data set specified. The CLIST user is prompted to reenter both the data set and member names and is given the same opportunity to terminate the CLIST by entering a null value. At this point, the CLIST user can enter any data set name and that data set name may or may not include a member name. If a value is entered for the data set name, a GOTO statement transfers control to the beginning of the CLIST where the newly entered information can again be checked.
Lines 27 through 36	These lines create the fourth of five WHEN conditions and includes logic for dealing with a situation where the data set name specified is invalid. This kind or error is created by using improper syntax to specify the data set name. This might include things like unbalanced parentheses or quotes as well as qualifiers that are too long or start with an invalid character. The CLIST user is prompted to reenter the data set name and is again given the opportunity to terminate the CLIST by entering a null value. If a value is entered for the data set name, a GOTO statement transfers control to the beginning of the CLIST where the newly entered information can again be checked.
Lines 37 through 47	These lines create the last of five WHEN conditions and includes logic for dealing with a situation where the data set name specified is sequential, but a member name was also entered. Since a member name cannot be specified with a sequential data set, the CLIST user is prompted to reenter the data set name. The opportunity to terminate the CLIST by entering a null value is again available. If a value is entered for the data set name, a GOTO statement transfers control to the beginning of the CLIST where the newly entered information can again be checked.

RELEASE 4 EXAMPLE *(Continued)*

```
    GOTO DSNCHECK                                               0046
  ENDO                                                          0047
OTHERWISE +                                                     0048
  DO                                                            0049
    WRITE &DSNTEST                                              0050
    WRITE RE EXECUTE THE CLIST WITH CHANGED DATA SET NAME.      0051
    EXIT                                                        0052
  ENDO                                                          0053
WRITE YOU WILL NOW BE PROMPTED TO ENTER THE START AND           0054
WRITE END POSITIONS OF DATA TO BE PRINTED. WHEN ALL             0055
WRITE COLUMNS OF DATA HAVE BEEN SPECIFIED, ENTER A BLANK VALUE. 0056
WRITE                                                           0057
WRITE ENTER THE START AND END POSITIONS OF THE                  0058
WRITENR FIRST COLUMN OF DATA TO BE PRINTED ===>                 0059
SET &SYSDVAL = GO                                               0060
DO UNTIL &SYSDVAL =                                             0061
REREAD: +                                                       0062
  READ                                                          0063
  IF &SYSDVAL NE THEN +                                         0064
    DO                                                          0065
      READDVAL &COL1 &COL2                                      0066
      IF &COL2 =   THEN +                                       0067
        DO                                                      0068
          WRITE ONE OF THE COLUMN VALUES WAS OMITTED.           0069
          WRITE PLEASE RE ENTER BOTH COLUMN VALUES.             0070
          GOTO REREAD                                           0071
        ENDO                                                    0072
      IF &DATATYPE(&COL1) = CHAR OR +                           0073
        &DATATYPE(&COL2) = CHAR THEN +                          0074
        DO                                                      0075
          WRITE ONE OR BOTH COLUMN VALUES CONTAINS NON NUMERIC  0076
          WRITE DATA. PLEASE RE ENTER BOTH COLUMN VALUES.       0077
          GOTO REREAD                                           0078
        ENDO                                                    0079
      IF &COL2 < &COL1 THEN +                                   0080
        DO                                                      0081
          WRITE END VALUE IS LESS THAN START VALUE.             0082
          WRITE PLEASE RE ENTER BOTH COLUMN VALUES.             0083
          GOTO REREAD                                           0084
        ENDO                                                    0085
```

Lines 48 through 53	The preceding five WHEN conditions account for the four most common errors as well as when the data set (and member, if any) is properly specified. The OTHERWISE section of the SELECT statement would then capture any unexpected error based on the &SYSDSN-derived value in variable &DSNTEST. Since the type of error is not known here, no attempt at recovery is made. WRITE statements are used to display the original &SYSDSN function error message and ask the CLIST user to reexecute the CLIST with a different data set name. The CLIST is then terminated.
Lines 54 through 59	These lines write information to the terminal that tell the CLIST user how to enter the start and end column numbers for the data that they would like to print. They are instructed to end the cycle by entering a null value. The last statement in the group of WRITE statements uses WRITENR to leave the cursor positioned after the text written to the terminal.
Line 60	This line sets the system variable &SYSDVAL to the value GO. This variable will be used in the DO UNTIL statement that controls iterative processing. This action serves as much to document the process as anything else, since a DO UNTIL loop must be executed at least one time, anyway.
Line 61	This line uses the DO UNTIL statement to loop through logic that will collect start and end column pairs. The condition test will fail when the CLIST user enters a null value.
Line 62	This line contains only a label. A continuation character is used to get to the executable code on the next line. This will provide a point to branch to when the column information entered is found to be invalid.
Line 63	This line reads the column information entered by the CLIST user. No variables are specified, so the data is placed in system variable &SYSDVAL. Remember, this is the same variable that is used to control loop processing.
Line 64	This line uses the IF statement to see if a value was entered. If a value was entered, a DO group is executed that attempts to validate the column values entered. If a value was not entered, the DO group is bypassed, reaching the end of the DO UNTIL loop. The loop condition test would then fail, bringing an end to iterative processing.
Line 65	This line defines the start of a DO group for validating the data that was entered.
Line 66	This line uses the READDVAL statement to parse the information that was entered. The first two pieces of information in variable &SYSDVAL will be placed in variables &COL1 and &COL2. These two variables will serve as the starting and ending column numbers respectively.

RELEASE 4 EXAMPLE *(Continued)*

```
WRITE YOU WILL NOW BE PROMPTED TO ENTER THE START AND          0054
WRITE END POSITIONS OF DATA TO BE PRINTED. WHEN ALL            0055
WRITE COLUMNS OF DATA HAVE BEEN SPECIFIED, ENTER A BLANK VALUE. 0056
WRITE                                                          0057
WRITE ENTER THE START AND END POSITIONS OF THE                 0058
WRITENR FIRST COLUMN OF DATA TO BE PRINTED ===>                0059
SET &SYSDVAL = GO                                              0060
DO UNTIL &SYSDVAL =                                            0061
REREAD: +                                                      0062
  READ                                                         0063
  IF &SYSDVAL NE THEN +                                        0064
    DO                                                         0065
      READDVAL &COL1 &COL2                                     0066
      IF &COL2 =  THEN +                                       0067
        DO                                                     0068
          WRITE ONE OF THE COLUMN VALUES WAS OMITTED.          0069
          WRITE PLEASE RE ENTER BOTH COLUMN VALUES.            0070
          GOTO REREAD                                          0071
        ENDO                                                   0072
      IF &DATATYPE(&COL1) = CHAR OR +                          0073
        &DATATYPE(&COL2) = CHAR THEN +                         0074
        DO                                                     0075
          WRITE ONE OR BOTH COLUMN VALUES CONTAINS NON NUMERIC 0076
          WRITE DATA. PLEASE RE ENTER BOTH COLUMN VALUES.      0077
          GOTO REREAD                                          0078
        ENDO                                                   0079
      IF &COL2 < &COL1 THEN +                                  0080
        DO                                                     0081
          WRITE END VALUE IS LESS THAN START VALUE.            0082
          WRITE PLEASE RE ENTER BOTH COLUMN VALUES.            0083
          GOTO REREAD                                          0084
        ENDO                                                   0085
      SET &COLS = &STR(&COLS &COL1:&COL2)                      0086
      WRITE ENTER THE START AND END POSITIONS OF THE           0087
      WRITENR NEXT COLUMN OF DATA TO BE PRINTED ===>           0088
    ENDO                                                       0089
ENDO                                                           0090
PRINTDS DA(&DSN) CLASS(&CLASS) NOTITLE COLUMNS(&COLS)          0091
```

Line 67   This line uses the IF statement to test for a value in the second variable. If none is present, then the CLIST user only entered one of the two required values (since this logic is bypassed when no values are entered at all).

Line 68   This line defines the start of a DO group for dealing with missing column information. Rather than guess which column number they were trying to enter, users will be requested to reenter both start and end column values.

Lines 69   These lines write a message to the terminal to let the CLIST
and 70   user know that one of the column values was omitted. This message will be followed by the standard prompt for column information after branching back to that section of code.

Line 71   This line uses the GOTO statement to branch back to logic that will issue the standard prompt for column information and completely process that new data.

Line 72   This line uses the character string ENDO to end the DO group for dealing with missing column information.

Lines 73   These lines contain a compound IF statement test using the
through 79 &DATATYPE function to see if either of the column values entered are not numeric. No attempt is made to determine which of the values contains character rather than numeric data. Like the previous validation test, a message is written to the screen describing the error and a branch is made back to logic that will restart the process of entering the next column pair.

Lines 80   These lines use an IF-statement test to be sure that the second
through 85 column number specified is not less than the first. This leaves the possibility that the same column value will be used for both a start and end value. This is an acceptable way to specify a single print position. No attempt is made to correct the values (by switching them) since this might instead be the result of a typographical error. Like the previous validation tests, a message is written to the screen describing the error and a branch is made back to logic that will restart the process of entering the next column pair.

Line 86   At this point, the column information has passed three checks and is considered to be valid. This line adds the latest column pair to the variable &COLS by setting the variable equal to itself and the two column variables. To create the proper PRINTDS parameter syntax, the two column values are separated from each other by a colon and from any other column pairs (that may already be stored in &COLS from previous executions of the DO UNTIL loop) by a space. Below is what that statement might look like each time it is executed. The column values entered from the most recent execution of the loop are in bold print.

```
SET &COLS = &STR( 1:15)
SET &COLS = &STR( 1:15 93:114)
SET &COLS = &STR( 1:15 93:114 20:37)
```

RELEASE 4 EXAMPLE *(Continued)*

```
WRITE YOU WILL NOW BE PROMPTED TO ENTER THE START AND          0054
WRITE END POSITIONS OF DATA TO BE PRINTED. WHEN ALL            0055
WRITE COLUMNS OF DATA HAVE BEEN SPECIFIED, ENTER A BLANK VALUE. 0056
WRITE                                                          0057
WRITE ENTER THE START AND END POSITIONS OF THE                 0058
WRITENR FIRST COLUMN OF DATA TO BE PRINTED ===>                0059
SET &SYSDVAL = GO                                              0060
DO UNTIL &SYSDVAL =                                            0061
REREAD: +                                                      0062
  READ                                                         0063
  IF &SYSDVAL NE THEN +                                        0064
    DO                                                         0065
      READDVAL &COL1 &COL2                                     0066
      IF &COL2 =  THEN +                                       0067
        DO                                                     0068
          WRITE ONE OF THE COLUMN VALUES WAS OMITTED.          0069
          WRITE PLEASE RE ENTER BOTH COLUMN VALUES.            0070
          GOTO REREAD                                          0071
        ENDO                                                   0072
      IF &DATATYPE(&COL1) = CHAR OR +                          0073
        &DATATYPE(&COL2) = CHAR THEN +                         0074
        DO                                                     0075
          WRITE ONE OR BOTH COLUMN VALUES CONTAINS NON NUMERIC 0076
          WRITE DATA. PLEASE RE ENTER BOTH COLUMN VALUES.      0077
          GOTO REREAD                                          0078
        ENDO                                                   0079
      IF &COL2 < &COL1 THEN +                                  0080
        DO                                                     0081
          WRITE END VALUE IS LESS THAN START VALUE.            0082
          WRITE PLEASE RE ENTER BOTH COLUMN VALUES.            0083
          GOTO REREAD                                          0084
        ENDO                                                   0085
      SET &COLS = &STR(&COLS &COL1:&COL2)                      0086
      WRITE ENTER THE START AND END POSITIONS OF THE           0087
      WRITENR NEXT COLUMN OF DATA TO BE PRINTED ===>           0088
    ENDO                                                       0089
ENDO                                                           0090
PRINTDS DA(&DSN) CLASS(&CLASS) NOTITLE COLUMNS(&COLS)          0091
```

Lines 87 and 88	These lines write information to the terminal that prompt the CLIST user to enter the next column number pair.
Line 89	This line ends the DO group that contains column information validation.
Line 90	This line ends the DO UNTIL structure that is used to collect column information.
Line 91	This line will execute at the termination of the DO UNTIL iterative structure. It contains the PRINTDS command that will be used to print the data set that was specified as positional parameter input. The value for the output print class was either specified as a keyword or left to default to the value coded on the PROC statement. The NOTITLE parameter is included to keep the PRINTDS command from inserting its own titles. The last parameter included specifies the column values that the CLIST user entered during loop processing.

Index

used as table entries, 95
used in I/O processing, 105
value length, 82
VERIFY command, 35
version 2 enhancements, 26
Virtual Storage Access Method:
 data sets, printing, 35
 define (example), 31
VOLUME parameter:
 of ALLOCATE command, 10, 43
 LISTDSI statement, 231
volume table of contents, 123
VSAM (*see* Virtual Storage Access
 Method)

VTOC, 123

WHEN command, 35
WHEN parameter, of SELECT
 statement, 255, 258
width of screen, system variable, 242
WRITE statement, 105
 for debugging, 220
WRITENR statement, 108
writing:
 to a file, 110
 to the terminal, 105
 (without carriage return), 108